Next Week—*East Lynne*

Next Week—*East Lynne*.

Domestic Drama In Performance

1820–1874

Gilbert B. Cross

Lewisburg
Bucknell University Press
London: Associated University Presses

© 1977 by Associated University Presses, Inc.

Portions of this work originally appeared as a dissertation, *Nineteenth Century Domestic Drama As Theatrical Communication* © 1972 by Gilbert B. Cross.

Associated University Presses, Inc.
Cranbury, New Jersey 08512

Magdalen House
136-148 Tooley Street
London Se1 2TT, England

Library of Congress Cataloging in Publication Data

Cross, Gilbert B.
    Next week—*East Lynne*.

    Bibliography: p.
    Includes index.
    1. English drama—19th century—History and criticism. 2. Theater—England—History. I. Title.
PR721.C7   822'.7'09   74-25573
ISBN 0-8387-1646-6

For Peggy, John, and Robert

CONTENTS

LIST OF ILLUSTRATIONS

9

ACKNOWLEDGMENTS

THERE ARE MANY PEOPLE I should like to thank for their help in preparing this book. Professor John Styan, formerly of the University of Michigan, encouraged me to undertake this study and was unfailingly patient and considerate with me at all times, as was his colleague, Professor Jack Bender. I am likewise indebted to my friend and colleague, Professor Alfred Nelson of Eastern Michigan University, who, besides helping with the proofreading, has taught me more about the theater than anyone else. I am grateful to Sarah and John Constant, who spent many hours singing and playing the score of *Black Ey'd Susan* for me, and to George Magee, who painstakingly copyedited the text and made invaluable suggestions.

I should also like to express my appreciation to Miss Harriet Jameson and her staff of the Rare Book Room at the University of Michigan Library, to Bill Cagle and his staff of the Lilly Library, Indiana University, and to George Nash and his staff of the Enthoven Collection at the Victoria and Albert Museum, London.

11

Finally, recognition is due to my long-suffering wife, Peggy, who helped at every stage and provided the support and encouragement necessary for the completion of the study. There are also several publishers that need to be mentioned for their help and assistance in providing illustrations and/or permissions to quote.

For the illustrations, the following sources have been most generous:

The Victoria and Albert Museum
The Lilly Library
Cherokee Books
Society for Theatre Research
Chatto and Windus.

Extracts from printed works still in copyright are published by the kind permission of the following:

Bobbs-Merrill Company, for J. O. Bailey's *British Plays of the Nineteenth Century* (c. 1966)

Random House, Inc., for J. B. Schneewind's *Backgrounds of English Victorian Literature* (c. 1970)

The University of Chicago Press, for David Grimsted's *Melodrama Unveiled: American Theater and Culture, 1800–1850* (c. 1968)

Yale University Press, for Walter Houghton's *The Victorian Frame of Mind, 1830–1870* (c. 1957).

BEFORE THE CURTAIN

So, if you want an evening's treat
O seek the Surrey side.

H. S. Leigh[1]

IN 1825 "PHILO-DRAMATICUS" wrote an open letter to the managers of Covent Garden and Drury Lane lamenting the state of English drama. "Who are your successful authors?", he demanded, "Planché and Arnold, Poole and Kenney; names so ignoble in the world of literature that they have no circulation beyond the green room."[2] His contempt has been a common attitude toward nineteenth-century drama, for no plays between Sheridan's *The Critic* (1779) and Tom Robertson's *Society* (1865) remain in the theater repertory.

1. Quoted in Allardyce Nicoll, *A History of Early Nineteenth-century Drama, 1800–1850*, 2 vols. (Cambridge, England: Cambridge University Press, 1930), 1:120.
2. Philo-Dramaticus [pseud.], "A Letter to Charles Kemble, Esq., and R. W. Elliston, Esq. on the Present State of the Stage," *Blackwood's Magazine* 17 (June 1825): 730.

13

Growing critical attention is being paid to the significant changes in the theater that were taking place by the turn of the nineteenth century, for during this period theater control was rapidly passing into the hands of the uneducated urban masses of London's slums. Dramatists were forced to choose between writing for the growing working-class audiences at the minor (or illegitimate) theaters or attempting "literary" dramas for the patent houses.

Those who chose to earn a precarious living as popular dramatists found that one type of play was in demand—its nature being largely determined by a combination of audience demands and legal restrictions. The word "melodrama" was loosely applied to such plays because the minor theaters of Paris and London initially presented them without dialogue and to a musical accompaniment. The term *melodrama* was derived from the Greek word *melos* and the French word *drame*, but the anglicized form *melodrama* soon replaced the French form *mélo-drame*, which was initially used. At first melodrama embraced Gothicism, with its wild and gloomy settings, its tortured heroes, and its impassioned rhetoric. The first play performed in England to be called a *mélo-drame*—Thomas Holcroft's *A Tale of Mystery*—was performed at a patent house, Covent Garden, in 1802, with considerable success. At this time there was nothing pejorative in the term *melodrama*. Holcroft's play was an adaptation of Guilbert de Pixérécourt's *Coelina; ou, l'enfant du mystère*. In *A Tale of Mystery* all the ingredients of Gothicism were found. The setting was Italy with the climactic scenes taking place in "the wild mountainous country called the Nant of Arpennaz," accompanied by the inevitable "storm of lightening, thunder, hail, and rain." Stalking throughout the play was the typical Gothic villain haunted by a secret in his past. The heroine, a helpless orphan, finally discovered her birthright, and the hero was honest, courageous, and clearly destined for the heroine in the last scene. Changes in mood and pace were signaled by appropriate musical accompaniment. The characters were types, virtuous or evil, and were to be repeated endlessly in countless melodramas.

Romantic poets seized upon the Gothic elements with a fervor equaling that of the melodramatists but with very different objectives in mind. Though the Gothic model was ever cheapened by the popular theater, in literary dramas its cruder elements were refined and sensationalism severely curtailed. While a "popular" writer like "Monk" Lewis could justify his inclusion of four huge black slaves on the grounds of the terror that they would produce, Wordsworth painstakingly employed Gothicism as a means rather than an end in *The Borderers*, (written 1795–96). Coleridge's *Remorse*, (Drury Lane, 1813), which brought verse-drama back to the stage, was a play whose Gothicism became a framework for a psychological investigation. Thus, in Romantic drama the conventions of the Gothic prototype were utilized, but the poet was primarily concerned with the study of the human psyche. Coleridge had followed the lead of Joanna Baillie, whose *Plays on the Passions*, (1798, 1802, 1812), were written around particular human emotions, by writing a play that sought to analyze remorse. Of all Romantic dramas, *Remorse* was the only play by a major poet to achieve anything like a popular success. Even so, Henry Crabb Robinson wrote:

> I have no hesitation, however, in saying that its poetical is far greater than its dramatic merit; that it owes its success rather to its faults than its beauties; and that it will have for its less meritorious qualities applause which is really due for its excellencies.[3]

A detailed analysis of the reasons why none of the major Romantics produced lasting drama is beyond the scope of this work; moreover, such studies already exist. In brief, however, it may be said that they "failed" because the "portrayal of internal reality was still the province of fiction."[4] They were clearly groping in the direction of modern drama but were severely handicapped since they knew almost noth-

---

3. Henry Crabb Robinson, *The London Theatre, 1811–1866* (London: Society for Theatre Research, 1966), p. 52.

4. Terry Otten, *The Deserted Stage* (Athens, Ohio: Ohio University Press, 1972), p. 40.

ing of the technical requirements of the stage. Only Byron had any connection with the theater; the rest were amateurs. Because the Romantics were determined to produce noble dramas, they were all too conscious of this self-appointed task. Looking for worthy models to emulate, they chose the Elizabethan dramatists at a time when the nature of contemporary theater was changing radically. None of them recognized that their famous predecessors were men who believed in "character in action" (as Browning put it in his preface to *Strafford* [Covent Garden, 1837]) rather than "action in character." Finally, and perhaps most significantly, the genius of the Romantics was poetic, their concern and interest lay in psychology and motivation. Unfortunately "the notion *ut pictura poesis*" [art as a "speaking" picture], while an important agent of imaginative creation in Romantic lyric and narrative verse, became an ultimately devitalizing one for Romantic drama."[5]

While the major Romantics failed to construct tragedy out of the materials of their own age—Browning's *A Blot in the 'Scutcheon*, (Drury Lane, 1843), was a dismal failure and may be taken as the end of the attempt by the Romantics to revive verse-drama—less prominent verse-dramatists were becoming increasingly aware that their future lay in taking the direction that the popular theater was pursuing. Those verse-dramas that gained any success on the stage did so by realizing that the age demanded plays that had a contemporary setting and injected excitement, idealism, humor, and domesticity, into some of the problems encountered by middle- and working-class Londoners. Even so, the legitimate dramatists all failed to achieve a lasting reputation. James Sheridan Knowles's *Virginius*, (Glasgow, 1820), was treated with respect initially—it was, after all, a domestic play in a Roman setting—but it later received short shrift. John Westland Marston handled verse well, but his brave attempt to regenerate verse-drama was unavailing. Of all the men of letters who wrote plays in the last century, only

5. Joseph Donohue, *Dramatic Character in the English Romantic Age* (Princeton, New Jersey: Princeton University Press, 1970), p. 185.

Edward Bulwer-Lytton achieved anything like a popular success. The year 1820 is chosen as the starting point of this study because in that year Moncrieff's *The Lear of Private Life* was performed at the Coburg Theater. This play may justly be called *the first domestic drama*—a genre that had already begun to lose some of its appeal in 1874 when T. A. Palmer's classic version of Mrs. Henry Wood's novel *East Lynne* was produced in Nottingham. Domestic drama became increasingly popular through the 1820s as audiences exerted pressure on authors to write to a well-tried formula. For their part, managers, as Dickens was quick to point out, knew only too well that in order to exist they had to please their patrons—the Mr. Whelkses of the world:

Accordingly, the Theatres to which Mr. Whelks resorts are always full; and whatever changes of fashion the drama knows elsewhere, it is always fashionable in the New Cut. . . . Heavily taxed, wholly unassisted by the State, deserted by the gentry, and quite unrecognized as a means of public instruction, the higher English Drama has declined. Those who live to please Mr. Whelks must please Mr. Whelks to live. It is not the Manager's province to hold the Mirror up to Nature, but to Mr. Whelks—the only person who acknowledges him.[6]

Audiences required plays with prescriptive morality. They wanted to see onstage a world that seemed real enough, but in which a perfect justice and morality would ultimately prevail. The sanctity of marriage and the preservation of the family unit were matters of the deepest concern. The dutiful regard with which a son or daughter held their stern-but-loving father was placed in an uneasy proximity with the revolutionary belief that inherent worth was not based on birth or rank. Out of these plays, and the domestic sentiment of Knowles, J. W. Marston, and Bulwer-Lytton, grew the social drama of Robertson, Pinero, and Shaw.

6. Charles Dickens, "The Amusements of the People," *Household Words* 1 (30 March 1850): 13.

East Lynne at the Alfred Theatre (LILLY LIBRARY)

While there are several significant studies of the literary dramas of the period[7] and an important analysis of Gothic drama,[8] comparatively little has been written about the popular stage,[9] and no full-length study of the domestic drama has yet been published despite the enormous influence of the genre on modern drama. This study is concerned only with domestic drama, and not with other types of "melodrama" *except* where they make a significant contribution to the study of domestic drama.

Reasons for the lack of scholarly criticism of domestic drama are not difficult to suggest. A major problem immediately confronts the researcher—that of finding texts. Paradoxically the moribund verse-dramas of the day are readily available, but of the thousands of illegitimate plays produced in the last century, comparatively few were ever published. There were several anthologies published serially during the last century. *Cumberland's British Theatre* was begun in 1826. Four volumes of *Richardson's New Minor Drama*, with prefaces by Moncrieff, appeared between 1828 and 1831. Ben Webster began editing a series entitled *Acting National Drama* in 1837. This series was published with the support of the Dramatic Authors' Society to forestall the wholesale piracy by Cumberland and other unscrupulous publishers.

The two most useful series of plays, often cited in this work, are John Dicks's *Dicks's Standard Plays* begun as late as 1875 and Thomas H. Lacy's invaluable *Acting Editions of Plays* (later French's), which were published from 1849 onwards. There are sixteen volumes in Dicks's set and

7. As, for example, Robert Fletcher, *English Romantic Drama, 1793–1843* (New York: Exposition Press, 1966), and Otten, *The Deserted Stage*.

8. Bertrand Evans, *Gothic Drama from Walpole to Shelley* (Berkeley, California: University of California Press, 1947).

9. David Grimsted's *Melodrama Unveiled*, (Chicago: University of Chicago Press, 1968) is a thorough examination of American melodrama. Frank Rahill's *The World of Melodrama* (University Park, Pennsylvania: Pennsylvania State University Press, 1967) deals with English, French, and American melodrama. There are two books for the general reader: Michael Booth's excellent *English Melodrama* (London: Herbert Jenkins, 1965), and Maurice Willson Disher's *Blood and Thunder* (London: Frederick Muller, 1949).

one hundred thirty-three in the series that French took over from Lacy. Over thirty more volumes were published by French before this series ended. Since the volumes in Lacy's and Dicks's series each contain about fifteen plays, well over two and a half thousand plays—many of them domestic dramas—are still accessible to the scholar. Were it not for these two series and library collections such as that of the Lilly Library at Indiana University, any serious study of domestic drama would be almost impossible in the United States.

The strongest deterrent to the scholarly study of domestic plays lies in the nature of the genre itself. Domestic drama does not lend itself to traditional literary analysis. Scholars, unwilling to describe repetitive themes, characters, and situations at length, are forced to investigate those ingredients of performance that account for the domestic drama's undoubted success on the stage. They must therefore try to explain to their own satisfaction why endlessly repeated characters, situations, and effects were so obviously popular. *Next Week*—East Lynne: *Domestic Drama in Performance 1820–1874* examines domestic drama on its own terms, without condescension, for only when the plays are treated with sympathy and understanding can we account for their extraordinary, popular success on the stage.

In order to understand how domestic drama became the dominant form of mass entertainment, it is first necessary to examine the theatrical conditions existing at the beginning of the nineteenth century. These conditions were unique. The "war" between the patent houses and the minor theaters, besides taking on the appearance at times of a vendetta, was a major reason why the melodrama, and later, the domestic drama, evolved as it did. Other factors, such as government censorship, the pitiful economic status of playwrights, and the absence of adequate copyright laws, all played a role in the evolution of domestic drama. So, also, did the audience, for its wishes constituted the most influential force exerted on the drama. As the Gothic genre moved into opera, so, too, was the aristocracy deserting the theaters. Soon the playhouses were under the control of an uneducated, unsophisticated, working class that insisted its dramas be written to a proven formula. The net result of all these forces was the domestic drama.

There are three main areas of concern in this examination of domestic drama itself. The first of these includes the observable characteristics of the genre, in particular: situation, character, setting, and spectacle. Attention is also paid to the character stereotypes and the significance of the process by which their popularity came to dictate much of the form and content of later dramas. The second area of concern is that of the dramas in performance and their manipulation of audience response by conventions of costume, make-up, and gesture. Finally, there is an analysis of the subject matter of the plays that reflected, however inadequately, England's change from a semifeudal to an increasingly democratic society.

It is only when these major aspects of domestic drama are given sympathetic consideration that many of the reasons for the popularity of these plays become clear. *Next Week—East Lynne* seeks not only to present insights into the nature of domestic drama, but also to recapture some of the thrills, vitality, humor, and excitement that were such an integral part of nineteenth-century theatergoing.

Next Week—*East Lynne*

1
THE CONDITION OF THE
THEATER QUESTION

Your Committee find that a considerable decline, both in the literature of the stage, and the taste of the public for theatrical performances, is generally conceded.

Select Committee, 1832[1]

SO LOW HAD DRAMA sunk in the esteem of its early nineteenth-century critics that a Select Parliamentary Committee was formed in 1832 to investigate the state of London's theaters. Edward Bulwer-Lytton was the chairman of this Select Committee, and he generally favored the cause of the minor theaters. Since the whole legal apparatus of theater control was subjected to careful scrutiny, the work of Bulwer-Lytton's committee gives a clear insight into the problems that beset both minor and major theaters and that brought about the conditions favorable to the rise

1. *Report of the Select Committee on Dramatic Literature* (London, 1832) paragraph 1.

of domestic drama. Of these conditions, none was more significant than the patent system that caused continuous warfare between theaters until about a decade before it was legally abolished in 1843.

It was during the third year of the Restoration that the system of theater monopoly began. In 1662 no one could have been expected to foresee the profound effect that the patent system would have on the drama and theater almost two centuries later. Charles II granted letters patent to Sir William Davenant and Thomas Killigrew who thought of a joint company, but this plan failed, and, as a consequence, two separate companies were formed. Killigrew established the King's Servants first at the Red Bull, then at Gibbon's Tennis Court. Meanwhile a new theater was under construction between Brydges Street and Drury Lane, and Killigrew's company occupied this theater on 7 May 1663.[2] Davenant took the Duke of York's Servants to the Duke's Theatre (first in Lincoln's Inn and later at Dorset Garden) and ultimately his patent was used by John Rich to open a theater in Covent Garden on 7 December 1732.

Thus for many years the two great theaters—Drury Lane and Covent Garden—enjoyed a monopoly of legitimate drama. All other theaters, except the Italian Opera House (which performed operas) and the Haymarket (which after 1766 received a patent for summer performances), had to give musical plays or dumbshow. It was from the attempts of the minors to circumvent the restrictions of the patents that domestic drama traces many of its most characteristic features.

The patents were not the sole form of control that the government exercised over theaters. Early laws, generally vagrancy acts, had been enacted, but in 1737 the first comprehensive act for licensing theaters and censoring plays became law. The Licensing Act was a very powerful weapon, and it strengthened the hands of the patent theaters. It also played a vital role in determining the form of

2. Alfred Harbage, *Thomas Killigrew: Cavalier Dramatist 1612–1688* (Lancaster, Pennsylvania: University of Pennsylvania Press, 1930), p. 118.

drama that would emerge at the nonpatent theaters. After 24 July 1737, no new play could be performed until a copy had been lodged at the Lord Chamberlain's office two weeks before its performance and it had received official approval.

The Lord Chamberlain's "Examiner of Plays" had the authority to require changes in a play or even to ban it entirely. The early nineteenth century was blessed by two of the most conservative examiners imaginable—John Larpent and George Colman. The latter held the office from 1824 until his death twelve years later. Some idea of the control the Examiner exercised can be gathered from a memorandum he sent Douglas Jerrold concerning *The Rent Day*. He asked that the underlined sections be omitted:

Act I, Scene I. "The blessed little babes, <u>God</u> bless 'em!" Scene III. "<u>Heaven</u> be kind to us, for I've almost lost all <u>other</u> hope." Ditto. "<u>Damn him.</u>" Scene IV. "<u>Damn business.</u>" "No, don't <u>damn</u> business. I'm very drunk, but I can't <u>damn</u> business—it's <u>profane.</u>" Ditto. "Isn't that an <u>angel?</u>" "<u>I can't tell; I've not been used</u> to such company." Scene V. "Oh, Martin, husband, <u>for the love of heaven!</u>" Ditto. "<u>Heaven help us, Heaven help us!</u>" Act II. Scene III. "<u>Heaven</u> forgive <u>you,</u> can you speak it?" "<u>I leave you, and may heaven pardon and protect you!</u>" Scene last. "Farmer, neighbours, <u>heaven</u> bless you—let the landlord take all the rest." Ditto. "They have not the money, and <u>heaven</u> prosper it with them."

G. Colman[3]

When questioned by the Select Committee, Colman admitted, with apparently genuine regret, that he had not been so punctilious as a dramatist himself.[4] Nevertheless, he was well aware that the standards of his youth had changed markedly, and indelicacy on the stage would no longer be tolerated. *The Literary Gazette* (20 July 1833) reported gleefully that *The Convent Belle*, (Adelphi, 1833), which Colman's office had licensed, had been condemned on its first appearance for "too much freedom of speech."[5]

3. Quoted in Dewey Ganzel, "Patent Wrongs and Patent Theatres: Drama and Law in the Early Nineteenth Century," *PMLA* 76, no. 4 (September 1961): 393.
4. *Report of the Select Committee*, paras. 860–61.
5. *The Literary Gazette* (20 July 1833), p. 460.

Under such a puritanical and scrupulous censorship, a comparatively innocuous drama was likely to emerge, and, as shall be seen in the final chapter, such was generally the case.

Any unlicensed play performed at a theater made the manager and each performer liable to a fifty-pound fine each time the play was performed. The Examiner of Plays, Colman, was questioned on this very point by the 1832 Committee. In reference to the theaters across the river he said:

> They are perfectly lawless; they only act under a common magistrate's license, which is to license music and dancing. . . .
>
> Do they bring pieces to you to be licensed or not?
>
> No, they set us at defiance; they are outlawed or at least lawless.
>
> Then have you no remedy?
>
> I suppose I have the same remedy as any common informer.[6]

Although the Lord Chamberlain could license all plays, Section V of the Licensing Act stated that "plays" could be performed only in Westminster and "places of His Majesties residence." For fifty years this was interpreted to mean that London dramatic performances could take place at Drury Lane and Covent Garden, and the patent theaters had had over a half century virtually free of competition. At rare moments, accommodations had been made.[7] In 1766, Samuel Foote was granted a patent for the Little Theatre in the Hay-Market, and was able to forego operating a chocolate house with "morning diversions." Foote's patent was restricted to the summer months (May 15 to September 15). Another accommodation had been reached in 1792, when, as a part of his attempt to secure Killigrew's patent, Sheridan entered into an agreement with the Opera House.

6. *Report of the Select Committee*, paras. 949–51.
7. Even so an act of Parliament had to be passed in 1752 giving local magistrates the power to license places of amusement for music and dancing (but *not* for drama). In 1787 John Palmer opened the Royalty on a magistrate's license with *As You Like It!*

The Opera House agreed that it would open only two nights a week to perform Italian opera.

The Patents, by their high-handed behavior and by their continued persecution of the minors, made many enemies. It was ironic, however, that they should suffer their first major setback from the Lord Chamberlain's office where they had traditionally found solid support. The Earl of Dartmouth had listened with a sympathetic ear to Henry Greville's idea for an English Opera House, possibly at the Pantheon. Though he had not felt able to approve the plan, especially since Greville had suggested that legitimate drama could be played two nights a week, he had revealed an inclination to weaken the monopoly of the patents. Dartmouth's partiality to the minors encouraged the opening of several theaters, who thus joined Sadler's Wells, Astley's, the Royal Circus, and the Royalty in catering to minor audiences. The Sans Pareil Theatre opened in 1806, and others followed suit. An article in *The Morning Chronicle* for 16 November 1807 gave a list of the various theaters preparing to open to the public (though some did not open as scheduled):

> The theatre, in Argyll-street;
> A theatre, in Tottenham Court-road;
> A theatre, in Berwick-street;
> A theatre, in Leicester-fields;
> Two theatres, at the Lyceum, in the Strand;
> The Pavilion in Wych-street. . . .[8]

Other theaters followed. In 1809, for example, the Lyceum received a license so the burned out Drury Lane Company could perform there. Prior to this, the Lyceum had been an exhibition room, a concert hall, and the home of Madame Tussaud's first London waxworks show.

The rising tide of minor theaters led to more strenuous efforts by the patent holders to close their rivals down. Magistrates were unable to act unless someone informed on oath that he had seen a performance contrary to the statute,

8. Quoted in Watson Nicholson, *The Struggle for a Free Stage in London* (Boston: Houghton, Mifflin and Co., 1906), p. 166.

and such informers were less common than might be supposed. It is believed that when he became lessee of Drury Lane, Robert W. Elliston, personally informed against the Coburg Theatre. Elliston was never one to do anything by halves. When lessee of the Royal Circus (renamed the Surrey Theatre) in 1809, he had produced *The Beaux' Stratagem* as a burletta and later *Macbeth* as "a grand ballet of action with music." The music consisted principally of a scarcely audible violin. Elliston also wrote to the Prime Minister and Parliament asking for a license and, interestingly enough, his reasons for wanting to operate a minor theater were excellent. However, when Elliston found himself lessee of Drury Lane in 1819, he changed his tune. Discovering that Junius Brutus Booth had given a few performances at the Coburg in late 1819 and early 1820, he filed an information against Joseph Glossop, its proprietor. Glossop issued a defiant retort in a playbill, which read in part:

> The Proprietors of the Two Patent Theatres taking Offence at the Attraction of this Gentleman [Booth], have thought proper to institute a PROSECUTION, by the way of INFORMATION, against the COBURG THEATRE for the *alleged offence of rationalizing their Performances*, and bringing them within that pale of Perfection which they would claim exclusively to themselves—how justly the public will decide—at all events, assured of their continued *Support and Patronage*, the Proprietors of the COBURG THEATRE will take every means in their Power to resist this attempt at abridging their sources of Amusement and instituting a Monopoly.[9]

Glossop's statement gained him many sympathizers, but he was still fined—half the money going to the informer, half to the parish. Such actions scarcely profited the patents, as the evidence of William Settle, a law clerk, revealed to the Select Committee. Asked what the cost of the proceeding against the Tottenham-street Theatre had been, he replied:

9. John Booth, *A Century of Theatrical History, 1816–1916: The "Old Vic."* (London: Stead's Publishing House, 1917), pp. 13–14.

About £700 or £800.

Do you know what they recovered from the defendant?

Not a shilling.[10]

Apart from fines, the power of the magistrates was very limited. Magistrates could always have a disorderly house suppressed, but a minor theater scarcely fitted the nineteenth-century definition of "disorderly." All a magistrate could do, in effect, was to refuse a license at the beginning of the year, and this was seldom done.

Legal restrictions, nevertheless, were steadily forcing the minor drama into a particular mold, and the drama that resulted was the ancestor of domestic drama. The mixture of dumbshow, music, and pantomine was frequently termed a *burletta*. The origin of the word *burletta* stems from the Italian *burlare*—to mock or jest; and the term *burla* was used to identify a piece of extended comic business in the *commedia dell'arte*. Dialogue was not permitted in the burletta at first, since dialogue was felt by the patents to be their sole preserve. They had shown their true colors when they haled Delpini, the Clown, before a magistrate for inadvertently saying "roast beef" in the middle of a pantomime, and the passage of time only confused the question of what could and could not be presented at a minor theater.

In many cases, it proved impossible to distinguish burlettas from melodramas or legitimate plays. J. B. Buckstone's *The Wreck Ashore*, (Adelphi, 1830), was licensed as a burletta,[11] yet it clearly possesses the attributes of a melodrama as defined by Madame Celeste, who became manager of the Adelphi in 1844: "Mystery, villainy, comic business, smugglers, caves, crossing of swords, firing of guns, lost daughters mysteriously recovered, shrieking their way into

10. *Report of the Select Committee*, paras. 3,539–40.
11. Minor theaters resorted to many expedients to prove that a musical entertainment rather than a dramatic one was taking place. At the Sans Pareil, for instance, a piano rose up occasionally through a trap to remind the audience that they were attending a musical performance.

Adelphi playbill describing Buckstone's *The Wreck Ashore* as a "domestic burletta" (LILLY LIBRARY)

their father's arms, hair-breadth perils, executions, reprieves."[12] As productions became more elaborate, it became increasingly impossible to distinguish a burletta from a play with music. As a result, songs were constantly added to versions of legitimate dramas in an effort to pass them off as burlettas.

From 1809 to 1818 the only question to be raised about a burletta was how much music was to accompany the dialogue. By 1818, it was generally believed that the Lord Chamberlain defined a burletta as having at least five songs per act.[13] The Select Committee questioned several witnesses to see if a definition of burletta could be agreed upon. Two witnesses defined a burletta as "recitative and music," but David Morris, part-proprietor of the Haymarket, was more specific. He stated that "Mr. Colman, the licenser, has established what is to constitute burletta; it is, I believe, five or six songs."[14] To earn a license for a play, all that a manager had to do was to send over a manuscript including any six songs that happened to be handy. When the play was actually performed, there was no guarantee that the songs would be included in the performance. During a normal production, a pretense could be kept up by the use of a piano accompaniment, or the striking of a few chords, but it was clear that, by 1832, the theatrical patents had proved to be as ineffective as the licensing laws of the day.

After the Select Committee had finished its work, Bulwer-Lytton introduced a bill to remove the legal restrictions on the minor theaters and to check the censorship powers of the Lord Chamberlain. A copyright provision was included. The bill succeeded in the Commons but failed in the Lords where the patent holders rallied more support. The defeat of the bill was, as it transpired, a victory for the minor theaters. The amount of popular support that had

12. Quoted in J. O. Bailey's *British Plays of the Nineteenth Century* (New York: Odyssey Press, 1966), p. 32.

13. Ernest Bradlee Watson, *Sheridan to Robertson: A Study of the Nineteenth-century London Stage* (Cambridge, Massachusetts: Harvard University Press, 1926), pp. 35. 39.

14. *Report of the Select Committee, para. 2,460.*

been forthcoming made it clear to the majors that they should not force a showdown with their rivals. Although legally the patent system dragged on until 1843, it was virtually a dead issue by 1832. After that date any serious playwright could give his plays to any theater he wished. Actors could then find homes in minor theaters and achieve star billing on the grounds of their own merit.

When Sir James Graham introduced and carried the 1843 bill, it was something of an anticlimax. The Patents lost legally what they had virtually already lost in fact. They retained the privilege of not having to secure an annual license, but Parliament had showed its power over royal patents. Minor-theater lessees were free to present the classics of the English stage. Many minor-theater managers perhaps foresaw the end of the melodrama, since the burletta was no longer legally necessary. They soon found themselves to be in error. A brief flirtation with Shakespeare soon revealed that audiences, forced to subsist on melodrama and local talent, had developed a definite taste for the lowly form. This was the most significant and far-reaching effect of the theater war; it created an audience with firmly established views on what was acceptable and what was not. Drama was in a straitjacket from which it did not free itself for fifty years. Only one theater manager, Samuel Phelps of Sadler's Wells, succeeded in making Shakespeare less than "caviar to the general." All other lessees turned their attention firmly to making an accommodation with melodrama and farce. Though extracts and even complete classics were not infrequently seen in minor theaters, there was no longer any illusion that the London working-class audience had a natural affinity with Shakespeare.

The nature of melodrama and consequently of domestic drama was also affected by the ease with which successful French plays could be "adapted" for the English audience. Plays of foreign dramatists especially of Guilbert de

Pixérécourt and August von Kotzebue at first dominated nineteenth-century English drama. Fully one half of the plays written between 1800 and 1850 were either suggested by Paris models or literally adapted by English playwrights.[15] While it is doubtful that Pixérécourt and his compatriots added anything original to English drama, they did popularize "type characterization, thrilling plot, contrast of dark villainy and purest innocence, [and helped] to establish definitely on the English stage all the tricks and devices of the melodramatic style."[16] A writer in *The Quarterly Review* presented a typical lament of the day:

> It is equally curious and mortifying to remark that, in most cases of the announcement of a new and successful piece, its French parentage is openly avowed and credit taken for the skill displayed in its adaptation to a British audience. Nor is it any defense or palliation of the debt that our elder dramatists were equally indebted to Italian or Spanish originals. They were indebted to Italian or Spanish novels doubtless, though seldom until such novels had passed by translation into popular belief and favour; but the dramatic treatment of the stories was original, and had not been anticipated by the librettos of the Variétés and Porte St. Martin.[17]

Economically speaking it made little or no sense for an author to slave away at writing an original work when he could get the same amount for two French translations done in a week or two. The effect on the dramatist's skill and the state of the drama can readily be seen. Dickens satirized the practice in *Nicholas Nickleby* in a scene where Nicholas protested to Mr. Crummles that he lacked the invention to produce a play. Originality was quickly dismissed:

> "Invention! what the devil's that got to do with it?" cried the manager, hastily.
>
> "Everything, my dear sir."

15. Allardyce Nicoll, *A History of Early Nineteenth-century Drama*, 2 vols. (Cambridge, England: Cambridge University Press, 1960), 1: 79.
16. Ibid., p. 81.
17. "Dramatic Register for 1853," *The Quarterly Review* 95 (July 1854): 40.

"Nothing, my dear sir," retorted the manager, with evident impatience.

"Do you understand French?"[18]

It was reported, less in jest perhaps than it should have been, that at the Princess's all the light pieces were translated from the French by a hack who was chained by the leg to his desk. Dion Boucicault, the most famous melodramatist of the day, learned about the economic woes of his profession early. When he offered a new play to a manager, he was told that a hundred pounds was all he might expect. Selling the play, Boucicault accepted a commission to translate three French plays at fifty pounds each, since he could not, at first, make a living by writing original dramas. It is small wonder that melodramas were written rapidly with little care and to an established pattern.

Everything was grist to the mill of the early nineteenth-century dramatists. Novels provided a ready source of plots. At first French sources were chosen, but native talent soon became popular. Isaac Pocock wrote several plays based on Sir Walter Scott's works. *Rob Roy MacGregor; or, Auld Lang Syne!* was presented at Covent Garden in 1818. The same theater saw *The Antiquary* in 1820, *Montrose; or, The Children of the Mist* in 1822, and *Nigel; or, The Crown Jewels* in 1823. The latter was quickly prepared in order to forestall a Drury Lane production from the same novel. Almost all the Waverley novels were presented on stage. *The Heart of Midlothian* appeared in versions by T. J. Dibdin, W. Dimond, Montague and Jervis, W. H. Murray, W. R. Osman, Archibald McLaren, D. Terry, and an unknown author. Captain Rafter's version was based upon a French dramatization of the novel. *Ivanhoe* was even more popular—five versions were played in 1820.[19]

Charlotte Brontë suffered a similar fate. Her novel, *Jane Eyre*, was published in 1847, and dramatized by John

18. Charles Dickens, *Nicholas Nickleby* (London: Oxford University Press, 1950), chap. 23.

19. The best book on the subject is H. A. White's *Scott's Novels on the Stage* (New Haven, Connecticut: Yale University Press, 1927).

Brougham within a few weeks. This play, called *Jane Eyre; or, The Secrets of Thornfield Manor House*, was licensed for the Victoria in January 1848. Another version, or perhaps the same one, was published by Dicks (number 400) and described on the title page as "first performed at Laura Keene's Varieties, New York in 1856." This play was also licensed for the Surrey in 1867. An anonymous version was licensed in 1877 for performance in Coventry. T. H. Paul's only play was called simply *Jane Eyre* and was licensed for the Adelphi, Oldham, in 1879[20] In this same year, J. T. Douglass (who used the not insignificant *nom de plume* "James Willing") finished a play for the Park Theatre entitled *Poor Relations; or, Jane Eyre*. Three years later yet another version, by William G. Wills, was licensed for the Globe Theatre.

Charles Dickens became a popular source of material from *The Pickwick Papers* onwards. He offered his readers a great deal more vital than the outworn conventions of the Gothic and the sentimental. Some working-class readers would read Dickens directly, but his characters became familiar from the innumerable stage adaptations. Dramatists paid little attention to the novelist's plots, concentrating instead on the characters. William Leman Rede began *The Peregrinations of Pickwick* after eight numbers of *The Pickwick Papers* had been issued, and the play itself made its debut at the Adelphi on 3 April 1837.[21] Expecting his novel, *Oliver Twist* to be popular, Dickens made a proposal to Frederick Yates, manager of the Adelphi, to adapt the work himself. Though this scheme fell through, at least eleven versions of *Oliver Twist* came out between 1838 and 1868.[22]

20. Ernest Reynolds, *Early Victorian Drama, 1830–1870* (Cambridge, England: W. Heffer and Sons, Ltd., 1936), p. 145.

21. Louis James, *Fiction for the Working Man, 1830–1850* (London: Oxford University Press, 1963), p. 49. James says that the play was performed in October 1836, but it was not licensed until April 1837.

22. Malcolm Morley noted that a speech from *Pickwick* turned up in a 1929 version of *Sweeney Todd*. See "Dickens's Contribution to *Sweeney Todd*," *Dickensian* 58 (Spring 1962): 94.

It appears that Dickens had supplied the manuscript of *The Cricket on the Hearth* to Albert Smith and was suitably rewarded. A skit by G. Bolton, *The Civil War of Poetry,* (Olympic, 1846), includes the lines:

> I'm working on an adaptation. . . .
> But, as we'd have it represented
> Before our rivals, we've succeeded
> In getting Boz's leave to read it
> In Manuscript (of course you know
> That golden reasons work'd him so).[23]

It thus appears that Dickens, always the businessman, had decided to make a virtue of necessity.

The constant adaptation of novels did not help the craft of playwriting. A type of drama arose that ignored subtleties of character and situation and concentrated upon stringing together a series of episodes. Incidents were ferreted out that would be both exciting and appealing, but no time was devoted to close examination of character and motivation. Eventually, the only element that mattered to the dramatizers of the classics of English fiction (and, indeed, English poetry) was plot in which stock characters could be set.

Even more exciting incidents were found in newspapers. The rise of mass-circulation newspapers and magazines was a notable feature of the nineteenth century, and dramatists found untold wealth in their pages. Among London sources for *Maria Marten; or, The Murder in the Red Barn* were *The Annual Register, The Gentleman's Magazine, John Bull, The Times, The Sunday Times,* and *The Morning Herald.* Press accounts lacked the detail found in novels, but this deficiency could be remedied by linking several incidents together in a continuous sequence. Colin Hazlewood's method of composition goes a long way toward explaining why so many plays were produced that were devoid of literary merit. It was Hazlewood's daily habit to read all the stories in the cheap penny magazines dealing with lurid crimes and the newspapers. He would cut out

23. Nicoll, 1: 99.

speeches and file them alphabetically by subjects such as "benevolence," "courage," or "loyalty." When dictating a play, he would judiciously throw in slips at the right moment. Charles Reade employed a similar method. Once a week he would spend a day with his scrapbooks. Armed with a pair of scissors, he would cut out pictures and articles. Then he would arrange them, paste them in his scrapbooks, and index them carefully. It is said that he could find any article he wanted because he had been so thorough in his indexing.

Virtually no form of artistic integrity could exist in the early days of the domestic drama. Boucicault modified the ending of *The Octoroon* to suit national prejudices. In the English version, the play ended happily in miscegenation, in the American, Zoë, the Octoroon, took poison. He even had some playbills announce that the last act of the play had been "composed by the public and edited by the author."[24] Boucicault was also particularly adept in borrowing a plot from one source and effects from another. He had few scruples and calmly borrowed the "sensation" scene from Augustin Daly's *Under the Gaslight*, (New York, 1867), which had the hero tied to the railroad tracks and rescued at the last moment. Boucicault stole this scene for his play *After Dark: A Tale of London Life*, (Princess's, 1868). When reproached on the matter, he pointed out that his scene was quite different because it was set in the new subway system of London. Needless to say, the significance of the change in settings was less apparent to others than it was to Boucicault.

A further prominent feature of early nineteenth-century drama was the rapidity and frequency with which plays were dashed off, for the playwright's concern had to be firmly fixed on the present and not on posterity. George Dibdin Pitt wrote twenty-five plays in 1847. Thomas J. Dibdin wrote forty-two pieces for the Surrey between 1825 and 1826. Plays were always in demand, for a run of one

24. Quoted in Maurice Willson Disher, *Melodrama: Plots that Thrilled* (London: Rockliff and Co., [1954]), p. 7.

month was considered good. Most plays never got beyond the manuscript stage, and all were liable to be changed around to suit the talents of a particular theater company. Therefore, there was never any guarantee that a play would be performed or published as it had been written by the author.

What the nineteenth-century dramatist needed most of all was financial independence. Authors were wretchedly paid, and many were happy to be resident hacks for a few pounds weekly. Douglas Jerrold, who wrote *Black Ey'd Susan*, (Surrey, 1829), received sixty pounds for a play that made thousands. Thomas Potter Cooke, the actor who played William in the play, got the same amount for one week's acting. R. W. Elliston, who had been lessee of the Surrey for less than two years,[25] found his fortune made yet had the effrontery to suggest to the playwright that his friends should buy Jerrold some silver plate! Edward Stirling learned the same bitter lesson:

> It occurred to me to try my hand at writing a piece for a benefit. The subject I chose was "Sadak and Kalasrade." It was beautifully placed on the stage, and the scenery painted by William Beverley, the eminent artist. Beverley cleared one thousand pounds by this piece: I received sixty. Fortune smiled; my pen now went at tip-top speed—pieces written and produced plentiful as blackberries—quantity rather than quality was the order of the day.[26]

Prices paid for dramatic pieces had plummeted since the eighteenth century, and they continued to fall throughout the first half of the nineteenth. In 1773, Goldsmith had received a handsome sum for *She Stoops to Conquer*, and even in the period 1800–1810, Frederic Reynolds was averaging four to five hundred pounds a play. James

25. For the story of Elliston's seven years as lessee of Drury Lane *see* Alfred L. Nelson and Gilbert Cross, eds., *Drury Lane Journal: Selections from James Winston's Diaries 1819–1827* (London: Society for Theatre Research, 1974).

26. Edward Stirling, *Old Drury Lane: Fifty Years' Recollections of Author, Actor, Manager*, 2 vols. (London: Chatto and Windus, 1881), 1: 76.

Sheridan Knowles got four hundred pounds for his famous *Virginius*, and Dion Boucicault three hundred for *London Assurance*, (Covent Garden, 1841). Admittedly patent theaters paid better than the minors, and they also followed the older practice of paying one hundred pounds to an author on the third, sixth, ninth, and fortieth nights. However, what the Patents professed to do was not always what they could do. James Kenney, who was the author of the very popular opera, *Masaniello*, (Covent Garden, 1829), received nothing because the theater went bankrupt.[27] For obvious reasons the minors paid much less than their great rivals. George Davidge, who was manager of the Coburg in 1832, said that he paid about twenty pounds for a new piece.[28] As has been already noted, Jerrold received only fifty pounds for *Black Ey'd Susan* and ten pounds for the copyright.

> The selling of the copyright for what it would fetch was rendered necessary as there was a dealer in new plays who provided provincial managers with copies of London successes at two pounds a play, by means of which, as he said, the authors were represented by mere skeletons of their dramas, and were, in fact, not only robbed, but murdered. His payment for *The Rent Day*, he said, was £150 paid on the twenty-fifth night of the performance.[29]

Clearly a first-rank literary drama could not emerge under such conditions. When dramatists are forced to write a play a month, it is quantity alone that counts. It appears that Dion Boucicault may have used a pen name in order to disguise the number of plays he was actually writing:

> Since only a pittance was paid to dramatic authors, Boucicault was forced to furious productivity. In 1844 under his own name he provided various companies with seven plays. The

27. Kenney claimed the theater was Drury Lane (*Report of the Select Committee*, para. 4,075), but the work was licensed for Covent Garden. Covent Garden had a receiver appointed in 1829.

28. *Report of the Select Committee*, para. 1,260.

29. Walter Jerrold, *Douglas Jerrold: Dramatist and Wit*, 2 vols. (London: Hodder and Stoughton, 1914), 1: 204.

appearance of *Judith* as by Lee Moreton may be laid to one of two motives—for some reason he did not wish his other managers to know that he was writing for the Adelphi, or, more likely, eight productions in a year might cause even the popular audience to suspect the quality of what it was seeing. The authors of detective stories in our own time have been known to resort to such stratagems. Certainly such early experiences, such desperate attempts to make a living from his chosen profession, had much to do with the reforms which Boucicault later instituted: royalties, the long-run system, etc.[30]

Adequate copyright protection would clearly have been of great significance in the first years of the nineteenth century. Authors could have written less, been much more independent, and could have produced better plays, but literary copyright did not protect plays, since a performance did not necessitate making a copy of a work. Common law theoretically protected an unpublished play, but once a play was published or printed, the common-law copyright expired.[31] Davidge was asked by the Select Committee if an author had a right to any remuneration from country theaters:

No; when once the piece is published, it becomes . . . (out of London at least) public property. All persons who can get a copy of the piece play it without advantage to the author or the person who holds the copyright.[32]

In any case, the law was of little help to the penniless. An author getting two to three pounds a week was not going to sue in the courts. A manager who was on the brink of disaster was scarcely worth suing, for he could not pay a fine. By the beginning of the nineteenth century, Parliament had recognized the right of the proprietors of a literary work to prevent others from copying it. However, such

30. Alan Downer, "The Case of Mr. Lee Moreton," *Theatre Notebook* 4, no. 2 (January–March 1950): 44.
31. Thomas Morton told the Select Committee that George Colman, Snr., had even lost an action because the judge ruled that a performance was a publication. *Report of the Select Committee*, para. 2,537.
32. *Report of the Select Committee*, para. 1,234.

protection did not help a dramatist because it was generally believed that performing a play was not the same as making a copy of it.[33]

Several dramatists, under the leadership of James Robinson Planché, joined forces to change their situation. Planché had been angered at the Edinburgh production of one of his plays from a stolen manuscript. He and his supporters persuaded Parliament to enact the Dramatic Copyright Act, which received the royal assent on 10 June 1833. To enforce the provisions of the Act, the Dramatic Authors' Society was founded. A similar practice already existed in France and was doubtless the inspiration for the English system. Henceforth, authors often published plays that proclaimed that they were members of the Dramatic Authors' Society. Additional warnings were sometimes added as, for example, on the title page to John Wilkins's *Civilization*, (City of London, 1852):

> Notice—This Play being the sole property of Messrs. Johnson and Nelson Lee, it cannot be acted without their permission; or the full amount allowed by the Copyright Act will be charged.

The law gave the dramatist, or his assignee, the sole liberty of presenting an unpublished play. A play published or printed since 1833 could only be produced if an author gave his permission. This last stipulation was limited to twenty-eight years from publication with a reversionary period to the author for the rest of his life. Penalties were established with a minimum fine of two pounds for each illegal performance.

Many problems arose. The Dramatic Authors' Society could not police all the theaters to check on illegal performances. Booksellers who purchased publishing rights also claimed to have bought dramatic rights. The act, of course, had no power outside Great Britain so that American pro-

33. Douglas Jerrold told the Select Committee that if the literary copyright extended to drama "it would induce men of original talent to write for the stage." *Report of the Select Committee*, para. 2,831.

ductions did not help British playwrights. Nevertheless, the 1833 Act did provide a measure of financial independence for an author and consequently improved the status of the drama. In 1842 copyright laws were further amended in an Act that specifically stated that the assignment of a copyright of a dramatic piece did not convey the right of representation. Thus, the right to "multiply copies" was separated from the right to give performances. Curiously, the Act did not prevent anyone from dramatizing a non-dramatic work, thus the wholesale piracy of novels continued unabated throughout the century.

It would be a mistake to assume that the dramatists' situation changed suddenly with the passage of a copyright act. Little or no money came from publishers' fees, for, as Douglas Jerrold had pointed out in 1832, "the public have ceased to look upon plays as part of the literature of the country."[34] Without financial independence, authors could never write to please themselves. They were totally at the mercy of managers and audiences, and the practical playwright wrote to please his masters. The failure of copyright acts to reduce significantly the dependence of authors upon others made it clear that the only lasting solution to the financial plight of authors was a system of royalties. In France, Beaumarchais had been instrumental in establishing royalty payments and had made a fortune out of *The Marriage of Figaro*. After the Revolution, the French theaters seem to have returned to individual arrangements. Vigorous action by the *Comité des Auteurs*, led by Pixérécourt, resulted in a standard ten percent royalty payment—an achievement that perhaps had something to do with the superiority of French drama over English. Dion Boucicault played a major role in winning royalties for British authors. After the success of *The Colleen Bawn*, (Laura Keene's, 1860), Boucicault offered it to Benjamin Webster at the Adelphi. The author-producer hired his own cast and arranged all the details. Webster cooperated because it was clear that if he did not, someone else would. The play ran

34. *Report of the Select Committee*, para. 2,833.

for three hundred sixty nights, the Queen visited the Adelphi twice, and Boucicault netted some ten thousand pounds. Following up on his success, Boucicault sent out his own road companies instead of selling the rights to provincial managers.[35] By 1870, royalties had become widespread, and Bronson Howard, the American, became the first playwright to make a fortune, in 1889, from the royalties of one play, *Shenandoah*. Henry Pettitt, who wrote between 1870 and the end of the century, left an estate of £50,000 upon his death.[36]

Royalties and copyright laws were of vital significance to the development of domestic drama. For the first time texts became fixed. Hitherto a playwright had sold his play outright and had no say in what happened to it. As has already been noted, Boucicault claimed to have edited the last act of *The Octoroon* after it had been "written" by the audience. In his memoirs, *Forty Years on the Stage*, J. H. Barnes wrote that in Boucicault's *London Assurance*, the moral lesson of the play, commonly referred to as a "tag," came from the character Sir Harcourt, an old roué and libertine: this state of affairs was brought about by the actor William Farren, who positively refused to play the part unless he spoke the honest man's tag. Boucicault offered no objection to assigning a speech wholly out of character to Sir Harcourt.[37]

It is not to be supposed that years of theater tradition changed overnight. One of the problems with a play was that it frequently traveled in manuscript. No "correct" published text existed. Often a play might be sent in "lengths" (of forty-two lines), or in parts. It was not unusual for a company to sit up all night trying to get a manuscript in shape for the next day's performance. However, a dramatist was now more willing to publish since some protection was

---

35. Frank Rahill, "Dion Boucicault and the Royalty Payment for Playwrights," *Theatre Arts* 23, no. 11 (November 1939), 811.

36. Ibid., p. 812.

37. J. H. Barnes, *Forty Years on the Stage: Others (Principally) and Myself* (London: Chapman and Hall, Ltd., 1914), pp. 43–44.

available. He had the legal right to insist that his text remained unmutilated, even if he could seldom enforce it.

Royalty payments made it increasingly possible for dramatists to make a living from the stage and, thus, to concentrate all their efforts on being successful in their chosen profession. Prior to the time when copyright made it possible for them to become full-time dramatists, many playwrights had held other jobs. Planché had worked in a government office; Tom Taylor was a journalist; Mark Lemon kept a tavern; Douglas Jerrold wrote for *Punch*. Even Boucicault found it necessary to become an actor for a time. There was no sudden enfranchisement; the process of becoming financially independent was a slow one. Most never achieved success. Charles Somerset, author of over thirty plays, was seen in his declining years wearing a placard inscribed, "Ladies and Gentlemen, I am starving."

As a profession, playwriting did not have much to offer the serious writer:

> There was no temptation for the poet or the novelist to turn playwright. Playwriting was an unhonoured, unrewarding, and unlucrative profession. Even to the journeyman playwrights who catered to the public taste for burlesque, the most popular form of dramatic entertainment, the theatre brought little financial benefit. J. R. Planché, author or part-author of fifty-seven extravaganzas and more than a hundred farces, melodramas, comedies, and opera libretti, was still in harness at the age of seventy-six and glad of a Civil List pension at £100. When Robert Brough, author of innumerable popular and often revived burlesques, died in 1860, although he lived laborious days and was chargeable with no improvidence, he left his wife and children dependent on the proceeds of a benefit performance at which five London companies that had been indebted to his pen took part.[38]

Even writers like Maturin abandoned the legitimate drama in favor of melodramas fetching fifty pounds at best. There *were* some dramatists who made a fair living from the stage. George Colman, J. M. Morton, "Monk" Lewis, and

38. Lynton Hudson, *The English Stage, 1850–1950* (London: Harrap and Co., [1951]), p. 24.

the Dibdins in the 1800s—Fitzball, Moncrieff, J. B. Buckstone, and Boucicault later—but they were exceptions rather than the rule, and bankruptcy was seldom far off.

As long as playwrights remained as resident dramatists at the various London theaters, it was to be expected that the quality of drama would be strained. Edward Fitzball was the resident playwright at the Surrey during the forties. Payments were low. John Wilkins at the City of London got thirty-five shillings a week and Colin Hazlewood sixty at the Britannia. Thomas Dibdin worked at Drury Lane for some time as an adapter of manuscripts. As a play came in, he examined it for possibilities of production. Frederic Reynolds was doing something similar at Covent Garden. He wrote:

> What was the name of my situation, however, I could never learn. Some called me "whipper-in to the tragedians," many "ferret to the painters and composers," and others "maid of all work" to the manager, who himself called me *thinker*, at the same time kindly allowing me, without injury to my morals, to be a *free* thinker. But though I cannot attach a name to the officer, I can say something of the office, which certainly was no sinecure, having to suggest or to execute through the whole year any project that might be conducive to the success of the treasury.[39]

This playhouse tinkering with texts to ensure that they would suit the actors available was another attempt to stave off financial disaster.

The patent theaters were even more financially hard pressed than most since they continued the disastrous policy, imitated by a few of the minors, of keeping three companies. As early as 1809, John Kemble had engaged three distinct companies at Covent Garden. One company was for comedy and farce, another for tragedy, and a third for opera and ballet. In the course of an evening, less than half of the actors would be engaged, but all had to be paid since they were contracted for the season. By 1841–1842, Covent Garden still kept a large staff, as George Vandenhoff noted:

39. Quoted in Dutton Cook, *On the Stage: Studies of Theatrical History and the Actor's Art*, 2 vols. (London: Sampson Low and Co., 1883), 1: 132.

GENTLEMEN

Acting and Stage Manager:

Mr. Geo. Bartley, acting and stage manager, with a great variety of business; the bluff, hearty old man, pères nobles, Falstaff, etc.

Light Comedy and Eccentrics:

Charles Mathews (Lessee), Walter Lacy, F. Vining.

Leading Business:

Geo. Vandenhoff.   John Cooper.

Old Men:

Wm. Farren.   F. Matthews.   C. W. Granby.

Low Comedy:

J. P. Harley.   D. Meadows.

Irish Characters:

John Brougham.

Heavy Business:

C. Diddear.   J. Bland.

Walking Gentlemen [i.e., beginners]

C. Selby.   A. Wigan.   H. Bland.

Pantomine and General Business:

Messrs. Payne.   Messrs. Morelli.
  ″   Honner.   ″   J. Ridgway.
  ″   T. Ridgway.

LADIES:

Mrs. Nisbett.   Madame Vestris.   Mrs. Glover.
Mrs. W. Lacy.   Mrs. H. Bland.   Mrs. Brougham.

Miss Cooper.	Miss Lea.	Mrs. S. C. Jones.
Mrs. Selby.	Mrs. W. West.	

Columbine:

Two Miss Kendalls, with a large Corps de Ballet.

Opera:

In addition to the above we had
regularly engaged to support

Miss A. Kemble,

Messrs, Harrison, Bynge, and Horncastle, *tenors*.
Mr. Stretton, *baritone*.
Messrs. Borrani and Leffler, *bass*; and a fine Chorus.[40]

With companies of this size, to say nothing of the army of
stagehands required to mount a production, authors were
forced to write or adapt plays that would use up as much of
the available talent as possible. Although the minors did not
have the right to produce legitimate drama until 1843,
they, too, were overstaffed. Heavy overheads dominated
managerial concerns. For scenic effects in a large theater,
as many as a hundred "carpenters" (mainly scene shifters),
thirty gasmen, and a dozen property men might be required. When Madame Vestris managed Covent Garden,
she had a payroll of almost seven hundred. Covent Garden
had not made a profit since 1820, claimed a witness before
the Select Committee.[41] Indeed, for several years prior to
1820, only the pantomine had kept the theater solvent. This
fact is hardly surprising considering that Covent Garden
then had over one thousand people directly dependent
upon it, and that this number often doubled at the height
of the season.

The constant struggle to remain solvent led to other prac-
tices inimical to artistic integrity. Any play that proved suc-

40. George Vandenhoff, *Leaves from an Actor's Note-Book* (New York: D. Appleton and Co., 1860), pp. 121–22.
41. *Report of the Select Committee*, para. 1,726.

cessful at one house was certain to attract the envious attention of other theaters. A play could be commissioned on the
same subject—four versions of *Oliver Twist* were licensed
in 1838–1839—or downright robbery was attempted by
means of a play-pirate. Such gentlemen led dangerous lives,
but often succeeded in taking down a garbled version of a
play from one or two performances. All that was needed
then, at most, was a change of name and setting. Charles
Mathews told the Select Committee:

> For instance, I have paid, in conjunction with my partner [of
> the Adelphi] a certain sum for a piece called *The Wreck Ashore*
> [by J. B. Buckstone, 1830], and I saw it advertised to be acted
> at the Queen's Theatre, *sans cérémonie*. It is true I sent a re-
> monstrance to them by a lawyer, and that particular piece was
> stopped, but that very night a piece of ours was played, called
> *The Bold Dragoons* [by Morris Barnett, 1830] which was acted
> under the title of *The Dragoons of Normandy*. They send short-
> hand writers into the pit of the theatre now, and instead of
> the prompter getting that which was formerly considered his
> perquisite, they steal it without any ceremony at all, and it has
> become a kind of property among book sellers and
> adventurers.[42]

Writing a rival play was only a shade more honest than
piracy. When Edward Fitzball wrote *The Red Rover; or,
The Mutiny of the Dolphin*, (Adelphi, 1829), it was followed
within three weeks by another version by R. T. Weaver
written for Sadler's Wells. Before the end of the year, a
version by an unknown author had been produced at the
Surrey. Sometimes little more than names were changed. A
provincial theater proudly announced a play called *The Red
Barn; or, The Murdered Maid*. This is clearly a rival version
of *Maria Marten; or, The Murder in the Red Barn*. The
name Marten was changed to Marlin, Corder to Corvill,
and some supernumaries added.

Compounding the problems that authors faced in the
nineteenth century was the problem of writing for a stock
company. Professional writers, since the time of Shakes-

---

42. *Report of the Select Committee*, para. 3,045.

The Red
BARN!

OR, THE

Murdered Maid!

Corvill, the Murderer .... Mr E. H. FAUCIT
Farmer Marlin .... Mr MASTERMAN
Francis .... Mr THOMPSON
Catchpole .... Mr YOUNG
Trap .... Mr YARNOLD
Officer .... Mr WILLIAMS

Peasants, Villagers, &c.

Maria Marlin, the Pride of the Village .... Miss SIBERY
Mrs. Corvill .... Mrs HOWELL
Dame Marlin .... Mrs MASTERMAN

The first Scene discovers Dame Marlin anxiously waiting the return of Maria from an

Interview with Corvill.

Dame entreats Corvill to repair the injuries by Marriage—he consents—appoints a meeting
with her, (disguised in Male attire) at

THE RED BARN,

Where he accomplishes his long premeditated design of murdering his

Unfortunate Victim.

ACT 2,—Dame discovered asleep—the ghost of Maria enters—invokes a blessing on her—conducts
her to the Red Barn, and vanishes

IN A FLAME OF FIRE

Dame entreats her husband to search the Barn, where the Murdered Body is discovered.

Corvill's Splendid Marriage.

When he is apprehended, and borne away to prison—Fatal Denument.

Tickets may be had of Mrs. Masterman, 5, Horner's-Square, and of the Printer.

☞ A Full and Efficient **Orchestre,** under the direction of **Mr. G. Leng**
is engaged, and will play several favorite Airs and Overtures.

Prices——Boxes, 2s.—Pit, 1s.—Gallery, 6d.   Half-price,——Boxes, 1s.—Pit, 6d.

J. HOWE, PRINTER, 3, SCALE-LANE (near High-Street) HULL.

Provincial theater playbill advertising a rival version of *Maria
Marten* (LILLY LIBRARY)

peare, had faced the problem of writing parts for available actors, but never to the extent faced by nineteenth-century playwrights. The *dramatis personae* of Colin Hazlewood's *Waiting for the Verdict; or, Falsely Accused*, (City of London, 1859), gave the parts to members of the company by "line of business."

Lord Viscount Elmore	—Second walking gentleman
Lieutenant Florville	—Juvenile [lead]
Humphrey Higson	—Second low comedy
Blinkey Brown	—First low comedy
Sir Henry Harrington	—Responsible
Jonas Hundle	—First heavy man
Jonathan Roseblade	—First old man
Jasper Roseblade	—Leading man
Rev. Owen Hylton	—Second old man
Grange	—Utility
Thorpe	—Utility
Lord Chief Justice	—Very responsible
Serjeant Stanley	—Second heavy man
Grafston	—First walking gentleman
The Sheriff	—Responsible
Martha Roseblade	—Leading lady
Sarah Sawyer	—Chambermaid[43]
Mrs. Burnly	—Utility[44]

Characters such as the Jew, the Irishman, the Frenchman, and the madman were all lines of business. Such characters were instantly recognizable upon their first appearance. As the irrepressible Vincent Crummles pointed out to Nicholas Nickleby, Smike's possibilities were limitless:

Without a pad upon his body, and hardly a touch of paint upon his face, he'd make such an actor for the starved business as was never seen in this country. Only let him be tolerably well up in the Apothecary in *Romeo and Juliet* with the slightest possible dab of red on the top of his nose, and he'd be certain

43. The "chambermaid" was better known by the French word *soubrette*.
44. Colin Hazlewood, "Waiting for the Verdict," *Lacy's Acting Editions of the Plays* 99 (London: T. H. Lacy, [1849–1917]): 2.

of three rounds [of applause] the moment he put his head out of the practicable door in the front grooves O. P. [opposite the prompter].[45]

A natural concomitant of the "stylized business" approach to acting was the concept of "stars and sticks." Under this system a starring role was merely supported by feeble utility roles. The Select Committee inquired of John Payne Collier:

> [Has] the star system that has been adopted by the two great theatres . . . been hostile to dramatic literature especially to any new plays?

> [Collier] Certainly, insomuch as it induces authors to write plays for particular actors, instead of composing them for a whole company capable of representing them, insomuch, too, as it induces managers of theatres to neglect all the inferior parts of plays, and to rely entirely on one performer.[46]

Theatrical jealousies were immensely strengthened by the stars-and-sticks philosophy, and again the drama and dramatist suffered, as Jerrold complained:

> Every puppet is his *own* manager! The playwright must propitiate, flatter, and succumb to—*actors!* To transmit a drama *direct* to head quarters is an unpardonable breach of theatrical etiquette; Mr. Jenkins must just glance his eye over it, to see if every character be made subordinate to *his* monopolizing ascendency . . . if [not] . . . forthwith [Jenkins] seizes his critical tomahawk, lops off the redundances and what he appropriates not to his particular use, like a loathsome weed, indignantly casts away. This mutilation of his scenes the playwright *must* submit to, if he would enlist the mirthmoving shrugs and grimaces of *Mr. Jenkins*.[47]

Inexorably playwrights were squeezed between the demands of audience and players. A whole generation of dramatists grew up who saw drama not in terms of the out-

45. Dickens, *Nicholas Nickleby*, chap. 22.

46. *Report of the Select Committee*, para. 363.

47. "Prefatory Remarks" to Douglas Jerrold's *The Bride of Ludgate* (Drury Lane, 1831) in *Lacy's Acting Editions of Plays* 93 (London: T. H. Lacy, [1849–1917]): 3–4.

side world, but of members of a company. Dramatists took pride in becoming known as "practical" men of the theater. As such they were expected to be able to write plays in which the same figures appeared over and over again, endlessly confronting the same problems.

The formula by which domestic dramas were written had evolved slowly. There are some earlier English examples of this type of drama, but they are rare. Thomas Heywood's *A Woman Killed With Kindness* (1603) is an example from the Elizabethan period. Nicholas Rowe had written an essentially domestic tragedy in *The Fair Penitent* (1703), and in doing so he prepared the way for George Lillo's *The London Merchant* (1731). Lillo's play was far more influential on the Continent than it was in England, where stage conditions at the patent theaters inhibited imitations. Nevertheless, the bourgeois spirit, the *comédie larmoyante*, and the blurring of comedy and tragedy are all essential components of the domestic drama. When the plays of Kotzebue, who had been strongly influenced by *The London Merchant*, were translated into English at the turn of the century, the domestic tragedy of Lillo found an even more receptive audience:

> Eighteenth-century sentimentalism and the early nineteenth-century trend toward the patriarchal Victorian family helped turn romantic verse-dramatists (as well as the writers of melodrama) toward domestic subjects. The domestic drama had a message: prescriptive morality . . . the morality prescribed by convention, sentiment, and contemporary manners. It was, so to speak, Sunday-school morality taught to make children docile and obedient. The plays presented idealized patterns of feminine marital behavior, Victorian-Christian gentlemanly sentiments, and family virtues. They idealized the relationship between the all-wise, ever-loving father and the dutiful daughter or son. . . . Eighteenth-century sentiments regarding female virtue had made the rebellious daughter "the equivalent of the defaulting solicitor." Besides affirming the virtues of the home, domestic dramas expressed the concepts that inherent worth is not dependent on birth or rank, and that the lowborn will rise.[48]

48. J. O. Bailey, p. 25.

At first domestic dramas embraced foreign settings rather than those of the English village. The emotions, sentiments, and situations, however, were perfectly familiar to the audience. A play set in Germany, but containing many of the essentials of domestic drama, was performed at Drury Lane in 1807. This play was James Kenney's *Ella Rosenberg*. Its plot was to remain generally unchanged in domestic drama for well over fifty years. The nobleman villain, Mountfort, falsely imprisoned the hero, Rosenberg, and abducted the latter's wife from the protection of Storm. Rosenberg and Storm were saved from death and Ella from dishonor only by the providential intercession of the Elector of Hanover. Though Mountfort proved repentent (a feature of domestic drama that all but disappeared within a short time), his pursuit of a fleeing innocent became a staple of domestic-drama fare. Another staple was the idealized village setting that became particularly significant after the success of John Howard Payne's *Clari; or, The Maid of Milan*, (Covent Garden, 1823). As Clari thought of her home, she sang the now-famous song, "Home Sweet Home." Before long such paeans to home and village life were to become standard features of domestic drama.

The first domestic drama having an English setting would seem to have been adapted by William Moncrieff. He was particularly adept at dramatizing novels, and, since many novels were serialized, Moncrieff gained a reputation for finishing some before their authors. All that can be said in Moncrieff's defense was that time was all important to him. In 1820, he wrote a dramatic version of Amelia Opie's novel *Father and Daughter* (a title he was to use for a later play). Opie's book was a somewhat melodramatized version of *The Vicar of Wakefield*. Moncrieff, apparently unaware that comparisons could be invidious, called his play *The Lear of Private Life*. A considerable number of the features of domestic drama were found in this adaptation. There was a seducer-villain (who hailed from the army rather than the squirearchy), and a heroine who left home with her babe in arms. There was that standard character, the father maddened with grief, and, of course, a last-minute righting of wrongs. Mrs. Opie shared Goldsmith's touching belief in the redemptive qualities of a marriage of villain and heroine; later dramatists did not.

By 1826, the direction of domestic drama had been clearly charted when John Baldwin Buckstone's *Luke the Labourer; or, The Lost Son* was produced at the Adelphi.[49] The action of this domestic drama was set in a country village of the type that was fast becoming a nostalgic memory to the London masses. The classes were polarized, with the local Squire Chase cast in the villain's role. His name, as was often the case, indicated his personality.[50] The heroine was Clara Wakefield, whose parents were reduced to direful straits by a series of misfortunes. Their domestic tranquility was in jeopardy, for a threat of eviction was ever present. The young farmer, Charles Maydew, whose kindness and honest intentions toward Clara mark him as the hero of the play, was obviously intended for the heroine. Squire Chase's attempts to gain Clara for himself became more importunate until the requisite scene where he physically attempted to force his attentions upon the hapless girl. All such "rapes" were foiled by the fortuitous arrival of assistance. In this case, help came in the person of Philip, a sailor. Such nautical figures were not at all rare in domestic dramas—even those that, like this, had absolutely no connection with the sea. After all the struggle and torments inherent in domestic drama had been overcome, a happy ending was made possible by the discovery that Philip was none other than Wakefield's lost son.

Buckstone was often ahead of his time, and briefly, in his characterization of Luke, whose story was only tenuously grafted onto the main stem, he voiced a protest against the injustices suffered by a man whom society would not forgive. Though Luke was dismissed by Wakefield for intem-

49. Winton Tolles said of this play that it "cut the pattern for native melodrama" (Bailey, p. 239).

50. Some versions of the play simply refer to the villain as "Squire," a surname being unnecessary after such a revealing title.

perance, he was repentent and willing to work. No one, however, would assist him and, as a result, his wife had died in his arms. Luke's pitiful tale hints at a criticism of society, but the mood soon changed as the formula was resumed. Luke was forced back into a familiar role, and social concerns and justification of attitudes were passed over in favor of thrills and dangers. Luke was killed at the play's end, and domestic tranquility was restored.

As a development of melodrama, the domestic drama inherited a great deal from its ancestor. The basis of domestic dramas was plot not character, and exciting incidents were strung together to provide a vehicle for stirring the emotions rather than the mind. Despite the apparent setbacks faced by the characters, virtue was always rewarded and vice resoundingly defeated by the final tableau. No ultimate issues were faced and danger was not real. Whatever disaster faced the hero or heroine, all would be set right in the final scene.

Because the emphasis was on plot, characterization was neglected, and characters were conceived of as stereotypes. They became dehumanized, personifications of economic categories, embodiments of the class relations existing between them. Behavior became symbolic. Unlike tragic figures, they had no conflict within themselves; they were essentially flat characters. The tragedy of a Lear, an Othello, or a Macbeth lies in the fact that they are all susceptible. They are complex figures and are divided within themselves, and in that fact lies their universality and the seeds of their destruction. In domestic drama people appear "whole," but in the real world, as in the world of tragedy, men remain divided. Though the characters of domestic drama looked real and seemed to come from related strata in society, they were not like real people. Because they were stereotypes, they could not develop, for they were devised to suit the exigencies of plot, and their actions revealed nothing of themselves nor of the human condition.

The stock characters of domestic drama were the hero, villain, heroine, old man (or woman, or both), comic man, and soubrette. Their presence was the one sure thing in an uncertain world. As Owen Davis said,

> Instead of avoiding the obvious, you must insist upon it first, last, and all the time. You must move up the ascending scale of emotions with directness. Your hero must be labeled at his first entrance. Nothing must be left to inference. . . . In the same easy way your comedian had to get a laugh as he came on. Instead of having your heroine pursued by some abstract thing such as fate, you must have her pursued by a tangible villain bent upon cutting her throat. . . . And the hero remained a hero, and the villain died as black as when he first came on.[51]

The eighteenth-century world of fainting heroines and men of sensibility adapted uneasily to the changed conditions of nineteenth-century London. Heroines gained a halo of virgin purity and this innocence was the polarity of the villain's nature and was just as absolute. It was, after all, the latter's desire for the heroine that set the action in motion. Even before her first entrance, or, at the latest, during her first scene, the heroine must be suffering. These trials and tribulations, however, the heroine faced with resignation. She possessed the Christian virtues of meekness, humility, and patience, but had unequaled powers of resistance and inflexible chastity.

All the better writers of melodrama had known that human nature was more interested in unrelieved vice than in unfailing virtue. Shakespeare's Richard III is of far more interest than the virtuous but colorless Richmond. Thus, the domestic dramatist's power lay in his ability to make his villain seem diabolical. He (or, less frequently, she) had to be a fiend in human shape, able to raise more fear in the audience than the circumstances seemed to warrant. Villains stirred that irrational fear in the auditors, even though they were all talk and little action. The villain, though a devil in his actions, concentrated on foreclosures rather than souls. His pursuit of the heroine showed a persistence that would be wholly admirable in a more worthy cause.

51. Quoted in Montrose J. Moses, *The American Dramatist* (Boston: Little Brown, and Co., 1925), pp. 299–300.

Not infrequently, he exhibited considerable courage and was seldom cowed by anyone. Even when defeated or rebuffed, he could confidently predict that his time would come. Occasionally he showed signs of repentance or remorse, but generally he did not, and, since villains generally hailed from the upper classes, their inevitable fate was seen as a victory by the proletarian audience.

Another stock figure was the old man or, less often, the old woman. Generally the heroine's father, he was frequently given to acting as a kind of Prospero-Polonius-Lear. His major function sometimes seemed to be solely to tell the heroine (and the audience) what had happened in the past to bring them to their current misfortunes. His next task was to caution the heroine about the snares of the world and the dangers to which a maiden's flesh was heir. At some time early in the play, he usually cursed his daughter for leaving with the villain or disregarding his advice. In the final moment of the play, he had a scene of recognition or reconciliation (or both). The old man also devoted a large part of his life to recalling happier times and imploring Heaven for forgiveness. Dickens mocked the old man in *Sketches by Boz*:

> By the way, talking of fathers, we should very much like to see some piece in which all the *dramatis personae* were orphans. Fathers are invariably great nuisances on the stage, and always have to give the hero or heroine a long explanation of what was done before the curtain rose, usually commencing with, "It is now nineteen years my dear child, since your blessed mother (here the old villain's voice falters) confided you to my charge. You were then an infant." Etc., etc. Or else they have to discover, all of a sudden, that somebody whom they have been in constant communication with during three long acts, without the slightest suspicion, is their own child . . . they fall into each other's arms and look over each other's shoulders and the audience gives three rounds of applause.[52]

The hero, of course, was designed to be exactly the opposite of the villain in every respect. He possessed generos-

---

52. Charles Dickens, *Sketches by Boz* (London: Oxford University Press, 1957), p. 109.

Stock melodrama figures (CHATTO AND WINDUS)

ity and faithfulness. As he lost his eighteenth-century "sensibilité," he became colorless and in general was relegated to the background where he was allowed to struggle manfully against vastly superior forces and the machinations of the villain whose treachery he never seemed aware of until it was too late. Nevertheless, the melodramatic hero was really "heroic" (whereas a tragic hero is flawed) and, therefore, he always did the right thing. Like the heroes of many a novel (Richard Carstone in *Bleak House* or David Copperfield, for example), he was all the context required but little else. He never knew the evil abroad in the world. His main function was always to rescue and marry the heroine and to present a picture of idealized virtue. An exception to the general rule of gullibility was the sailor-hero, who was much less easily hoodwinked and recognized the villain for what he was. Nevertheless, all types of heroes usually reached a moment of supreme danger—only to be saved at the last moment.

Melodramas would not be complete without the two comedy figures. The comic man (often identified by his waistcoat) and the comic maid (soubrette) often parodied the love theme of hero and heroine. The comic man usually did more to foil the villain than the hero, and always supported the hero even when the evidence against him was at its blackest.

These stock figures, then, were a popular means of shorthand. Immediately recognized by the audience, they made prolonged explanations unnecessary: melodrama had enough of them already, and they told the audience where matters stood at a glance. It does not take much imagination to see what effect the stock figures had on drama as a literary art, for any hack could mix the established ingredients and produce something palatable.

Be this as it may, a dramatist frequently found the problems of writing to a formula complicated by the high-handed way he was dealt with by theater managers. The treatment that Jerrold received from Elliston at the Surrey was no isolated example. Other instances of high handedness are not hard to discover. Boucicault, who suffered at the hands of a cabal of managers, wrote of them:

> As a low state of health is liable to let in a score of maladies, so a low state of the drama has developed the *commercial manager*. This person in most instances received his education in a barroom, possibly on the far side of the counter. The more respectable may have been gamblers. Few of them could compose a bill of the play where the spelling and grammar would not disgrace an urchin under ten years of age. These men have obtained possession of first-class theatres, and presume to exercise the artistic and literary functions required to select the actors, to read and determine the merit of dramatic works, and [to] preside generally over the highest and noblest efforts of the human mind.[53]

Theater managers had different points of view, of course. John Forbes of Covent Garden was asked by the Select Committee:

> Do you not know that Tobin's *Honey Moon* remained sixteen years without being read?

> I do not know the fact, . . . we frequently have only the first act[s] of plays and we are anxiously awaiting for the second and third.[54]

On the whole it seems reasonable to suppose that theater proprietors were anxious to obtain the best plays that they could as often as possible. It made no sense to reject a good play that might be brought out by a rival house.

One of the major concerns of the Select Committee was to account for the decline of theater attendance. The patents naturally enough laid the blame on the minor theaters and other forms of rival attractions. Charles Kemble told the Committee that minor theaters like the Strand and the City lured away their pit and gallery audience.[55]

Another reason cited was the immensity of the patent

---

53. Dion Boucicault, "The Decline of the Drama," *North American Review* 125 (September 1877): 243.

54. *Report of the Select Committee*, para. 1,984.

55. *Report of the Select Committee*, para. 622.

theaters and such minors as the Coburg. Drury Lane could seat three thousand people, of whom only three-quarters could hear and see properly.[56] The size of theaters was leading inevitably to spectacle and song rather than subtlety of thought, expression, and action. Sarah Siddons referred to Drury Lane as "the tomb of the drama," and when it is considered that theaters were lighted at first by candles, it was remarkable that anything was seen by those beyond the first few rows. Covent Garden held two thousand people before the second theater opened in 1809. In 1809, the capacity had risen to three thousand. Coleridge said of London's major theaters, "they are too large for acting and too small for a bull-fight." John Payne Collier, testifying before the 1832 Committee, traced all the theater's problems to size:

> Do you not consider that the public taste has been considerably deteriorated by the quality of the representations that have been given at the large theatres?

> Decidedly. I think the great theatres have owed their present condition partly to their magnitude, partly to the representations which have taken place in them, and partly to the difficulty of hearing, understanding, and enjoying representations of a more regular and legitimate character. In fact, it all resolves itself into magnitude.[57]

The lavish expenditures of the patents and other large theaters made it necessary to attract bigger audiences that were by nature less discriminating. The quality of drama naturally suffered as the playwrights attempted to please everybody:

> The galleries gained control; paying the piper, they insisted on calling the tune. And what a tune it was! These new patrons of the art of drama, addicted hereditarily to cock-fighting, pugilism, and bull-baiting (not outlawed until 1820) in their diversions, demanded something more lively than refinement of character development, beauty of language, or subtlety of

56. *Report of the Select Committee*, paras. 1,137–1,138.
57. *Report of the Select Committee*, para. 295.

wit. A show was what they wanted—the louder, gaudier, and longer it was, the better they liked it.[58]

Size of theater did, however, permit lavish spectacular effects that lay at the heart of much of the popular appeal of melodrama. Nineteenth-century dramatists taught their twentieth-century successors just how powerfully theatrical effects could reinforce the words and ideas of a dramatist. It may have been even more than this. The 1970s have seen the return of the Hollywood spectacular. In periods of financial depression, the human spirit longs for something grand and imposing—ocean liners overturning, hurricanes, buildings burning or collapsing during earthquakes, and so forth. Assuredly spectacular events caught the attention of the nineteenth-century theater audience. *The (London) Times* (2 August 1821) said of the Westminster scene in R. W. Elliston's *Coronation*, (Drury Lane, 1821):

> A most splendid scene it is in every point of view. Whether we consider the manner in which it is painted, the brilliancy with which it is illuminated, . . . it strikes us as being one of the most superb scenes ever exhibited in a theatre.[59]

In some instances, productions were remarkably ahead of their time. Edward Fitzball wrote a scene in *Jonathan Bradford*, (Surrey, 1833), in which four rooms of the inn were shown simultaneously.

Quite often a play had a spectacular scene (usually at the climax of the action), and later plays tended to be written around this scene. The playbill of J. B. Buckstone's *The Last Days of Pompeii*, (Adelphi, 1834), proudly proclaimed that the play would end with "the awful and magnificent eruption of Vesuvius" and "one wide sheet of flame."

58. Frank Rahill, *The World of Melodrama* (University Park, Pennsylvania: Pennsylvania State University Press, 1967), p. 112. Cruelty was commonplace. The real-life murderer of Maria Marten was sentenced to death. After his execution, his skin was tanned for bookbinding and his skeleton (less his skull) is still in use at West Suffolk Hospital. (See Donald McCormick, *The Red Barn Mystery* [London: John Lang, 1967].)

59. *The (London) Times* (2 August 1821), p. 2.

It is often said that Dion Boucicault was the first to use spectacular scenes in domestic drama. His popular play, *The Colleen Bawn*, contained a famous water-cave scene. Boucicault's use of the technical facilities of nineteenth-century theaters led to increased realism in a drama that ironically was becoming less realistic. It was Boucicault who brought the working-class audience into the theater, but he also encouraged the "realistic" school of Robertson that accompanied the return of the middle and upper classes to the theater.

In the movement toward novelty and effect, actors as well as dramatists suffered at first. Scenic artists and stage technicians rose in importance. Even by the end of the century, the position often remained unchanged in the provinces. Jerome K. Jerome commented that the manager of a theater was a first-rate fellow who treated the actors "as if we were stage carpenters."[60] Scenic workers became increasingly important, and the status of writers was correspondingly diminished. A large number of stagehands were required to put on the spectacular scene. In Fitzball's ballet, *Hans of Iceland*, (Covent Garden, 1841), well over fifty carpenters were needed to shift the last scene. (This piece played at a loss!) Clearly the advent of spectacular scenes could not fail to diminish the art of dramatic writing:

> As scene painters became more important than poets, it began to seem that Thomas Carlyle was right in dismissing the stage for attempting to achieve by mechanical means what poetic genius alone could accomplish on the printed page.[61]

The effect on the dramatic experience can be imagined, but also involved was the status of the dramatists themselves. As has been pointed out previously, first-class drama can only come when the dramatist is free to choose a mode of expression best suited to his own particular talents. The

---

60. Jerome K. Jerome, *On the Stage and Off: The Brief Career of a Would-Be-Actor* (New York: Henry Holt and Co., 1891), p. 103.

61. Leonard Ashley, *Nineteenth-century British Drama* (Glenview, Illinois: Scott, Foresman, and Co., 1967), p. 3.

emphasis on spectacular scenes and effects further reduced the status of the dramatists. All kinds of novelties were introduced with the stock-authors writing plays around them. Most of the worst excesses were found at the patent theaters, but some minor theaters were just as bad. The Coburg decided to impress its patrons with a sight that would interest them beyond all others—themselves. The indefatigable Glossop purchased a mirror curtain that measured thirty-six feet by thirty-two feet. It consisted of over sixty mirrors in which everyone in the audience saw himself reflected. The cost of the curtain was enormous; it served no real purpose, and the danger caused by its weight (over five tons) necessitated its removal.[62]

Thus, drama in the nineteenth century found itself at the mercy of external forces that forced it into a particular mold. The expansion of the London population created a rising demand for popular theaters. Three theaters were not enough, and minor theaters began springing up all over London in defiance of the law. By various maneuvers these theaters stayed open, but those who wrote for them were ill paid and their work was ephemeral. Each play was more than simply a play. All sorts of accommodations had to be made by the dramatists, and extraneous material was added to keep up the pretense that the play was *not* the thing. Music was added since it afforded some legal protection. Dancing, spectacle, performing animals, and other additions helped persuade the Lord Chamberlain and his informers that no legitimate drama was being presented. Such shifts led to a drama that could not concern itself with any of the important issues confronting the intelligent minds of the day. Added to all these problems was the lowly status of the dramatist who was unable to exercise his own talents. He had either to become a resident-employee

62. Mirror curtains were used at the Surrey, the Marylebone, the Standard, and at the Queen's, Manchester. The mirror curtain at the Coburg was installed in 1822. See N. M. Bligh, "Mirror Curtains," *Theatre Notebook* 15, no. 2 (Winter 1960–61): 56.

of a theater or to find employment elsewhere because he could not make a living solely as an author.

Conditions improved as the century progressed. Licensing laws were relaxed. Authors secured both copyright protection and royalties for their plays that meant a degree of artistic independence. None of these improvements would have meant much, however, had not they been accompanied by a growing refinement of audience taste—a move away from bread and circuses. Indeed, the study of nineteenth-century drama is, in many ways, a study of popular imagination, and no study of nineteenth-century domestic drama would be valid without an examination of its audience, for the nature of domestic drama was virtually dictated by those for whom it was intended. It is, therefore, upon the London audience that attention must next be focused.

2
THE DRAMA'S PATRONS

The drama's laws the drama's patrons give,
For we that live to please, must please to live.

Dr. Johnson[1]

THERE WAS SCARCELY ANY serious devotee of the Victorian theater who did not acknowledge the veracity of Dr. Johnson's aphorism when applied to the theater audience of his own day. Occasional voices were heard exhorting managers and writers to elevate public taste, but even they agreed that in the first fifty years of the nineteenth century the influence of the audience was stronger than it had ever been. Playwrights found it very convenient to explain away shoddy work and escape criticism by complaining that they were not allowed to write as they might wish. Managers, of course, blamed all failures and second-rate plays on their patrons. Since patronage had disappeared with the aristocratic audience and state subsidies were an unrealized

1. Samuel Johnson, "Prologue at the Opening of Drury Lane Theatre," 20 September 1747.

The Boxes by Thomas Rowlandson (1809) (VICTORIA AND ALBERT MUSEUM)

dream, the manager was in the market place, and like all merchants he was forced to sell what his customers demanded. It is no surprise to learn that a play's commercial appeal was often inversely proportionate to its literary and artistic merit. Melodrama, as the most popular dramatic form of the poorer classes, was the most influenced by public opinion. Plays were not so much the works of individual authors as they were a combination of elements long familiar in the theater. It became as foolish to look for the individuality of the average melodramatist as it would be to seek out the author of a traditional ballad or folk tale. The playwright knew that going against tradition was simply an act of theatrical suicide and that while changes and innovations were sometimes successful, on the whole it was safer not to take unwarranted risks.

Audience control was particularly effective because the Londoner generally lived and worked in the neighborhood in which he found his theater. Until after midcentury, no adequate means of transportation was generally available to the London worker. No omnibus service of note existed before 1850, and the Metropolitan (Underground) Railway only began operations in 1863. Lack of readily available, cheap transportation meant that when new theaters opened they secured a virtual monopoly of local patronage, but the cost was high. Minor theaters had to suit the "style" of their particular locality or take the consequences. The East End theaters preferred melodrama with a more intense and more prolonged activity than was customary in the West End. Domestic drama predominated in the East as it did elsewhere, but Gothic melodrama persisted there long after it had died in the West. The "Brit.," the Standard, and the Pavilion were also supplying drama of a type largely unavailable elsewhere in London. Their players achieved considerable local fame and flourished under the patronage of devoted supporters. Indeed the Britannia presented the most notable example of local support in London during the reign of the Lane family. Sarah Lane, known affectionately as *the Queen of Hoxton*, ruled the Britannia alone for the last thirty years of the century. She instituted the famous annual Britannia Festival, during which the local inhabitants were invited to present the actors with tokens of appreciation. These same presents, it should be remembered, also constituted a warning as to who was the ultimate source of the "Brit.'s" continuing prosperity. The exceptional relations existing at the Britannia pointed to the success that could result when the audience's wishes were given due consideration.

An equally popular theater manager, Samuel Phelps, succeeded in convincing his audience that their taste should aspire to something more than the melodramas and aquatic spectacles they had been used to at Sadler's Wells. He produced legitimate dramas and made a reputation for Shakespearean productions. His audience was largely working class since the large pit could seat a thousand spectators at a shilling each. *The Illustrated London News* (26 October 1844) praised the exertions of Samuel Phelps, recalling that

> When we visited Sadler's Wells last year to see some tremendous melodrama, or piece of *diablerie,* we forget which, nothing could exceed the tumult of the house: now all is quiet, orderly, and attractive, although at the same prices . . . so long as the plays of Shakespeare are performed with merit, and at a price within the means of the million, there need be no occasion to lament the decline of popular taste for the legitimate drama.[2]

Across the river the Surrey tried briefly to emulate Phelps, but clientele of this theater preferred the old melodramatic fare. The popular audience at this house munched its boiled-bacon sandwiches, its fried fish, and hot saveloys. No heartier laughter was heard than at the Surrey, but when the exciting moments of the drama approached, gossip ceased and jaws were stilled.

Audiences came to regard the special relationship existing between the front and back of the house as governed by its own system of laws with the audience usually having the power to damn or save. On occasions this power was

2. *The Illustrated London News* (26 October 1844), p. 267.

abused, but on the whole the Victorian audience withstood
the onslaught of mediocrity with unparalleled fortitude. As
the drama's patrons, audiences deeply resented managers
who tried to ignore their wishes or curb their powers. Examples of contests of will between audience and manager
are as old as theater itself. For instance, R. W. Elliston,
that Barnum of nineteenth-century theater, once tried des-
perately to persuade an audience that Andrew Cherry's *The
Village; or, the World's Epitome* was worth hearing out. He
went down on his knees before his masters to beg that they
allow the actors to finish the performance. It was

> An appeal powerful as that of Lord Brougham himself, who no
> doubt had treasured up the effect, at the concluding sentence
> of his celebrated speech on Reform. The petition was
> granted . . . but [the play] was damned on the first reading,
> and the curtain fell amidst the yells and hootings of an
> indignant audience. . . . [Elliston withdrew] the play at the
> sentence of the house, which had so emphatically announced
> there should be no two bites at a *Cherry*.[3]

Creating a disturbance was only one of the many ways in
which an audience could show its power. Other methods
were equally effective. Actors' benefits showed very clearly
what the actor's status was. Benefits seem to date back to
that given to Mrs. Barry at the command of King James II.
This compliment soon became widespread, but in Victorian
times it was a constant reminder to the actor of his dependent status. Almost every contract of a major actor contained a clause specifying a benefit. It was the proud boast
of certain provincial actors that they seldom *lost* more than
a few pounds at their benefits. Some London figures even
made money from them, but the cost in self-esteem could
be quite telling, as "Peter Paterson [James Bertram]," a
strolling comedian, claimed:

> I never myself took a benefit, but I cannot help saying that I
> think the benefit system a bad one; it quite destroys an actor's

3. George Raymond, *Memoirs of Robert William Elliston Comedian*, 2 vols.,
2nd ed. (London: John Ollivier, 1846), 1: 270–71.

independence; and the taking of a benefit is one of the great causes of an actor being so frequently seen in the public houses—it is in these places he "makes" his ben. He is obsequiously civil to all whom he sees, and appears profoundly grateful when anyone takes a pit ticket from him; in fact, he has to sink his independence in order to sell his tickets. Then he torments all his friends to sell for him; if he is slightly in debt to his baker or butcher, these unfortunate tradesmen are at once saddled with a score of pit, a dozen of stall, and fifty gallery cards. He must sell most of them, it is the best chance he will have of obtaining payments of his little debt.[4]

The audience had an opportunity to "have it out" with theater managers because all new plays were followed by an announcement of when they would next be presented. The moment when a play was "given out" could be one of dread to any manager. An expensive production costing thousands of pounds could die after only one performance at almost a total loss. This was the time when the audience sat in judgment on the combined efforts of author, manager, and actors:

> The ferocity with which the public pronounced sentence was a major cause for diffidence on the part of the literary men who might otherwise have written for the stage. . . . The verdict rendered by the audience was final and without appeal. No manager with safety could disregard it. . . . Elliston, as we have already observed, attempted frequently to defy the popular judgment.[5]

Conspicuously lacking from this audience were members of the aristocracy. Since the Restoration, members of the *beau monde* had been the mainstay of the drama. The rise of opera, however, had provided a rival attraction to drama and had wooed away members of the aristocracy from the theater. It was also clear that the French Revolution had shaken the complacency of the English nobility, frightening a few of them into a much-needed repentance for their self-

4. James Bertram, *Glimpses of Real Life* (Edinburgh: William Nimmo, 1864), p. 46.

5. Ernest B. Watson, *Sheridan to Robertson* (Cambridge, Massachusetts: Harvard University Press, 1955), p. 107.

ish pursuit of pleasure. This awakened sense of religious duty, however, could not account for the attitudes of the vast majority of the aristocracy which frankly found the new drama too innocuous, lacking in any kind of intellectual appeal. Even the classics of theater repertory were bowdlerized to suit the puritanical taste of the proletarian audience. Managers constantly bemoaned the loss of their staunchest supporters, even announcing the fact in their playbills, and it was the ambition of every theater proprietor to bring them back to the theater. Success in doing this was slight in the first part of the century, and it was a common complaint of dramatic writers, such as Fitzball.

> The highest people, I regret, give little encouragement to their own [talent]. No national impulse brings them to our theatre, and while that is the case, we can expect no *rising* native talent. Genius which presents itself under the barbarous names of Brown, Green, or Smith, be it ever so violetlike, is left to pine under the nettles at the corner of the garden of misfortune, while the exotic, under whatever name it assume, is carefully trailed, pampered, hot-housed, and nurtured with gold dust.[6]

Various reasons were given at the time by actors and managers for the lack of support that the aristocracy gave to the theater. Charles Mathews dismissed them as mere excuses: "And those persons who do not go [to see regular drama] will tell you they dine too late or the theatre is too large or what you please; but they are all excuses."[7] How aesthetically committed the aristocratic society was to opera is hard to determine. There were those who felt that operagoing was a social tyranny under which the leaders of fashion groaned for generations. The poor were different:

> Folks like them would not pay for admittance, unless they had souls for the drama, and employed the entertainment for its own sake. This is not by any means the case at the more

6. Edward Fitzball, *Thirty-five Years of a Dramatic Author's Life*, 2 vols. (London: T. C. Newby, 1859), 1: 87.

7. *Report of the Select Committee on Dramatic Literature* (London: 1832), para. 3,088.

pretentious houses, where . . . it would be found that a considerable proportion of any given audience had come there in secretly mournful compliance with fashion, or for some other as pitiful a reason.[8]

The opera, which began much later in the evening than the drama, flourished in the first part of Victoria's reign. It was understandable that theater managers should cite the late dining hours as a reason why their theaters were scorned by the fashionable. Though the argument that the nobility wished to dine before seeking an evening's entertainment has some validity, it has been very much exaggerated. *The Theatrical Examiner* (London) dismissed the thesis without reservation:

With respect to the fashionably late hours at which the genteeler classes of society dine being also a cause of complaint, we would only remark, that in the plentitude of Mr. Kean's fame the same objection might have been urged, and yet every night of his appearance saw the same large house crammed with all distinction of people to the roof. Where there is attraction, then even Englishmen will waive etiquette, and compromise the tardy devotion to their diaphragms.[9]

Queen Victoria was very fond of private theatricals, but, like other members of the aristocracy, gave little support to the public theaters. Fanny Kemble's wry comment in 1847, "all the theatres throughout the country—are Theatres Royal; and with very good reason, for they are certainly all equally patronized by royalty," was essentially accurate.[10] The Queen went to see Van Amburgh's animal show several times, but her visits to the theater were few and far between. She did revive the office of Master of the Revels, but the command performances of works by Morton, Jerrold, and Boucicault took place at Windsor Castle, not in London

8. Twynihoe W. Erle, *Letters from a Theatrical Scene-Painter*, 2 vols. (London: privately printed, 1859–62), 1: 106–107.

9. *The Theatrical Examiner*, Sunday, 28 June 1829, p. 405.

10. Frances Kemble, *Records of Later Life* (New York: Henry Holt and Co., 1883), p. 513.

theaters. Later in life, the Queen did signal the return of respectability to the acting profession by conferring the first theatrical knighthood upon Henry Irving, but this event did not take place until 1895.

The middle class, though still a supporter of the drama, had turned its attention to other pastimes. Reading aloud to the family had become popular, for novel reading had much to commend itself. It involved no hazardous journeys through the slums of London, which were the haunts of thieves, footpads, and prostitutes. Novels could be more readily censured than the drama, and they could be read without fear of contamination from contact with the lower orders. The growth of circulating libraries and serialized novels was very rapid. For only a pound or so, a reader could have several novels during a quarter. Serialized novels were even cheaper, and there is no doubt that reading fiction became very fashionable. As social conversation became oriented toward the latest novels, perusal of them became a social obligation. However, though the thesis that the rise of novel reading hastened the decline of the drama was supported by contemporary critics, it has the ring of the *post-hoc* fallacy. Such a thesis has to be based on the shaky belief that the majority of London's middle class was so sophisticated that it preferred reading a novel of Dickens to seeing it represented on the stage. Furthermore, there is little clear evidence that those who take up novel reading lose their interest in theatergoing.

Yet another counterattraction to the professional theater grew up—this time much nearer home. Amateur theatricals excited a passionate following and many private theaters sprang up throughout London. A list, certainly not complete, was given in a pamphlet written by J. G. Burton entitled *The Critic's Budget; or, A Peep into the Amateur Green Room*, which listed the following:

Berwick Street Theatre (of High Holborn)
The Minor Theatre (Catherine St., Strand)
The Dominion of Fancy (Bologna's Theatre, Strand)

Pymm's Theatre (Wilson St.)
Gloster Street Theatre (Gloucester St.)
Bury Street Theatre (near the British Museum)
The Southampton Rooms (Bagnigge Wells)
Chiver's Rooms (Picket Place, Strand)
Mitchell's Rooms (Portsmouth St.)
The Kean's Head or O. P. (Russell Court)
The Coal Hole (Fountain Court, Strand)[11]

The interest that Dickens had in amateur theatricals is
well known, but lesser luminaries were even more violently
attracted to the amateur stage. It is ironic that this interest
in amateur theatricals should have led to a lessening of interest in the genuine article. Such was the case, however.
One particularly avid amateur group was the Pic Nic Society. The name indicated the arrangement whereby each
member contributed food for his supper. Sheridan had
them attacked in the press on the grounds they were in-
fringing his patent. The newspapers failing to do his dirty
work for him, Sheridan took personal control and, dressed
as Harlequin, invaded the society's "theatre" and put them
to flight. Shortly after this disgraceful episode, the Pic Nic
Society collapsed.

Even those who were prolific workers, such as Douglas
Jerrold, seem to have taken an active part in amateur theatricals:

It may well be wondered how Jerrold, engaged during the day
in a printing office, energetically completing his education in
his spare time, and turning his attention to dramatic writing as
well, could have found time also for such work as is suggested
by an amateur dramatic company that gave from one to three
performances a week for five years. The extent of the
performances may possibly have become exaggerated by
memory. There were a number of such amateur companies
performing at private theatres in the 'twenties, but the
performances received only occasional paragraphs in the

11. J. G. Burton, *The Critics' Budget; or, A Peep into the Amateur Green Room*
(London: J. Onwhyn, [1819]), pp. 47–49.

Blowing Up the Pic Nics by James Gillray (1802) (VICTORIA AND ALBERT MUSEUM)

dramatic periodicals of the day, and of this particular company I have found but bare mention.[12]

Managers also lost the support of the genteel classes by continuing the old practice of half-price admission. The procedure was built upon the premise that a large audience could be expected to come to see the farces or afterpieces—if not the main attraction. The last part of the show was supposed to attract its own particular audience. What generally happened was that some of the lowest riff-raff of London assembled outside the doors of the theaters. When the half-price time arrived, the new arrivals entered and disrupted whatever was in progress. In *Alton Locke*, the hero described the half-price audience at the Victoria and its effect upon him:

> We were passing by the door of the Victoria theatre—it was just half-price time—and the beggary and rascality of London were pouring in to their low amusement from the neighbour-ing gin-palaces and thieves' cellars. A herd of ragged boys, vomiting forth slang, filth, and blasphemy, pushed past us, compelling us to take good care of our pockets . . . From that night I was a Chartist, heart and soul.[13]

Many theater disturbances could be traced to this half-price admission practice and it was eventually abolished. The old Olympic was the last theater of note in London to give up the arrangement.[14]

It was the tendency of much of the middle class, swept up as it was by evangelical fervor, to look upon the theater as the devil's instrument. A wave of puritanism accom-panied the accession of Victoria, and the theater was strongly criticized for its immoral tendencies. There was noth-

12. Walter Jerrold, *Douglas Jerrold: Dramatist and Wit* (London: Hodder and Stoughton, [1914]), 1: 53.
13. Charles Kingsley, *Alton Locke* (London: Cassell and Company, Ltd., 1967), pp. 106–8.
14. Errol Sherson, *London's Lost Theatres of the Nineteenth Century* (London: John Lane, the Bodley Head Ltd., 1925), p. 354.

ing new about this, of course. A sample of the type of warning that the middle class heard from the pulpit is found in Thomas Best's *Sermons on the Amusements of the Stage*:

> And now, whether you will avoid and forsake these sinful and dangerous Amusements, and act consistently with your professions and your prayers, remains to be tried. Bear in mind that you will never again attend the Theatre, in ignorance, unadmonished, and unwarned. You cannot therefore attend henceforward without deeper guilt and condemnation. May God give you grace to withstand this and all other temptations; and enable you to decide and to act now, as all those who turn away from such counsel will wish, in the bitterness of unavailing remorse, that they had decided and acted, when nothing shall remain of the pomps and vanities and pleasures of the world, but the stinging remembrance of their folly and their guilt![15]

The same spirit was enshrined in the "unco guid," a particularly fanatical group who seized upon the collapse of the Brunswick Theatre as a sign from God. Fifteen people were killed, and it is known for a fact that as the fifteen bodies were being removed, and the injured treated, a sermon was preached on the evils of actors and those who supported them. All of the more than two hundred sects on nonconformity were agreed that the theater and public house were the two great moral enemies of the public good. They were assiduously providing free and comfortable diversions which ultimately resulted in Young Men and Young Women's Christian Associations.

Methodist opposition to the theater, per se, was particularly strong, and certain plays were singled out for special disapprobation. The 1821 Adelphi production of *Tom and Jerry; or, Life in London* by Moncrieff was a case in point. This was a story of "low life" based on Pierce Egan's sketches and was particularly offensive to the more vociferous of Wesley's followers. Accordingly the doors of the

15. Thomas Best, *Sermons on the Amusements of the Stage* (Sheffield, Yorkshire: George Ridge, 1831), p. 81.

Adelphi were picketed and startled theatergoers found pious tracts thrust into their hands. The Bow Street magistrate, Sir Richard Birnie, reported to the Secretary of State, Peel, that the number of people taken into custody since December had doubled. This phenomenon he attributed to the performance of *Tom and Jerry.*[16]

The opposition of middle-class Methodist families to the theater was often remarked upon. As Max Schlesinger wrote in his *Saunterings In and About London*, which was published in 1853:

"Adventure No. 2," said Mr. Baxter, when the friends had gained the street. "That tall young fellow with the red whiskers is a Mr. Brimley; he is twenty-five years of age; he manages his father's business in the city; he is likely to have £200,000 or £300,000 of his own, and he trembles like a school-boy lest his papa should hear of his secret escapades."

"What escapades are those? If it is a fair question."

"Perfectly fair. His great crime is, that this evening, for the first time in his life, he has gone to the theatre."

"Impossible!"

"But fact. I know Peter Brimley, Esq., and Mrs. Brimley, and the whole family. A set of more honest, respectable people does not exist between the Thames and the Clyde; but if they were to understand that Mr. Ebenezer Brimley, their son, had crossed the threshold of frivolity, and placed himself on a seat of ungodly vanity, there would be more lamenting and howling among the uncles and aunts of Brimley House than there would be over a bankruptcy of the firm of Brimley and Co. These people are Methodists, and yet Ebenezer the Bold has taken the first step."[17]

Although it is clear that members of the upper-middle class, and even some Methodists, *did* attend the theater,

16. Alfred Nelson and Gilbert Cross, eds., *Drury Lane Journal: Selections from James Winston's Diaries, 1819–1827* (London: Society for Theatre Research, 1974), p. 46.

17. Max Schlesinger, *Saunterings in and About London* (London: Nathaniel Cooke, 1853), pp. 272–73.

the vast majority of minor-theater audiences was working- or lower-middle class. The 1851 Census classified over three-quarters of the 3 million population of London as working class. A small portion of this group attended West End theaters, but a report of a Parliamentary Committee in 1866 revealed that almost one-half of the available theater seats were in working-class areas.[18] It was many years before the West End attracted substantially more theatergoers than the East End. It follows that as the theater was so uniquely dependent upon public support, that the course of theatrical history in the nineteenth century was profoundly affected by the nature of the London worker. Any theater that hoped to survive had to take into account the background and education of its particular audience. No working-class audience could be expected to be enamored of psychological subtleties after twelve hours of hard, physical labor. The inevitable result of the particular circumstances existing in the early nineteenth century meant that the minor-theater audience brought all its prejudices and limitations to the theater with it. Audience members were largely illiterate. A Select Committee on the Education of Poorer Classes in England and Wales found an average of only one in twenty-seven children receiving an education of any significance.[19]

A large proportion of working-class London was involved in trade. Many of these trades involved immigrants or their descendants. The Huguenots in Wandsworth practiced their skills in hat making; other French Protestants established silk manufacture in Spitalfields. Dutch settlers brought with them brewing skills to Southwark, Whitechapel, and Holborn. Thus, certain areas of London became the neighborhoods of particular nationalities and the local theaters had to take this fact into consideration. In Whitechapel, plays often contained a kindly Jew since this part of the East End was the home of many Jews. As the century advanced audi-

18. See Michael Booth, "East End Melodrama," (Paper delivered at the Conference of Nineteenth-century British Theatre, Amherst, Mass. 11 May 1974), p. 4.

19. Quoted in Charles Knight, *London*, 6 vols. (London: Henry G. Bohn, 1851), 6: 20.

ences became more and more cosmopolitan. A. E. Wilson
quotes the *Referee* on a Pavilion audience in 1883:

> It is perhaps the most cosmopolitan pit in the metropolis.
> Here may be seen the bluff British tar; the swarthy foreign
> sailor fully arrayed in a picturesque sash, a red mop-cap and a
> pair of earrings; the Semitic swell in glossy broadcloth and the
> rorty coster, a perfect blaze of pearly buttons artistically
> arranged in an elegant suit of corduroy with a natty bird's-eye
> neckerchief tied in an imperceptible knot; the sallow, callow
> youth in the shortest of jackets and the largest of stand-up
> collars; the sallow youth's sweetheart; the respectable
> tradesman accompanied by his wife, five children, and a large
> bag of provisions and a bottle of enormous dimensions, a trio
> of artless maidens who giggle and weep torrents—no mean
> tribute to Mr. Charles Dornton and Mr. Rignold who are
> playing in the ever popular *Two Orphans*. [20]

In such a bustling, lusty city, it was to be expected that
the crime rate would be high, and it was. Charles Knight
noted in *London* that "the number of persons taken into
custody by the metropolitan police was equal to the whole
population of some of our largest towns, being 65,965." [21]
Knight also reported that the proportion of known bad
characters in the metropolis was 1 to 89 (more than Liverpool, Bristol, Bath, Hull, or Newcastle) with several districts being particularly notorious. In a parish in Southwark,
for example, one in thirty-three adults was "known" to the
police. [22] From such stuff audiences were made.

The slum conditions that prevailed throughout large parts
of London led inevitably to a great deal of death and dis-
ease. Another prominent social ill was begging:

> The right thing to do here [at Her Majesty's Theatre] is to
> leave the play before the end, and never was I more willing to
> conform to custom. On my way home I was accosted by a
> beggar woman. . . . Begging in London reaches alarming
> proportions. There are 15,000 professional beggars, a large
> percentage of whom are Irish. . . . As a general rule the

20. Albert E. Wilson, *East End Entertainment* (London: Arthur Baker, 1954),
p. 89.
21. Knight, 5:321.
22. Ibid., p. 324.

working classes are filthy beyond description. Their clothes are positively caked with a layer of shining grime so thick that it is solid.[23]

The truth of the matter was that no one received much in the way of money. The London laborer was not a lazy fellow; he worked extremely hard for his pittance. Those who were unwilling to work a twelve-hour day, six days a week, had the choice of turning to crime or seeking the grim comfort of the workhouse:

> Hard, solid work: work that makes millionaires, and leaves the worn-out fingers of the heroic honest man cold upon a pallet—work is the key to London. In the serried legions of the distressed battling for an independent crust, and loathing the unearned crumb, there is a spectacle of moral grandeur which covers all the crime and vice and drunkenness. There are a hundred daily heroes for one coward at his bench.
>
> Those who can and do work are emphatically—London; and the great city is their inheritance from countless generations of toilers stretching back to those rich English merchants whose fame reached Tacitus.[24]

It is only to be expected that men who worked so long and hard would seek a boisterous type of entertainment. The London worker had no time for the slow development of character nor for the introspection of pseudo-Shakespearean verse tragedy. Not for them the part of a passive spectator—they wanted to play a role in the drama unfolding before them. Should they feel they had anything to say, members of audiences said it. If they felt the urge to converse aloud or "chaff" the actors, they were not restrained by any false sense of propriety. Above all, the Londoner remained cheerful and optimistic.[25] The Eastender, even more so than his somewhat more fortunate

23. Francis Wey, *A Frenchman Among the Victorians* (New Haven, Conn.: Yale University Press, 1936), pp. 115–16.

24. Gustave Doré and Blanchard Jerrold, *London: A Pilgrimage* (New York: Harper Brothers, 1890), p. 19.

25. Richard Hoggart notes in his *The Uses of Literacy* (London: Chatto and Windus, 1957), p. 78, that such cheerfulness is typical of the working-class outlook on life, "in most the note is of cheerful patience: 'y've got to tek life as it cums' yes; but also 'y've got to get wi' it best way y' can' ".

neighbor to the west, had a life-style that was lusty and
alive:

> A certain joyousness has always been the keynote of London
> life. A volume might be written on the cheerfulness of
> London; it is not gaiety—Paris or Vienna is a city of gaiety; it
> is a more valuable possession; the citizen of London is not
> lighthearted; he is always, in fact, possessed with a wholesome
> sense of individual responsibility; but he is cheerful, and he
> loves those amusements which belong to the cheerful
> temperament.[26]

The liveliness of London life was one reason for the behavior of London theater audiences before the 1870s, but
there were others. As prospective "gallery gods," many
youths underwent an apprenticeship at the penny theaters
that flourished in London during Victoria's reign. There
were at least a hundred of these theaters before the Theatres
Act of 1843, and virtually all of them were situated in
the poorest sections of London.[27] Two of the areas that
boasted many of these theaters, commonly referred to as
"gaffs," were the Ratcliff Highway (east of the Docks) and
Whitechapel—two of the most unsavory areas of London.
The audiences at the penny gaffs were almost exclusively
young people between the ages of eight and sixteen. The
vigorous exchange between audience and players was
continuous. No standards of behavior were expected from
the audience, which was as well since none were
forthcoming. It was at the gaffs, however, that those whom
David Garrick referred to as the gallery "gods" first formed
their dramatic taste and behavior. After several years of
apprenticeship at a gaff, no member of a London theater
audience could be expected to exhibit signs of refinement.

The gallery at the Victoria was typical of many:

> The gallery of the Victoria was a huge amphitheatre, probably
> containing about fifteen hundred perspiring creatures; most of

26. Walter Besant, *East London* (New York: Century Company, 1901), pp.
287–88.

27. The best account of the penny gaffs is found in James Grant, *Sketches in
London* (London, 1838); the gaff material has been reprinted in a pamphlet by the
Society for Theatre Research, 1952 (*Penny Theatres*, Pamphlet Series no. 1). *See
also* Appendix *infra*.

the men in shirt-sleeves, and most of the women bare-headed, with coloured handkerchiefs round their shoulders, called "bandanna wipes" in the slang of the district, and probably stolen from the pockets of old gentlemen who were given to snuff-taking. This "chickaleary" audience was always thirsty— and not ashamed. It tied handkerchiefs together—of which it always seemed to have plenty—until they formed a rope, which was used to haul up large stone bottles of beer from the pit, and occasionally hats that had been dropped below.[28]

Of all the elements that constituted the Victorian audience, prostitutes excited the most comment. The patent houses, for all their posturings, had accommodated prostitutes at a special rate, selling, for a nominal sum, special tickets that entitled their owners to an entrance for the whole season. In his *London Labour and London Poor,* Henry Mayhew commented on a convenient arrangement at the Lyceum Theatre:

> There is a coffee-house in Wellington Street, on the Covent Garden side of the Lyceum Theatre, in fact adjoining the playhouse, where women may take their men; but the police cannot interfere with it, because it is a coffee-house, and not a house of ill-fame, properly so called. The proprietor is not supposed to know who his customers are. A man comes with a woman and asks for a bedroom; they may be travellers, they may be a thousand things. A subterranean passage, I am told, running under the Lyceum connects this with some supper-rooms on the other side of the theatre which belongs to the same man who is proprietor of the coffee and chop house.[29]

Following the example of the patents, many minor theater managers, instead of fighting prostitution, decided to make money from it. Some went so far as to issue prostitutes free tickets (*orders*) so that the empty boxes could be filled. A sordid trade thus flourished in the theaters for many years. Some houses built special entrances for women of the town in hopes of shielding the decent part of the au-

28. John Booth, *A Century of Theatre History, 1816–1916:* The "Old Vic." (London: Steads Publishing House, 1917), p. 50.
29. Henry Mayhew, *London Labour and London Poor*, 4 vols. (London: C. Griffin and Co., 1861–62), 4: 238.

dience from the parade of vice. There were frequent attempts to have these "Cyprians" banned from theaters, but it was William Charles Macready who took it upon himself to rid Drury Lane of them.[30] In defending himself from charges made in *John Bull*, he stated in *The* [London] *Times* of 31 January 1842 that, although he could not refuse admission to anyone who bought a ticket, he had excluded prostitutes from

> the first two circles, the rooms, halls, passages, and lobbies attached to those circles. I confined such as might still for a time persevere in coming to the third circle, which they could enter by a separate pay-office, and by passing through a dismantled lobby, where the walls were purposely left unpainted and unpapered, in which no seat of any kind was placed, and which was constantly patrolled by a policeman.[31]

Though the problem was alleviated at Drury Lane, prostitution continued to plague the theater districts. In the sixties the Haymarket and the Strand were thronged with prostitutes.

Accompanying the squalor and crime of nineteenth-century London was a great deal of alcoholism. It is not difficult to account for the enormous consumption of spirits. Gin was cheap and effective. It brought about a pleasurable release from a long, hard day of physical work and millions of pounds was spent annually on spirits. Dickens saw to the heart of the problem:

> Gin drinking is a great vice in England, but wretchedness and dirt are a greater, and until you improve the homes of the poor, or persuade a half-famished wretch not to seek relief in the temporary oblivion of his own misery, with the pittance which, divided among his family, would furnish a morsel of bread for each, gin-shops will increase in number and splendour. If Temperance Societies would suggest an antidote against hunger, filth, and foul air, or could establish dispensaries for the gratuitous distribution of bottles of

30. *See* Alan Downer, *The Eminent Tragedian: William Charles Macready* (Cambridge, Mass.: Harvard University Press, 1966), pp. 209–10.
31. *The* [London] *Times* (31 January 1842), p. 5.

Lethe-water, gin palaces would be numbered among the things
that were.[32]

Drinking took place in theaters during the course of a performance. At Sadler's Wells, for instance, wine was served,
and there were special ledges for bottles built in the backs
of the seats. Since an evening's entertainment could last up
to five hours, drunkenness was not uncommon.[33] Actors
sometimes found themselves targets for bottles, and on several occasions, members of the audience were injured and
even killed by flying bottles.

It is scarcely necessary to stress that the art of acting did
not profit from its competition with food vendors who
seemed particularly oblivious to the necessity of permitting
the players to be heard. The greatest exertions of an aspiring actor might frequently be accompanied by the sound of
popping corks and shouting food sellers. The Surrey and
the Britannia did tremendous business in food and drink.
At both, huge trays of food were passed around and an
enormous supply of drink was consumed. The Britannia
gave its patrons an opportunity to eat a full supper (called
in local parlance a *tight'ner*). Great quantities of beer were
pumped up from the cellars by sweating barmen, and gin
and spirits were rapidly dispensed to the thirsting mul-
titudes while the local brew, "pongolo," was hawked around
in pewter mugs and tin cans.

The consumption of such quantities of inflammatory
spirits led to another problem in audience behavior. Drunken members of the audience were a frequent nuisance and
provided yet another excuse for the middle and upper classes to desert the theaters. Many accounts can be found in
theatrical literature of the grave consequences of intoxication. According to one account, a young man was pushed
over the rail of the gallery during the mad scramble for
seats. He had been drinking and was unable to recover his
balance. On another occasion, a bottle was thrown onto the

32. Charles Dickens, *Sketches by Boz* (London: Oxford University Press, 1957),
p. 187.
33. Wilson, *East End Entertainment*, p. 101.

stage of the Coburg and narrowly missed the leader of the orchestra. Davidge, the manager, offered a reward of five guineas for the name of the offender. It was the third outrage of its kind that season. In a prior incident, someone from the gallery had thrown a bottle that killed a fifteen-year-old girl sitting below.[34]

More humorous interruptions became associated with sailors. They remained among the strongest supporters of the drama—and among the lustiest. On one occasion at Sadler's Wells a dispute arose between sailors in the gallery as to whether real water was being used in one of the naval scenes. One of them proved his point by climbing from the gallery onto the stage and promptly sinking out of sight. For several days afterwards, the play was interrupted by other sailors anxious to emulate their messmate's triumph.

It would be foolish, however, to assume that the Victorian audience was only peripherally interested in what was happening on stage. Despite the boisterous and unrefined behavior of the gallery gods, they were stalwart followers of the drama—certainly more so than the upper and middle classes whose attendance became less and less frequent as the century progressed. The London populace looked upon theatergoing as more than merely watching a play; it had a much broader appeal. The interaction of audience and stage was part of the whole theater experience. Audiences regarded their local theaters in a proprietary manner and had no hesitation in offering gratuitous advice to managers and players. The sovereign power of the hiss or the cheer belonged to those who sat in judgment in pit and gallery. The judges remembered years of tradition and convention, and they seldom approved of change. For the first fifty years of the nineteenth century, the theater was forced, as never before, to cater to popular taste. The size of theaters, the style of acting, and the type of drama, were all dictated by the drama's patrons. The principles by which

34. John Booth, p. 23.

the popular audience judged a play were never explicitly formulated, but in most cases they could not be ignored. The patrons of British drama were not always consistent in what they said or did, but their main criteria of evaluation depended upon precedent. Sometimes exceptions were possible, as when Kean refused to play Shylock in *The Merchant of Venice* in the traditional red wig, but flying in the teeth of tradition generally led to failure. As a consequence, it became an inflexible rule for Dion Boucicault and others, that their plays must be "written" by the audience and conclude as the consensus of the audience would have them end. One should not be too critical of this, since try-outs precede all Broadway productions today.

One can only account for the undoubted hold that melodrama had over the popular mind by seeing it in a larger context; for melodrama became not only the prevailing form of popular entertainment, it became the dominant modality of nineteenth-century life:

> The aesthetic category of melodrama becomes a modality of the nineteenth-century mind, which emancipated itself only with difficulty from over-simplified premises, a fatalism theatrically effective, and a displacement of moral responses into the universe. The declamatory language, the violent and symbolic gestures, the animation of polar opposites to the point of caricature are evidence of a psychic crisis. . . . Melodrama cannot admit exceptions . . . the types must behave with a decorum of extremes: the resolution must be vividly schematic. The tensions must concentrate toward a last, overwhelming tableau, a final stasis beyond which one must not think.[35]

The audience's sympathy was for a hero beset, like themselves, by forces over which he had no control. Indeed, the very arbitrariness of the suffering inflicted on a morally upright hero or heroine produced that irrational fear or paranoia, which was such a crucial element in the appeal of domestic drama. Try as one might to impose a rational ex-

35. Wylie Sypher, "Aesthetic of Revolution: The Marxist Melodrama," *Kenyon Review* 10, no. 3 (Summer 1948): 436–37.

planation upon the catastrophe that had overtaken him, he failed to do so. This failure accounted for the strong hold that melodrama had over the imagination, particularly the popular imagination. It also explained the "overpowering sense of reality that the form of melodrama engenders even when on the surface it seems so patently unreal. For melodrama's greatest achievement is its capacity to give direct, objective fear to our irrational fears."[36] The statement, "we have nothing to fear but fear itself," is "not a cheering slogan because fear itself is the most indestructible of obstacles. Therein lies the potential universality of melodrama."[37] Because domestic drama stressed the identification of "there but for the grace of God go I," it produced in its listeners a self-pity. "Having a good cry," because it produced a kind of catharsis, made the struggle for survival in a hostile world more bearable.

Self-pity was closely allied to another emotion that became an integral part of the domestic drama —sentimentality. Death scenes had grim relevance in an age when half the population died in childhood. Millions have wept at Lady Isabel's famous lines in *East Lynne*: "I care not, for my life's sands will soon be run. Oh, Willie, my child, dead, dead, dead, and he never knew me, never called me mother!" (act 4, scene 3). But sentimentality (though denigrated today) was a hopeful sign. It was a deliberate overvaluing of the humble and the domestic in opposition to the undervaluing of them that a capitalistic economy encouraged.

It was only to be expected that the popular audience of the last century would have little stomach for poetic tragedy or genteel comedy. These types of theater were banished forever from the sight of those whose struggle for daily subsistence led them to demand a stage picture of a more thrilling world. In that world there was excitement, action, spectacle, and laughter. It was a place where dreams came

36. Robert W. Corrigan, *Laurel British Drama: The Nineteenth Century* (New York: Dell Publishing Co., 1967), p. 9.
37. Eric Bentley, *The Life of the Drama* (New York: Atheneum, 1964), p. 201.

true and where virtue was triumphant. In the theater they could laugh uproariously and weep unashamedly. They did not ask dramatists to write great works of literature but to depict a world in which no explanations were necessary —where an audience could tell at a glance how things stood. So villains always looked and acted like villains, heroines were always pure and faithful, and heroes were consistently heroic. It was not necessary to develop character by slow progression, for the nuances of a person's character were insignificant when compared with his actions. Bernard Shaw felt that

> the ordinary man's life-struggle is to escape from reality, to avoid all avoidable facts and deceive himself as to the real nature of those which he cannot avoid. . . . Hence the more unnatural, impossible, unreasonable, and morally fraudulent a theatrical entertainment is, the better he likes it. He abhors the play with a purpose . . . because it says to him, "Here, sir, is a fact which you ought to attend to." This, however, produces the happy result that the great dramatic poets, who are incorrigible moralists and preachers, are forced to produce plays of extraordinary interest in order to induce an audience of shirkers and dreamers to swallow the pill.[38]

It would be foolish to condemn the Victorian working-class audience or the dramatists who wrote for it any more than one should criticize Restoration dramatists or their audiences for supporting a style of drama that suited their particular taste. It is no disgrace that the Victorian dramatist gave his audience clear signals so that they knew when to applaud and when to hiss. Unfortunately, however, the very nature of domestic drama resulted in laying it open to burlesque and ridicule. A modern audience, for instance, may regret that such plays as Douglas Jerrold's domestic melodrama, *The Rent Day*, (Drury Lane, 1832), start out as a promising comedy of manners but fall prey to the absurdities with which innumerable melodramas were filled. Jerrold, however, knew his audience well. The days

38. Quoted in Martin Meisel, *Shaw and the Nineteenth-century Theatre* (Princeton, N.J.: Princeton University Press, 1963), pp. 90–91.

of comedies of manners were over; he had another job to do, and he did it well.

The patent houses still nursed the hope that Society would return to the theater and save them from ruin. This illusion continued to blind them to the fact that their own incompetence was in large part responsible for their financial plight. Fashionable society *did* attend theaters on important occasions such as royal visits, but these events were all too rare. It should have been clear that legitimate dramatists could not save them from ruin, but patent managers remained generally oblivious to the fact that audience taste had altered. In one area, however, attempts were made to pander to a depraved taste. Animal acts became popular. Quadrupeds did better than bipeds and the term "dog-stars" was facetiously used to refer to animal acts. A German visitor to England commented on a visit to a playhouse:

> But back to the play. It concluded with a melodrama in which a large Newfoundland dog really acted admirably; he defended a banner for a long time, pursued the enemy, and afterwards came on the stage wounded, lame and bleeding, and died in the most masterly manner with a last wag of the tail that was really full of genius. [39]

It was a troupe of performing lions and a domestic drama that made the most money for years at Drury Lane. Van Amburgh's lions appeared at that theater for over one hundred successive nights, and the Queen attended several performances. William Dunn, treasurer of Drury Lane, was asked by the Select Committee:

Did [Van Amburgh's] lions draw money?

[Dunn] The lions certainly paid their expenses.

39. [Hermann Pückler-Muskau], *Tour in England, Ireland, and France in the Years 1826, 1827, 1828, and 1829,* trans. Sarah Austin (Zurich: Massie Pub. Co., 1940), p. 58.

FIRST APPEARANCE OF

M_{R.} VAN AMBURGH

And his unrival'ed collection of

TrainedAnimals

Who are Engaged for **SIX NIGHTS** only at an

ENORMOUS EXPENSE.

And who was received on his first appearance last evening with enthusiastic applause, by an audience crowded in every part of the Theatre.
This extraordinary and highly classical performance was given for up-
wards of One Hundred successive Nights at the Theatre Royal, Drury-
lane, and several times

BY COMMAND OF HER MAJESTY.

This present **TUESDAY**, May 14, 1839,

The performances will commence with the Comic Piece of a

DAY AFTER the WEDDING

Colonel Freelove, Mr. CHUTE   Lord Rivers, Mr. HOUGHTON   Davis, Mr. DUFF
Mrs. Davis, Mrs. GARTHWAITE   Lady Elizabeth Freelove, Mrs. EDWIN YARNOLD

AFTER WHICH, AN INTERLUDE IN WHICH

Mr. VAN AMBURGH

WILL EXHIBIT HIS

FEARLESS AND EXTRAORDINARY PERFORMANCES

WITH HIS

LIVING LIONS,

TIGERS, LEOPARDS, &c.

The Duet " I've wandered in dreams" by the Misses A. & J. HYLAND.

A PAS SEUL BY MISS COOKE, pupil of Miss Raine.

To be followed by the Comic Piece of

TURNING THE TABLES.

Jeremiah Bumps, Mr. CHUTE   Jack Humphries, Mr. REES
Edgar De Courcy, Mr. HUDSON   Knibbs, Mr. DUFF   Thornton, Mr. HOUGHTON
Miss Knibbs, Miss CHALMERS   Mrs. Humphries, Mrs. GARTHWAITE.   Patty Larkins, Miss EGAN

A PAS SEUL BY MISS RAINE.

The entertainments will conclude with the Melodrama of

MARY STUART.

Lord Ruthven, Mr. EATON   Lord Lindsay, Mr. F. COOKE   Sir Robert Melville, Mr. COLEMAN
George Douglas, Mr. HUDSON   Dryfesdale, Mr. BARRETT   Candy, Mr. DUFF
Roland Græme, Mr HOUGHTON   Lady Fleming, Miss SULLIVAN
Mary Stuart, Queen of Scotland, Mrs. EDWIN YARNOLD
Lady Douglas of Lochleven, Mrs. BARRETT   Catherine Seyton, Miss CHALMERS

TO-MORROW WEDNESDAY,

M_{R.} VAN AMBURGH

Will make his Third Appearance with his Trained Animals, and will perform

EVERY EVENING throughout the WEEK

☞ **During the Summer Season the Doors will Open at Seven
o'Clock, and the Curtain will rise at Half-past Seven precisely**

Dublin Theatre playbill announcing Van Amburg's trained animals (LILLY LIBRARY)

Did any other piece pay the expenses?

A legitimate [*sic*] drama called *The Rent Day* was, I think, the most profitable of anything that was played.[40]

The legitimate theaters faltered; circus acts could not keep them solvent. The managers' prayers for the return of aristocratic patronage remained unanswered. Without an appreciative audience, actors could not play, and managers could not make ends meet. Macready recognized the importance of an audience to a player and spoke with unwonted gratitude of the ties that bound both sides of the curtain together in a working partnership:

> "I have little more to say," [said Macready in his farewell speech]. "By some the relation of an actor to his audience is considered as slight and transient. I do not feel it so. The repeated manifestation, under circumstances personally affecting me, of your favourable sentiments towards me will live with life among my most grateful memories; and because I would not willingly abate one jot in your esteem, I retire with the belief of yet unfailing powers rather than linger on the scene to set in contrast the feeble style of age with the more vigorous exertions of my better years."[41]

"Favourable sentiments" of an audience were expressed via applause. However, unlike the modern audience that seldom applauds except at the entrance of stars and at the fall of the curtain, the Victorian audience felt called upon to show its approval throughout the course of a production. The result was that most plays were accompanied by running applause.[42] There were many critics who felt that too much was lost by the frequent interruptions, but applause had been the symbol of success since Nero invented the claque. Victorian managers followed the Emperor's lead by

40. *Report of the Select Committee*, paras. 1,168–1,169.
41. William C. Macready, *Macready's Reminiscences and Selections From His Diaries and Letters*, 2 vols., ed. Sir Frederick Pollock (London: Macmillan and Co., 1875), 2: 370.
42. Owen Davis states in *I'd Like to Do it Again* (New York: Farrar and Rinehart, Inc., 1931), pp. 106–107, that he learned to engineer laughs or applause so that scene changes could take place while the audience was preoccupied.

distributing "orders" to those they could rely on to approve a play.

Applause often occurred at the most inappropriate moments, but it was less of a disruption than the practice, which first took root at the Italian Opera House, of calling for the repetition of a particularly pleasing moment in a production. These calls often necessitated the rising of souls from the dead so that the audience could have the pleasure of seeing them perish once more. Writers of the period frequently criticized this absurdity and similar ones, such as the calling for the repetition of a song by gallerites who could scarcely hear a syllable of it in their gloomy loft.

It was customary for nineteenth-century audiences to greet their idols in a manner that would shock the well-behaved audiences of the modern theater. On the occasion of Macready's farewell performance as Macbeth, all the house rose at his first entrance. Handkerchiefs and hats were waved; there was stamping and shouting and a crescendo of applause. Any popular actor could expect his audience to meet him more than half way. If he gave a good performance, his spectators would applaud him loudly. Part of the reason for this support was the normal desire to express sympathy for virtue in peril and a loathing for vice. Coupled to this moral judgment was the urge to enjoy a play to the full and to enter into it to the utmost—to become, for a few hours, part of the play itself. Actors came to look on applause as both a stimulus to their performance and an ingredient of the total theatrical experience. Mrs. Siddons's acting, for example, was a direct assault on her spectators' emotions, and a silent audience disconcerted her above all things. The same was true of Frederick Yates, who stopped a performance in a provincial town to tell his audience:

> "Ladies and Gentlemen, I am Frederick Yates. Possibly I may be unknown to you; in town, at my own theatre, they do recognize me; applause always accompanies my acting, in fact, it would be dull and vapid without; it is like salt to meat to an actor. The house tonight is badly supported—I am a loser; let

me ask you to applaud and I will act, thus accommodating each other." They clapped their hands at everyone and everything after this appeal.[43]

All actors of note learned to control their applause. Kean had developed a little trick of using a sound like a half-laugh as a cue for applause from his claque.[44] There were other ways of exciting applause. Joseph Jefferson recalls in his autobiography that many actors, once they had made a "point" (a particular piece of business) of which they were proud, would take a series of large steps to left or right to indicate that applause was in order.[45]

No actor was more adept at audience control than Henry Irving, who left nothing to chance. He employed applause as a springboard. Upon his first entrance as Mathias in *The Bells*, he measured the length of the applause by shifting his right foot and, as the noise finally began to weaken, he clipped it off by seeming to awaken from a long ordeal. Gordon Craig even suggested that the applause Irving received was a necessary catharsis on the part of the spectators:

> I am entirely in accord with this opinion—it is a good rule, "no applause." Irving is the exception here. In *The Bells*, the hurricane of applause at Irving's entrance was no interruption. It was no boisterous greeting by an excitable race for a blustering actor. . . . It was a torrent while it lasted. Power responded to power. . . , for though Irving endured and did not accept the applause, he deliberately called it out of the spectators. It was necessary to them—not to him; it was something they had to experience, or to be rid of, or rather, released from, before they could exactly take in what he was going to give them.[46]

The ultimate triumph of an actor's performance was when the pit "rose at him." This was the greatest honor an audi-

43. Edward Stirling, *Old Drury Lane: Fifty Years' Recollections of Author, Actor, Manager*, 2 vols. (London: Chatto and Windus, 1881) 1: 165.

44. Macready, 1: 136.

45. Joseph Jefferson, *The Autobiography of Joseph Jefferson* (New York: The Century Co., 1890), p. 65.

46. Edward Gordon Craig, *Henry Irving* (London: J. M. Dent and Sons, 1930), p. 54.

ence could pay an actor. Edmund Kean knew that it was
the audience at Drury Lane, not the directors, who made
the decisions that mattered. To his anxious wife's query as
to what Lord Essex thought of his debut at Drury Lane, he
replied characteristically, "Lord Essex be damned—the pit
rose at me." Such compliments were rare and what occurred far more frequently were keen encounters of wit between audience and players. Such events were often of
more interest than the plays themselves. As late as 1879,
J. H. Barnes was playing in Palgrave Simpson's *Zillah*
when the audience decided to "guy" the play by interrupt-
ing the performance with "witty" sallies at the actors' expense.

> One of the characters said, "Ah! I see it all!" Voice from the
> pit: "Do you, by gad! we don't!" Some papers had been
> lowered into a well in a bucket. A character said: "If I could
> only find those papers!" A gallery wit responded: "Look in the
> bucket, you old fool, and get it over." . . . Later on [Tom
> Mead] forgot the hero's name, which was Paul de Roseville,
> and dwelling on the Christian name, like the tolling of "Big
> Ben," he said, hesitatingly: "Paul—Paul—Paul—." A wit in the
> front said: "Paul—Paul, why persecutest thou me?" Of course,
> a yell of laughter followed.[47]

Endless examples are recorded of interruptions arising
because spectators were so involved that they took events
on the stage for reality. Joe Jefferson, touring in the provinces, reported that in a production of *The Lady of Lyons*
an old lady insisted that the lovers should be "allowed to go
their own way" and a farmer threatened the villain.[48]

It was often the villain of melodrama who gave the audience scope for much of their participation. It was a grand
effect in *Oliver Twist* when Bill Sikes dragged Nancy
around the stage by the hair, after which he

> always looked up defiantly at the gallery, as he was doubtless
> told to do in the marked prompt copy. He was always
> answered by one loud and fearful curse, yelled by the whole

47. J. H. Barnes, *Forty Years on the Stage: Others (Principally) and Myself*
(London: Chapman and Hall, 1914), pp. 96–97.
48. Jefferson, pp. 56–57.

mass like a Handel Festival chorus. The curse was answered by Sikes dragging Nancy twice round the stage, and then, like Ajax, defying the lightning. The simultaneous yell then became louder and more blasphemous. Finally when Sikes, working up to a well-rehearsed climax, smeared Nancy with red-ochre, and taking her by the hair (a most powerful wig) seemed to dash her brains out on the stage, no explosion of dynamite invented by the modern anarchist, no language ever dreamt of in Bedlam could equal the outburst.[49]

It was all part of theatergoing and audiences loved it.

There was, of course, another side to the coin. At times, audiences felt that their cherished rights were being infringed, and their reaction was often violent and destructive. It was every manager's nightmare that he might find himself at odds with the audience. Should the offense be minor, such as the performance of a displeasing actor, the weapon resorted to was generally a loud hiss, becoming more strident and prolonged if the offense were more serious. Actors were continually exposed to critical scrutiny, unlike managers who were out of the public eye for most of the evening. Box, pit, and gallery were the self-appointed protectors of years of theatrical tradition, and they regarded themselves as the guardians of that tradition. Any radically new touch added by an actor might enrage them, and once aroused it was almost impossible to win them back. Many an actor suffered at their hands—some for years for one offense. An audience seldom tolerated a direct challenge to its authority. Clement Scott once criticized the pit and gallery for their capricious hissing of the actor, James Mortimer. In doing so, Scott challenged the audience's sovereign will and brought down upon Mortimer's head "the most horrible persecution that [had] ever befallen a public man in my time."[50] Scott's reproach had challenged the foundations of that relationship that was so dear to the Victorian audience, and the unfortunate Mortimer suffered as a consequence.

49. John Booth, p. 51.
50. Clement Scott, *The Drama of Yesterday and Today*, 2. vols. (London: Macmillan and Co., 1899), 1: 544.

It is only fair to point out that the members of the audience could sometimes be persuaded that they were in the wrong. When Davidge had a boy ejected from the Surrey in 1837, he would not accede to the audience's demands to restore the youth. Davidge took a very bold line by claiming that he intended to be master in his own house. His obvious sincerity and determination won him the day. Another possibility was to use a humorous approach—as John Diprose reported:

> He sang, and was hissed; but, without being disconcerted, he looked steadfastly at the pit and said, "Gentlemen, I don't understand this. Do you think that for 600 livres per annum [i.e., £36], which I receive, I can afford to give you a voice worth 2,000?" The audience was so pleased with this sally that the actor was allowed to proceed with great applause.[51]

Unlike all other characters, villains exulted in the hissing they received, since it was a tribute to their skill. However, for all others, the sound of hissing was often the prelude to serious trouble. The hiss was a potent weapon, and the sound of it in the auditorium was sometimes a death knell to the management. Should the situation out front worsen, it might well be necessary for the manager to go out and face his accusers. The manager's form of address, "What is your pleasure?", revealed quite clearly his status vis-à-vis that of the drama's patrons. If a manager could not satisfy the audience, the disturbance might degenerate into a riot. The first signs of trouble generally manifested themselves in cries of, "Off! Off!", and assorted catcalls. The galleries took up the pit's disaffections and discharged volleys of orange peels. By the early nineteenth century, audiences had hit upon the idea of throwing pennies at the chandeliers. At this point, the luckless manager was "called for" and had to face his tormentors. It was no accident that the most severe theater riot in English history took place in the nineteenth century. After Covent Garden was rebuilt in 1809, prices in

---

51. John Diprose, *Diprose's Book of the Stage and the Players* (London: Diprose and Bateman, 1877), p. 145.

the pit rose from three shillings and sixpence to four shillings, and those of the boxes were raised by a shilling. While it is clear that the causes of the ensuing riot were far from noble, the disturbance did show a classic confrontation between management and audience. It was a determined effort on the part of the patrons of drama to exert their sovereign will. The cry of the rioters became, "Old prices! . . . Old prices!", and the disburbance became known as the *Old Prices Riot*. The battle also took on the overtones of a class struggle. It was claimed that John Kemble, the manager, had changed the arrangement of some private boxes to allow the aristocracy to indulge in immoral behavior. It was further charged—anathema to the patriotic English heart—that Kemble preferred foreign to native talent.

The O. P. Riot was a decisive struggle between management and audience. It lasted almost seventy nights in 1809, and, when it was over, popular rule was firmly established in the London theater. The lengths that both sides went to in order to prevail illustrate graphically the seriousness with which each side regarded the struggle. Kemble made the mistake of hiring a group of Jewish "bruisers", under the leadership of a fellow called *Dutch Sam*, to cow the audience by force. After one defeat, the "pittites" regrouped and hoisted a placard bearing the inscription, "And it came to pass that John Bull smote the Israelites sore." The wording is significant because, despite all their selfish reasons, the audience did harbor a belief that John Bull *was* fighting for a cause. Kemble's indiscretion cost him several broken windows at his home, and his pregnant wife was greeted with a placard proclaiming, "No more little Kembles." Forms of disturbance became steadily more outlandish. Cartoonists had a field day; even a dance was invented called the *carmagnole*. The name was taken from a dance popular during that other great expression of the people's will—the French Revolution. The carmagnole was performed with the most ludicrous gravity and became one of the most effective torments that the management had to

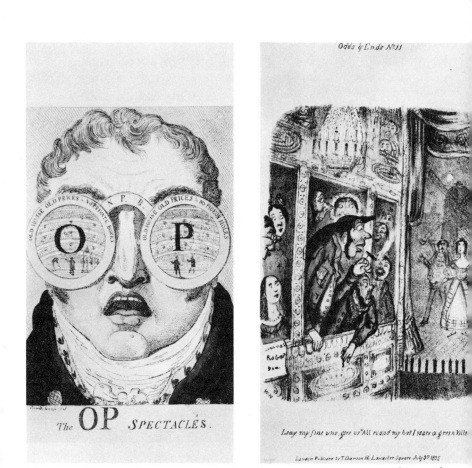

The O. P. Spectacles by Cruikshank, and a patron advises the players (VICTORIA AND ALBERT MUSEUM)

face. Special "O. P." medals were worn, and "O. P." hats became fashionable—to be replaced later by nightcaps and false noses. An "O. P." waistcoat was designed that had an *O* on one lapel and a *P* on the other. After some time, it dawned upon the rioters that they were paying the new prices and keeping the theater going. It was decided to wait for the half-price time, usually around nine o'clock, and then enter. Thus, for the first part of the evening, things went fairly calmly, but at half-price time, war was resumed. The rioters emphasized the noble and patriotic nature of their cause at the end of each evening by singing the National Anthem.

A compromise of sorts was finally reached. The pit prices were rolled back, but the boxes remained at the higher figure. There was no mistaking the real victors, however. The drama's patrons had clearly established that their will was law, and the effect on English drama was far-reaching and decisive.

The absolute power exercised by the Victorian audience raises the question of just what critical standards its members possessed. Clearly these standards exerted a telling influence on the nature of drama. It is known that, despite all the noises and counterattractions present, an audience was often deeply involved with the action onstage. Macready put such force into his delivery that audiences sat spellbound—entirely carried away by the player's performance. When O. Smith (Richard John Smith) played the part of a drunkard, he

> upset a cup of liquor; with a cry of horror he cast himself upon the stage and ravenously licked the spilled drink. It was one of those daring bits of business that only a strong actor, confident in his own powers, would have dared attempt; had it been weakly done it would have raised a laugh; as he did it, it sent a shudder through the house.[52]

It is pointless to multiply examples of audience involvement; it is clear that the workers of London took their

52. Henry B. Baker, *The London Stage: Its History and Tradition, 1576–1888*, 2 vols. (London: W. H. Allen and Co., 1889), 2: 91–92.

drama seriously. They wanted to be involved and they worked hard at meeting the actor more than half way. It would be very foolish to assume that the Victorian audience did not know the difference between tragedy and melodrama. Spectators had developed their own way of enjoying each, but they preferred to watch melodrama and were prone to resentment if anything was offered to them under false colors. Thus, when a revival of Sheridan Knowles's *Brian Boroihme; or, the Maid of Erin* was offered as a play at Covent Garden in 1837, the audience was displeased when they found it to be, despite its blank verse, almost melodrama.

The critical standards of the average London theatergoer were not high, but they were firmly held. As a costermonger told Henry Mayhew:

> Love and murder suits us best, sir; but within these few years I think there's a great deal more liking for deep tragedies among us. They set men a thinking; but then we all consider them too long. Of *Hamlet* we can make neither end nor side; and nine out of ten of us—ay, far more than that—would like it to be confined to the ghost scenes, and the funeral, and the killing off at the last. *Macbeth* would be better liked, if it was only the witches and the fighting. The high words in a tragedy we call *jaw-breakers*, and say we can't tumble to that barrikin.[53]

Mayhew's costermonger-informant was certainly exaggerating when he implied that tragedies were generally incomprehensible to the audience, and it is important to note that his informant was familiar with the classics, even though from the working class. It was, after all, at the Britannia, Hoxton, that the first real Shakespeare festival took place in 1846. The continuing success of Samuel Phelps at Sadler's Wells was equally noteworthy. For all their cloth caps and unrefined manners, the gallery at the Wells delighted in the classics of their drama, while their well-dressed "betters" were politely applauding Italian opera singers and performing dogs. The Victorian minor audience was unsophis-

53. Mayhew, 1: 15.

ticated, its members were not afraid to let themselves go. They did not wish merely to observe an imaginary world, they wished to be part of it. It was not, despite its superficial resemblances, their everyday world, but they were at home in it. It was a world full of signals that instantly told the spectator how things stood—where surface appearances were accurate reflectors of character and situations. The next task is to examine these signals and explain how they worked.

3
VISUAL AND
AURAL SIGNALS[1]

If you attempted to *think* you would be requested to look out for another shop at once. The slightest naturalness or originality would be put down to ignorance. You must walk through each part by the beaten track of rule and tradition.
                                                            Jerome K. Jerome[2]

AUDIENCES OF MINOR THEATERS, as has been seen, were notorious in regarding themselves as guardians of a large number of precedents and conventions—some of them relatively new, others dating back hundreds of years. Many conventions of costume and make-up that became stereotyped in the nineteenth century were regarded by audiences as absolutes to be ignored only by the foolhardy or the inept.

The unsophisticated nature of Victorian audiences led to

1. I am particularly indebted to my colleague, Alfred L. Nelson, for his help with the pages of this chapter dealing with costume and make-up.
2. Jerome K. Jerome, *On the Stage—and Off: The Brief Career of a Would-Be Actor* (New York: Henry Holt and Company, 1891), pp. 143–44.

a heavy reliance upon outward appearance to indicate moral character. By means of costume and make-up alone, an actor could immediately reveal the type of character he was playing. "Instant" characters made it possible for actor and playwright to press on to the next action-filled situation. It is obvious that melodrama made no claim to present subtle, ambiguous natures, for where action is the prime *raison d'être*, characterization is certain to suffer. Thus, the Victorian audience perceived the nature of a character or situation from universally accepted visual and aural signals, or conventions, that preceded or accompanied the delivery of any lines and influenced the way they were to be interpreted. Undoubtedly one of the reasons for the standardization of costume lay in the fact that underpaid actors, required by management to dress themselves for all the parts they were to play, could not afford to purchase, maintain, or transport a large number of elaborate costumes. The actor, Edward Elton, told the Select Committee in 1832:

> The highest salary I know paid in a provincial theatre of the very first class is three guineas a week, a very few receive so much as that, and have to pay their own travelling expenses from town to town, and frequently to provide their own stage dresses; yet it is expected a man receiving that salary shall be able to embody the first characters of Shakespeare.[3]

Most minor theaters lacked the financial backing for major productions, and economic realities encouraged the development of the stock company. Under this system actors and actresses were hired for their "lines of business" rather than for their all-round abilities. Dramatists writing for such companies produced innumerable variations of the same theme. In each of these melodramas were stock figures, the most important of whom were the hero, heroine, villain (or villainess), old man (or old woman), comic man, and soubrette. It was economically prudent to standardize wherever possible, and an actor specializing in villains

3. *Report of the Select Committee on Dramatic Literature* (London: 1832), para. 4,169.

needed only one basic costume and make-up. Some theaters did have wardrobes of sundry articles, but no theater
could be relied on to furnish costumes for all. Elaborate
costuming was kept for the annual Christmas pantomine
—the only production generally guaranteed to make a profit.

There were, of course, notable exceptions. The Olympic
Theatre had been an insignificant minor theater until
Madame Vestris took over the lease in 1831. She planned a
small intimate theater without the Cyprians and roaring
boys who plagued the less fortunate minors, and she persuaded James Robinson Planché, an expert on costume, to
be her advisor. Charles Kean took the Princess's Theatre in
1850 and endeavored to produce dramas that were historically accurate and pleasing to the eye. Naturally as the century progressed costuming improved, but even late in the
century Jerome K. Jerome received an offer of twelve shillings a week at one theater simply because he owned a
dress suit and could play a "swell!" It was all very well for
Charles Kean and Madame Vestris to urge reforms in costume, but few theaters could meet the additional cost and
certainly most actors couldn't. Later in the century, it became a familiar sight to see a theater displaying a sign "cer-
tifying" that a production was accurate in every detail, but
these notices themselves were not above suspicion. While
advertisements in copies of plays indicate the availability of
suppliers of everything from tights to armor, it is foolish to
think that the average minor theater or strolling player
could afford to buy many such items. [4]

Actresses were expected to furnish their entire wardrobes; no small requirement as can be seen from a complete list of costumes required for "melo-drame" given by

4. Walter Donaldson in *Recollections of an Actor* (London: John Maxwell and
Co., 1865), p. 166, recalls a Scottish production of *Macbeth* in 1815 where Macbeth was dressed in a "red officer's coat, sash, blue pants, Hessian boots, and a
cocked hat." The love of extravagance is often a reaction to the squalor of actual
living conditions, and theatrical portraits that could be colored or tinseled were
quite popular with working-class families.

Leman Thomas Rede. It reveals much about the type of dresses worn on stage and the expectations they would raise. The list is as follows:

> Scarlet stuff dress, with blue ribbons, pocket made in
> dress; French cap, white muslin apron trimmed.
> Buff dress with blue or green ribbons.
> Black velvet body made with stomacher.
> Black ribbon and cross.
> Gipsy hat, black mits, white mits.
> Black shoes with buckles or clasps.
> French head dress.
> Black velvet body with long and short sleeves.
> Boy's dress.[5]

Whatever the style of dress might be, there was little doubt that the heroine would be dressed in white. White, of course, has traditionally symbolized purity and innocence. A heroine was thus instantly recognizable by her attire, and the audience responded accordingly. Many of the heroines of melodramas were dressed in white with handkerchief and bonnet to match. Three of the four dresses of Agnes Fitzarden in Moncrieff's *The Lear of Private Life*, were basically white. Her first dress was a white muslin, full-trimmed dress; her second was a white net with satin slip; and her final dress was of white satin. Clara Wakefield, the heroine of John Baldwin Buckstone's *Luke the Labourer; or, the Lost Son*, (Adelphi, 1826), wore a white gown, a colored handkerchief, black mittens, and straw hat.

The heroine's bonnet was almost as common a signal as her white dress. Jerome K. Jerome mocked the convention:

> The stage heroine's only pleasure in life is to go out into a
> snowstorm without an umbrella, and with no bonnet on. She
> has a bonnet we know (rather a tasteful little thing), as we
> have seen it hanging up behind the door of her room, but

5. Leman Thomas Rede, *The Road to the Stage: Contains Clear and Ample Instructions for Obtaining Theatrical Engagements* (London: J. Onwhyn, 1835), p. 26.

when she comes out for a night stroll, during a heavy snowstorm (accompanied by thunder), she is most careful to leave it at home. Maybe she fears the snow will spoil it, and she is a careful girl.[6]

When Eliza entered at a tense moment in Dion Boucicault's *After Dark*, (Princess's, 1868), her distress was signaled by the fact that her hat had fallen from her head and was supported by its ribbons. Such touches, apparently insignificant in themselves, were nevertheless important signals for the audience, which was equally able to perceive a flirt or a trollop by the type of bonnet worn.

A naval uniform was as clear a signal of heroic and democratic virtues as a heroine's white muslin dress was of purity. The appearance of a "Jolly Jack Tar" was greeted by enthusiastic approval reflecting the high esteem in which naval figures were held. This was, after all, the period of history that included Trafalgar. Moreover, many Londoners worked on the docks:

> their stage idols were watermen and sailors like themselves, with names positively smelling of salt water and courage: Jack Gallant, Jack Stedfast, Bill Bluff, Union Jack, Ben Billows—all characters played by the inimitable Thomas Potter Cooke, the creator of William [hero of *Black Ey'd Susan*] . . . the brave sailor was so popular that he kept appearing in non-nautical melodrama.[7]

As was pointed out earlier, there was no reason why Philip Wakefield in *Luke the Labourer* should have been dressed in naval uniform, for this drama is purely domestic, yet the entrance of a naval figure (to be accompanied by the inevitable "naval" jargon) established at once the nature of the new character. We can find several depictions of naval figures in illustrations and in the cardboard cut-outs of the juvenile drama—an untapped source of nineteenth-century dramatic history. These "strips" and cut-outs were often drawn from

6. Jerome K. Jerome, *Stage Land: Curious Habits and Customs of Its Inhabitants* (London: Chatto and Windus, 1889), pp. 16–17.

7. Michael Booth, *English Plays of the Nineteenth Century*, 5 vols. (Oxford: Clarendon Press, 1969–76), 1: 154–55.

life and show many of the great Victorian actors in their most famous parts. One of the cardboard figures depicts T. P. Cooke in one of his greatest roles—Harry Hallyard in John Haines's *My Poll and My Partner Joe*, (Surrey, 1835). Cooke posed

> in heroic attitude, his face fringed with black whiskers, a quaint little straw hat perched on his head, his right hand brandishing a cutlass and his left grasping—heaven knows to what purpose—a Union Jack.[8]

There was a less marked but still perceptible tendency to employ an army uniform as a sign of villainy. The army suffered from unpopularity throughout the century, though at times, such as the Crimean War or Waterloo, the animosity lessened. The lack of sympathy for the army was a result of Britain's historical dependence on its army to still social unrest. Before the founding of the metropolitan police force by Robert Peel in 1829, the army was virtually the only force that authorities could call on at short notice to maintain order. Despite their remarkable restraint on numerous occasions, the Life Guards were familiarly known as the *Piccadilly Butchers.* Memories of army brutality during the Gordon Riots, the Peterloo "massacre," and throughout the "hungry forties," left an indelible mark. The navy, on the other hand, remained popular, especially with audiences such as those of the Surrey, because they were mainly composed of dockworkers, chandlers, and shipbuilders whose livelihoods depended on British maritime supremacy. They also mingled on a friendly and informal basis with sailors, heard their tales of adventure, and shared the democratic feelings of those who lived a hard life with cruel taskmasters. And although it was unthinkable that Agnes Fitzarden should be seduced by a Jolly Jack Tar dressed in a blue jacket edged with white, a striped shirt, white trousers, and a straw hat perched upon a pigtail, no audience was surprised when the seducer turned out to be a despised redcoat.

8. A. E. Wilson, *Penny Plain, Two Pence Coloured: A History of the Juvenile Drama* (London: George Harrap and Co., Ltd., [1932], p. 94.

An equally positive signal to the audience was the entrance of one whose fortunes had declined. A growth of stubble merely added to what was already perceived by the audience from the costume. Thus, the notes to Douglas Jerrold's *Fifteen Years of a Drunkard's Life*, (Coburg, 1828), described Vernon's final costume as "a dress of mere rags." The use of rags to indicate moral (and financial) collapse was standard. Stock posters of the day reflect the conventional signals of the dissolution of sobriety—the rags, the unkempt hair, and the quarrelsome disposition. Such grim warnings were bread and butter to the unsophisticated audiences of the minors. The sight of rags and patches was sufficient to indicate the downfall of a person, but other signals existed—especially the use of a cloak. Twynihoe W. Erle, as a frequenter of minor theaters, observed:

> That the husband has seen better days is indicated (to those at least to whom a revelation of the conventional significance attached to various properties at minor theatres has been vouchsafed) by his envelopment in a long black cloak, which imparts to his general effect the appearance of an animated extinguisher.[9]

The upper classes were symbolized by the usual devices. Maltby in Tom Taylor's *The Ticket of Leave Man*, (Olympic, 1863), looks off and sees "carriage company," which he described as "heavy swells on the lark, white ties, and pink bonnets." Erle, discussing the profligate aristocrat of Alfred Rayner's *The Foundling of the Sea*, (Victoria, 1859), said that he was distinguished by the "accredited tokens of a peer as known to minor theatres . . . a glossy white hat, a light paletôt with sky blue cuffs."[10]

Of all stereotypes in melodrama, none was so well known as the villain. He needed no time to explain his evil character (though he frequently undertook to announce it gratuitously in his first soliloquy), since it was immediately per-

9. Twynihoe Erle, *Letters from a Theatrical Scene-painter*, 2 vols. (London: privately published, 1859, 1862), 1: 59.
10. Ibid., 1: 16–17.

ceived. A villain was enshrouded in black, given a black moustache (in early days it was made from burned cork), and a cane. Even that standard signal of the villain, the opera hat, is found as early as 1820. Alvanley's second dress in *The Lear of Private Life* included a dark blue coat, black breeches, black silk stockings, and an opera hat. Emissaries of landlords, lawyers, and other stigmatized characters were frequently dressed in suits of solemn black. Grafton, a villain from T. E. Wilks's *The Dream Spectre*, (Victoria, 1843), wore the traditional black suit that stood out in marked physical and symbolic contrast to the heroine's white. This symbolism was retained even when the "gentleman-villain" became popular. Chandos Bellingham in Boucicault's *After Dark* is typical. He had a black moustache, a black hat, and black suit and gloves. The gentleman-villain as a type was mocked by William S. Gilbert in *Engaged*, (Haymarket, 1877). In this light comedy Belrawney was dressed in a black cloak, black frock coat, black trousers, black wig, and green spectacles. The latter, while intended to shield his dreadful eyes, are reminiscent of the stage convention used in *East Lynne*, where Lady Isabel returns to the bosom of her family disguised *solely* by a pair of blue glasses. Gentleman-villains preferred, on the whole, to sport monocles and to don patent leather boots, especially at The Britannia, where patrons were known to prefer melodrama in which "the village maiden was pursued by the libidinous squire in sticking plaster boots."[11]

Villainesses did not become a marked feature of domestic melodrama until after the middle of the century. Whether they were partners in crime with villains or whether they worked alone, they soon became indispensable to melodrama plots. For a brief period following the success of Colin Hazlewood's *Lady Audley's Secret*, (Victoria, 1863), red hair marked the adventuress, but the normal state of affairs dictated that the villainess should have raven black hair, snakelike eyes (later in the century assisted by a lorgnette),

11. H. Barton Baker, *The London Stage: Its History and Tradition, 1576–1888*, 2 vols. (London: W. H. Allen and Co., 1889), 2: 267.

and showy dresses. Henry James Byron's *The Lancashire Lass; or, Tempted, Tried, and True*, (Amphitheatre, Liverpool, 1867), described Kate Carstone as "black haired with black eyebrows and slightly browned complexion, supposedly of gipsey descent." Her costume was described as, "Prologue: Cheap striped shawl, dark dress, bonnet with showy ribbons, earrings. Act II: Black shawl and dark dress, ragged, torn shoes, hair in disorder, no bonnet."

Even such relatively insignificant creatures as the "Walking Gentleman" and the "Walking Lady" adopted conventional dress. Erle mocked the former for his appearing with

> a bran-new hat which he carries in his hand, as ladies do lace pocket handkerchiefs, with a view to decorative effects only, since he never puts it on. . . . His face is as luminously clean as that of a wax doll at a bazaar; his coat is fresh and glossy, and his boots polished to that degree that they form a pair of lustrous mirrors.[12]

Other stock-character types were equally recognizable. The farcial nature of melodrama's comic scenes demanded its appropriate costume. Originally more a comedy figure, the rustic gradually became an admirer and protector of the heroine and the archenemy of the villain. The arrival of the rustic was signaled by his flowered waistcoat. The association of a waistcoat with comic figures was, of course, a very old convention. A firm tradition had gradually developed that in performances of *Hamlet* the First Gravedigger should divest himself of several waistcoats while digging. This piece of stage business disappeared around 1830, but it was the most obvious example of the association of waistcoats with comic figures in the early nineteenth century. The tradition was transferred to melodrama and became well established. In *Luke the Labourer*, Gilbert Bachelor changed his costume but wore his flowered waistcoat throughout the play. In *The Dream at Sea*, (Adelphi, 1835), Buckstone again employed a waistcoat—this time as a hiding place for Tommy Tinkle's fortune, and, in *Black Ey'd Susan*, Gnatbrain's inherent goodness was shadowed forth

12. Erle, 2: 57–58.

by his waistcoat. As Dutton Cook put it, "Red hair [on a man] is always associated with comicality, and, when combined with a chintz waistcoat, invariably signifies rustic integrity."[13]

The use of make-up in the English theater has had a relatively short history. In Elizabethan England make-up was used by women as a cosmetic (Hamlet talks of paint an inch thick), but it was not employed much in the theater. Certain characters were traditionally made-up—Negroes and Moors were played as blackamoors for two hundred years. By the eighteenth century the overuse of make-up was being deplored by writers. In 1789, Waldron produced a new edition of John Downes' *Roscius Anglicanus* in which he stated that painting the face and using dark lines to indicate age had been carried to excess, until Garrick set an example in subtlety. However, the advent of the nineteenth century found make-up still in its infancy, and throughout the first half of the century the art of make-up remained more or less conventional. Little heed was paid to time, place, or setting:

> Neither the social position, age, or country of the character, nor the historical period of the play affected the clothes or the makeup of the actor and actress. With the beginning of the Twentieth Century there came about a slow but gradual change.[14]

The revolution in make-up came with the discovery of greasepaint, for before that date all stage make-up, even if used with grease, was basically a powder supplemented by black crayons used as underliners. The first use of greasepaint in the English theater was in 1877, although it had been used on the continent for some years prior to this, and by 1890 greasepaint was in universal use.

Added to the actor's problems in using make-up effectively was the tendency of the lights to distort his features.

13. Dutton Cooke, *On the Stage: Studies of Theatrical History and the Actor's Art,* 2 vols. (London: Sampson Low and Co., 1883), 1: 236.

14. Ivard Strauss, *Paint, Powder, and Make-up* (New Haven, Conn.: Sweet and Son, 1936), n.p.

A writer in the *Theatrical Observer* (London) complained bitterly of this:

> If the footlights and lustres in front do not reduce the features of the performers to one unmeaning blank . . . they do worse, for, by the predominance of light at the feet of the performer, the shadows are necessarily thrown upwards, and the effect is, therefore precisely contrary to the intentions of nature.[15]

Most of the actors fought back by employing strong coloring. The basic work on make-up available to actors in the period 1820 to 1870 was Leman Rede's *The Road to the Stage*. Generally manuals of acting followed Rede's lead, which stressed, among other things, the need for an emphatic make-up because of gas lighting:

> Chinese vermillion boiled in milk and then suffered to dry, and afterwards mixed with about half the quantity of carmine [a powerful red derived from the cochineal insect] is decidedly the best colour an actor can use . . . especially as the late introduction of gas into our theatres has rendered a more powerful colouring than that formerly used decidedly necessary.[16]

Since members of the audience could see very little detail unless they were in the front seats, an exaggerated make-up and style of acting were felt to be necessary. Naturally some problems could be alleviated if the audience was told how to react by means of a traditional signal. Conventions in make-up complemented those of costume in revealing immediately, upon his first appearance, a character's true nature and intent. Manufacturers' advertisements of the period reveal that standard products were employed for certain character-types or situations. White was used in plays where sickness or fainting was to be represented (even though the lack of make-up in itself would

15. Quoted in E. B. Watson, *Sheridan to Robertson: A Study of the Nineteenth-century London Stage* (Cambridge, Mass.: Harvard University Press, 1955), p. 94.

16. Rede, p. 32.

produce the same effect). Percy Fitzgerald described some of the other materials available to the actor:

> *Blue.*—For unshaven faces. This is *very necessary in low comedy characters.*
> *Prepared Burnt Cork.*—For Negro Minstrels. This we can recommend, as it can be taken off as easily as put on.
> *Carmine.*—For the face, and to heighten the effect of burnt cork in Negro characters. A most brilliant colour.
> *Prepared Dutch Pink.*—For pale, sallow, and wan complexions.
> *Email Noir.*—*To stop out teeth for old-men characters,* witches, &. (that is, give the appearance of a cavity).
> *Prepared Fuller's Earth.*—To powder the face before "making up."
> *Hare's Feet.*—For applying powders to the face, &. . . .[17]

Wigs were, of course, one of the most visible indicators of character. Jerome K. Jerome had to purchase seven of these to further his acting career—" a 'white Court,' a 'brown George,' a 'flowering ringlets,' a 'scratch,' . . . a 'comic old man,' a 'bald,' and a 'flow' for every thing that one was not quite sure about."[18] John Hammerton in *The Actor's Art* (1897) deplored the persistence of stage conventions in regard to wigs:

> It is the face and head that give the index to character. To this end a knowledge of physiognomy ought to be acquired; that is the physiognomy of life . . . [because] black hair is not a necessary badge of villainy, nor are golden curls the *sine qua non* of virtue, or a carroty wig the cause and effect of comicality or stupidity.[19]

Even the parting of an actor's hair could be used to indicate character or situation. "Old Stager" talked of every change in hair style being related to a different mood:

> Now parting [the hair] down the centre and curling it (if long enough) after the fashion of a love-sick youth or a gay cavalier,

17. Percy Fitzgerald, *The World Behind the Scenes* (London: Chatto and Windus, 1881), p. 124.
18. Jerome K. Jerome, *On the Stage and Off*, p. 97.
19. John Hammerton, *The Actor's Art* (London: George Redway, 1897), p. 53.

or flat to the side of the face, with a puritanical lengthening of
countenence . . . now brushing it under in rolls after the
fashion known a few years ago as "The Newgate Knocker,"
being of a rakish medical student aspect . . . or thieflike (Jack
Sheppard cut).[20]

An innovative actor had to overcome years of tradition to
present a character in a fresh light, but it goes without saying that the average stock-company actor neither wished
nor dared to alter the traditional signals of character. Audiences at the minors wanted characters who could be recognized on sight, and they tolerated little interference with
the established conventions. For example, as late as the last
quarter of the nineteenth century, when F. A. Scudamore
tried to play a villain with flaxen locks, the audience would
have none of it, considering this novelty to be a dangerous
innovation leading to unnecessary complexities of character.
Even though the melodrama villain continued into this century and became much more sophisticated, elegant in
dress, and suave in his villainy, his hair remained as black
as his soul.

Considering the importance of make-up in melodrama, surprisingly little has been written about its use.
Hints can be derived from the few available accounts
and from suggestions in printed versions of plays. In
George Dibdin Pitt's *The String of Pearls; or The Fiend of
Fleet Street,* (Britannia, 1847), the villain's make-up included "iron gray scratch-wig—heavy eyebrows—repulsive
make-up." Just what the "repulsive make-up" involved can
only be guessed, but it was effective, for when Sweeney
Todd asked Jonas Fogg if he remembered him, Fogg replied pointedly, "True sir: You are not easily forgotten." In
Dion Boucicault's *Arrah-Na-Pogue,* (Dublin, 1864), Michael
Feeny was directed to: Make-up the face very repulsive,
unwashed, two-days growth of black beard, lines of face
marked prominently. He wore a "black close-crop wig." His
face was "rusty black" with "battered high crown hat." T.
W. Erle gave a graphic account of make-up in the melo-

20. Old Stager [pseud.], "Dramatic Directory," *A Practical Guide to Private
Theatricals* (London: Thomas Scott, 1875), p. 43. Jack Sheppard, the highwayman,
was a popular figure in romantic melodrama.

drama *Adelbert the Deserter; or, The Robbers of the Black Forest*:

> The make-up of the several accomplices forms each a tableau in itself. . . . One of the villains displays the result of a guilty mind by such dark furrows across his brow that he looks as if his forehead had been subjected to the action of a dirty rake. Another betokens the deep stains upon his conscience by so wholesale an outlay of burnt cork upon his face, that his features are almost as black as Ira Aldridge's or those of your unhappy Cinderella, . . . and the consumption of Berlin wool required to form the long sable locks of the whole party taken together must have been such as to have imparted a feverish impulse to the worsted trade.[21]

These villains Erle called "black." They were bold in their make-up and villainy. Some villains, though much rarer, were "white." A white villain was described by Erle as having: "Pink bloodshot eyes like a white mouse's and on every alarm of detection they start out of his head like a scared rabbit's or a prawn's. . . . He is as pale, through guilty apprehension, as plaster of Paris or a parsnip indisposed."[22] Several plays do contain cowardly villains—generally accomplices of "black" villains. Though no make-up was suggested for Caleb, the runaway watchmaker's apprentice in Edward Fitzball's *Jonathan Bradford; or, The Murder at the Roadside Inn*, his every action suggested a frightened white-faced villain. It is also significant to note that Caleb wore a tawdry, flowered waistcoat indicating faded rustic integrity, and a long curling wig indicative of youth and frivolty.

Minor-theater audiences were both eclectic and conservative in their ideas of how certain characters should appear and behave, and they had come to expect that their precepts would remain inviolate. They did not ask dramatists to write great works of literature but to paint a world in which no explanations were necessary and where it was possible to tell at once how things stood. Heroes were consistently heroic, heroines were always virginal and faithful,

21. Erle, 1: 25–27. No record of this play remains.
22. Ibid., 1: 95–97.

and villains always looked and acted like villains—
verisimilitude was not in demand. As Augustin Filon
lamented:

> The "man about town" . . . represents the selfishness, the
> folly, and the insolence of the higher classes, as imagined by a
> man who never had been inside a drawing-room. Did he know
> Society at his finger-ends, the man would never think of
> painting it. He never paints from nature. He copies for the
> thousandth time from the old models, Sheridan and
> Goldsmith, or his new masters, Scribe and d'Ennery.[23]

The move toward realism in the latter part of the
nineteenth century and the growing sophistication of audiences led to the end of the stock company and the domestic
drama it had performed—though the end was long in com-
ing.

Costume and make-up were vital adjuncts to the actor's
physical movements. Naturally, acting styles changed not
only with the passing of time but also from theater to theater. It would be a great disservice to regard all minor theaters
as inflexibly bound to convention or their audiences as
monolithic. Nevertheless, several traditions were widespread well into the latter part of the century. This persistence was just as evident in acting as in everything else.
Victorian styles of acting were not based, as those of today
are, upon an attempt to appear as realistic as possible. The
grandiose nature of early melodrama required a comparable
style of acting. As the Gothic prototype was steadily driven
out by the domestic drama, so the style of acting became
more restrained. It is clear that many actors and audiences,
particularly after midcentury, were increasingly aware of
the absurdity of their histrionics, but innovations were only
slowly approved. Actors like Henry Talbot who attempted a
more realistic style were soundly criticized for merely be-
having as they would at home and not acting at all.[24] Until

23. P. M. Augustin Filon, *The English Stage: Being an Account of the Victorian
Drama*, trans. Frederic Whyte (London: John Milne, 1897), p. 81.
24. J. H. Barnes, *Forty Years on the Stage: Others (Principally) and Myself*
(London: Chapman and Hall, 1914), p. 32.

the Fechter revolution, acting theory was based on the premise that an actor's task was not to hold a mirror up to nature but to reflect the sublime. A normal tone and behavior were, *ipso facto*, incapable of doing this, and since there were virtually no schools for actors in the first half of the Victorian period, an actor learned his craft by imitating his elders. Later in the century, acting schools became more numerous, and the founding of the Royal Academy of Dramatic Art helped change the actor's method of learning his craft and encouraged innovation.

Nineteenth-century acting went through various phases.[25] The style of Kemble was the basic style before Fechter introduced a deeper subtlety and restraint. Kemble's influence on traditional acting was marked. There is no denying that later players gave their art a great deal more variety, but that artificial gesture and declamation lay at the root of their style, too. Kemble's school of acting was irreverently referred to as the "teapot" school. The name derived from the tendency of the players to extend one arm before them and to declaim in this stance. Women pressed their other hand to their breast; males placed it on their hips. One leg was often thrust forward and, for variety, it could be reversed. Edmund Kean was hailed as a "natural" actor after he burst upon the London stage. However, his naturalness consisted of abandoning the Kemble stiffness and unemotionality. Kean infused violence into his roles and in doing so gave an impetus to the newer melodramatic acting that was to gain a firm hold at the minor theaters until the end of the century. So explosive could Kean become that he once summoned Marie Wilton to a private rehearsal so that she should not be frightened by him during the performance. Kean's style of acting was undoubtedly more "lifelike" than most, but he did not seek to imitate natural behavior. Macready took his violence from Kean and his declamation from Kemble. So violent was he that he once

25. Alan S. Downer, "Player and Painted Stage: Nineteenth-century Acting," *PMLA* 61, no. 2 (June 1946): 522–76, is the best brief study of the various acting styles of the century.

Robert Dighton's drawings of Charles Kemble and Mrs. Siddons in "tea-pot" poses (VICTORIA AND ALBERT MUSEUM)

broke a finger of Fanny Kemble in a stage rage. He was also capable of subtler touches and had a tendency to grunt and groan throughout his part. Such mannerisms and defects were marked among nineteenth-century actors. Kean sounded as if he had a head cold. Samuel Phelps was always examining his chest and picking at it, and Macready adopted a style of walking that was imitated by innumerable "supers" at his theater. The contempt that critics felt for the sight of a whole company walking in the distinctive manner of their idol was justified. It is highly probable that actions of this type delayed the arrival of the natural school of acting for years.

It was Charles Albert Fechter who prepared the way for Henry Irving, but the acting of neither was what could be called *realistic*. Fechter made it clear that the *comparative* naturalness of his style of acting was not a lower form of the art, but a marked improvement over the staginess of tragic declamation. *The Illustrated London News* (13 April 1861) said that "the English actor declaims too much, and M. Fechter's quiet and familiar delivery will go far to arrest that tendency; at the same time he will learn from the English actors the value of certain 'points.' "[26] On 4 May the same paper proclaimed:

> What we see in M. Fechter's Hamlet is the poet's manner of expression, not the actor's. The performer no more acts the part than Hamlet himself would, but conducts himself with princely courtesy, gives vent to his outraged feelings, dallies with his revenge, and is at last hurried to the issue just as the young and overtried Prince of Denmark would have done in his uncle's Court.[27]

Henry Irving knew that he would have to work hard to make plays like *The Corsican Brothers* and *The Bells* successful. His movements were not natural in the everyday meaning of the word, but every movement he made was significant and part of a language that communicated every nuance of character.

26. *The Illustrated London News,* 13 April 1861, p. 333.
27. Ibid., 4 May 1861, p. 410.

Throughout the century, but particularly during the first half, acting was dependent upon making "points" and creating "effects." Edmund Kean was particularly fond of points. All plays of the period could be broken down into many pieces of stage business that had become as famous as the texts themselves. A famous point of Kean's was his reaction to Wilford in the library scene of George Colman the younger's play, *The Iron Chest*, (Drury Lane, 1796). When appearing in Croyden, it was the only scene Kean bothered to rehearse. In this scene, with

> Wilford's utterance of the word "murder" the chord was struck that seemed to vibrate through every fibre of his frame, the internal struggle to regain his self-possession quite thrilled the audience. His trembling hand turned over rapidly the leaves of the book he held, as if to search its pages, that were evidently a blank to his bewildered sight, till the agony of his feelings overbore all efforts of repression, and with tiger fury he sprang upon the terrified youth. . . . His terrible avowal of the guilt that had embittered existence to him brought, as it were, the actual perpetration of the deed before us; the frenzy of his vengeance seemed rekindled in all its desperation, as he uttered the words—"I stabbed him to the heart." He paused as if in horror at the sight still present to him, and, following with his dilated eye the dreadful vision, he slowly continued— "And my oppressor rolled lifeless at my foot!"[28]

At the lowest minor theaters it was not uncommon for an entire performance to rest on one particular point or effect that the audience held especially dear. The nearest modern parallel to this situation might be found in the tremendous emphasis placed on Hamlet's third soliloquy. Points were scored and something of a running tally of an actor's performance was kept. The harm this system did to the craft of acting was formidable. Most of all, originality was severely curtailed. Kean was fortunate when he made his debut as Shylock in a black wig rather than a red one; other actors had been hissed off for far less. New effects were seldom tolerated, but certain "improvements" of accepted effects

28. William C. Macready, *Macready's Reminiscences and Selections from his Diaries and Letters,* ed. Frederick Pollock, 2 vols. (London: Macmillan and Co., 1875), 1: 136–37.

were less harshly judged. So essential were points and effects that when Macready introduced a new one in which Hamlet danced with a handkerchief to reveal his antic disposition, the American actor, Edwin Forrest, seized the opportunity to show his displeasure with Macready by hissing.

Actors in domestic drama were particularly prone to pointmaking. One series of points obviously grew out of the stage directions to a piece of business in George Dibdin Pitt's *The String of Pearls*. Jarvis Williams ("a lad of no small appetite") found himself alone in Mrs. Lovett's bakehouse where he sampled her pies:

> *(Jarvis takes a pie off tray R., and eats voraciously.)*
> JARVIS. . . . Beautiful! delicious! lots of gravy!
> *(He suddenly discovers a long hair, views it mysteriously, and winds it around his finger.)*
> Somebody's been combing their hair. I don't think that pie's a nice 'un.
> *(Puts part of the pie back, and takes another.)*
> This is better! Done to a turn! Extremely savoury!
> *(Puts his hand to his mouth.)*
> What's this? A bone? No, a button? I don't think I like pies now (act 1, scene 4).

That such points were consistently made, with perhaps certain individual embellishments, is clear from an eyewitness account by T. W. Erle of the same scene:

> A series of effects are produced by the successive discovery in the pies of what may be called "internal evidence" of the true nature of their ingredients. Thus, one of the consumers finds in the first instance a woman's hair. . . . The discovery of the hair is followed by that of a thumb nail. . . .The startling revelation of a brass button attached to a fragment of material substance of some kind or other which bears the aspect of having once formed a constituent portion of somebody or other's leather breeches proves what is called "a staggerer."[29]

After making an important point of which he was particularly proud, an actor might signal to the audience that ap-

29. Erle, 2: 20–22.

probation was in order. He could turn triumphantly to the audience or rush into a corner of the stage.[30] The actor's movements, as shall be seen later, were exaggerated, amounting at times to a stylized pattern something like a ballet. It is absurd to criticize such acting for being unnatural; it was not intended to be anything else. The lines of *Sweeney Todd* could not be delivered in the normal conversational manner required of a play such as *Hedda Gabler*. Domestic drama required a certain style; it was a form of dramatic communication ideally suited to its medium and message. It was a style that was designed not to overtax the mind but to appeal to the emotions.

Bold, extravagant, unsubtle acting was needed to conduct the Victorian audience into the gaslight world of love, loyalty, and elemental morality. The very origins of melodrama in dumbshow and the particular theatrical conditions that existed in the nineteenth century made it necessary for actors to achieve their effects through an exaggerated technique. The stage saw many mute characters in plays at the beginning of the nineteenth century. Such characters were descended from dumbshow plays, and from stage directions we can gain an insight into the type of acting at this time. Here, for example, are the movements in act 1 of Barnabas Rayner's *The Factory Assassin; or, The Dumb Man of Manchester*, (Astley's Amphitheatre, 1837):

> *Edward proceeds to strike Jane—Music—Tom rushes forward, catches him by the arm, struggles with him, and wresting the knife from him, dashes it to the ground. Edward wrestles with Tom, who is ultimately thrown down, and Edward escapes over the balcony. Tom rises and goes and shakes Jane violently as before. Tom then rushes to the window, rings the alarm bell, the rope of which is attached to the balcony—his mute cries become frightful. Voices respond below—the R. door is burst open, and all the characters rush in. . . . Music very marked—Tom falls on his knees and calls on Heaven to witness his innocence. The workmen rush to seize him—Mr. Palmerston*

30. Joseph Jefferson, *The Autobiography of Joseph Jefferson* (New York: Century Company, 1890), p. 65.

interferes between them. Tom seems almost frantic, and dashes himself on the ground.—Tableau—Drop descends slowly (act 1, scene 3).

As has been seen, the melodramatic style of acting was necessitated both by the theatrical conditions existing and by the nature of domestic drama itself. This acting style constitutes one of the reasons why a great deal of the drama of the nineteenth century can no longer be played seriously to audiences today. Without the exaggerated style of acting, much domestic drama seems flat and stale, yet with the melodramatic style of playing, domestic drama appears ludicrous to a modern audience. There was another reason for the style also. It was a matter of necessity in many cases. A stock actor had little time to devote to the development of realistic characters. Instead he had to have a set of signals with which he could embellish any character with a minimum of rehearsal. Nuances of character were not possible under the pressures of playing several different characters each week. The quickest way to depict a hero was to exaggerate the stately poses of Kemble; a villain had the passion and evil of Kean's crookbacked Dick.

The postures and movements of nineteenth-century actors were accompanied by appropriate gestures. These gestures can now only be seen in pictures, posters, books, and the sheets of the toy drama. Many nineteenth-century actors, such as Ducrow, Munden, John Kemble, Edmund Kean, and Mrs. Siddons, appeared in their most florid poses. Since the early sheets were drawn from life during a performance, it is likely that the juvenile drama does show the type of gesture employed on the adult stage.

There were, of course, various books published on the subject, for gestures constituted a great deal of what was referred to as "the art of acting." A prominent American publication, *The Thespian Preceptor*, described many of the prominent signals employed by actors to tell their audiences how things stood. Joy, for example, "when sudden and violent, is expressed by clapping of hands, and exulting looks; the eyes are opened wide, and on some occasions, raised to heaven."[31] "Old Stager" listed and described some forty-six emotions ranging from "aversion" to "intoxication."[32] The standard nineteenth-century work on gesture was published by Henry Siddons in 1822.[33] Here some sixty-nine "expressions of the various passions" were listed and illustrated. The idea that any combination of emotions could be communicated by standard gestures lasted well into the nineteenth century, and even, in rare instances, into the twentieth.

The heroine, though this fact is often overlooked, had to portray a greater range of feelings than any other character in domestic drama. Consequently her gesture language was more taxed than that of the other characters. In the last moments of John Baldwin Buckstone's *The Dream at Sea*, Anne Trevanion "staggers back and falls," "sinks to the earth—a shot is heard—she rises, and rushes to the mouth of the cave," "kneels to assist Launce," "falls into Trevanion's arms," "points to Ralph," and "kneels at the feet of Richard." In Douglas Jerrold's *Fifteen Years of a Drunkard's Life*, when Patty discovered that her brother had lost all their money, she "runs up to the farm, is about to enter, when she falls upon her knees at the door, in the attitude of prayer." Such supplicatory gestures are found throughout domestic dramas. At the conclusion of *Lady Audley's Secret*, for example, "Talboys kneels beside her covering his face with his hands."

Villains, it appears, had developed special ways of walking. Indeed, it seems that special "walks" were a standard signal of character. Bart Kennedy classified them as follows:

> The light comedian must have . . . a walk that is quick and decided and a bit bustling . . . it ought to be the male counterpart of the mincing trot of the soubrette. On the other

31. *The Thespian Preceptor* (Boston: Joshua Belcher, 1810), p. 27.

32. Old Stager [pseud.] "Art of Acting," pp. 18–24.

33. Henry Siddons, *Practical Illustrations of Rhetorical Gesture and Action Adapted to the English Drama*, 2nd edition (London: Sherwood, Neely, and Jones, 1822).

hand, a low comedian may choose the walk that takes his particular fancy. He may, so to speak, steal the walking thunder of the tragedian, and get laughs thereby; or he may hop, skip, or strut, or if he feels that the occasion calls for it, walk even upon his hands. . . . The walk of the villain must fit the brand of villainy he is portraying. It may be sneaking, or it may be aggressive, or it may be a walk that is a blend between the two.[34]

A villain was particularly noted for his movements on stage. He frequently entered as if retribution lurked all around. Grafton in *The Dream Spectre* entered cautiously. *"He goes round the stage observingly and beckons off. Enter Van Doone and Hoole."* It is unnecessary to emphasize the point that in his desire for secrecy, the villain generally behaved in a manner most likely to attract attention. Not only did he endow entrances with a style peculiarly his own, but he even developed a unique method of traversing the stage:

> His gait is a combination of the strut of a bantam with the hop-over-nothing of a string-halt horse and consists of alternate brandishings of his legs, each of which manoeuvres constitutes in itself a separate and gymnastic exploit. His strides are so high.[35]

Should any of his machinations have a temporary success, he adopted "a swagger mainly executed by a series of alternate swoops of his shoulders as he steps."[36]

An entrance was employed by an actor as a telling means of communication. An entrance is always significant for a character, but some actors had trained their audiences so well in the art of communication that even opening a door could become a significant means of communication. George Arliss, writing as late as 1928, noted that a fellow actor "banged open the door with the flat of his hand . . . a signal for great resounding clapping and stamping."[37]

34. Bart Kennedy, *Footlights* (London: Henry Walker, 1928), p. 80.
35. Erle, 1: 95.
36. Ibid., 1: 8.
37. George Arliss, *On the Stage: An Autobiography* (London: John Murray, [1928]), p. 61.

Various articles were essential in portraying certain gestures. A handkerchief was an essential prerequisite of many emotional scenes ever since Addison complained of its overuse in his day. Edmund, in T. W. Moncrieff's *The Somnambulist*, (Covent Garden, 1828), was so moved at the thought of Ernestine's betrayal that he took "his handkerchief and covered his face to hide his emotion." If no handkerchief were available, the hands served just as well. When all seemed lost in Tom Taylor's *Ticket of Leave Man*, Brierly complained that he can fight no longer and "throws his head on his hands in despair." Similarly there are few heroines who have not "wrung their hands in despair" at one time or another. Other attitudes such as astonishment were frequent and well known to the gallery gods. An actor could stand "transfixed" or he could react in what today would be termed a *melodramatic fashion*. This was the way that Launce reacted when he discovered, in *The Dream at Sea*, that Anne Trevanion was still alive:

> *Launce, attracted by the sound, starts up; he looks toward the pallet, and stands in wonder. His hands are thrown back; as if in search of some support, his head thrust forward regarding the object with wild but joyous terror.*

An almost identical position was assumed in the famous depiction of Henry Irving as Mathias in Leopold Lewis's *The Bells*. Here Irving's head was thrust forward, his hands reached behind him, clutching at a curtain, and his whole face was transfixed with a look of terror. T. W. Erle described the melodramatic style of a scene of powerful emotion played in the conventional way:

> Powerful-emotion-business by a tender-hearted sergeant, executed in the orthodox fashion, namely by putting his head against some one else's neck and then waggling his shoulders about.[38]

Acting as an art suffered under severe handicaps that tended to require the most exaggerated of styles of playing.

38. Erle, 1: 31.

Henry Irving as Mathias in *The Bells* (VICTORIA AND ALBERT MUSEUM)

Because of poor lighting only those on the front rows could see any facial movements of a delicate nature. Kean was criticized by a newspaper critic because he placed too much faith in facial expression—most of which was visible only to those close to the stage. Facial expressions are mentioned in stage directions but far less than other movements and gesture. In Jerrold's *The Rent Day*, Crumbs, the steward, "looks fiercely around him" at one point, and "exchanges a look of contempt with Jack and Hyssop." Other plays demanded gnashings of teeth and twisted countenances, such as Sweeney Todd's terrible "grimaces."

The use of gas as a means of illumination made exaggerated facial movements necessary. Subtle facial gestures were impossible as long as stage lighting lagged so far behind domestic advances in illumination. It became necessary for actors to use large amounts of make-up in order to be seen by distant spectators. Irving was apparently more successful than most, but his achievements began in the last quarter of the century. Steady improvement had been made in stage lighting throughout the nineteenth century, but it was 1881 before a theater (the Savoy) became entirely lit by electricity. It is clear that electric lighting was undoubtedly a contributing factor in the rise of the more natural style of acting that arose in the last quarter of the nineteenth century.

An examination of the style of acting in the minor theaters of the last century should not blind the reader to the fact that no period in English theatrical history has produced so many renowned players—but unsophisticated audiences had made unfortunate demands upon actors:

> Many of them might have been good actors; but from long experience in bad plays before primitive audiences, they had come to accentuate the mechanism of the art of acting instead of concealing it. It was the revealing of the mechanics that taught the gallery boy when to *take up his cue in the responses*. (My italics.)[39]

"Boz" commented disparagingly on the influence that "the Theatrical Young Gentleman" had on the style of acting by

39. Arliss, p. 63.

his desire to know all the modes of communication that were involved:

> He is likewise very accurate in judging the natural expressions of the passions and knows precisely the frown, wink, nod, or leer, which stands for any of them, or the means by which it may be converted into any other; as jealously, with a stamp of the right foot becomes anger; or wildness, with the hands clasped before the throat, instead of tearing the wig, is passionate love . . . the theatrical young gentleman assures you with a haughty smile that it always has been done this way, and he supposes that they are not going to change it at this time of day.[40]

So well-known did the visual signals of the stage become that they could be transferred to the popular literature of the day. Louis James pointed out that the illustrations in the "penny dreadfuls" often employed the gesture language of the theater:

> These woodcuts and the stories perfectly supplement each other. The outstretched hands point to the power of destiny, the falling curve of the heroine's body illustrates her helpless innocence; the villain's enormous eyes—Sala as a woodcutter was told to make them larger—show devouring lust. They convey the conventional poses of both actor and stock characters, *designed to evoke a crude but precise response from the back of the "gods,"* or a semi-literate reader struggling to understand the story. The illustrations were more than ornament. Today, when we are deluged with pictorial art, it requires an effort to imagine the impact of pictures on early nineteenth-century readers. The appreciative Wilkie watched in tears a stage representation of his picture, *The Rent Day,* and Cruikshank's series of etchings, *The Bottle,* were twice made into penny-issue novels. (My italics.)[41]

Audiences and critics alike were moved by pictures or tableaux. There was a certain aesthetic pleasure in seeing a picture made into a stage tableau. This may be difficult to comprehend in today's world, surrounded by pictorial art on all sides, but in the early nineteenth century, things

40. Charles Dickens, *Sketches of Young Gentlemen* (London: Chapman and Hall, 1838), pp. 54–55.

41. Louis James, *Fiction for the Working Man, 1830–1850* (London: Oxford University Press, 1963), p. 150.

were very different. The sight of Sir David Wilkie's two
pictures *Rent Day* and *Distraining for Rent* on stage was
greatly applauded by the audience. *The Theatrical
Examiner* (London) was loud in its praise too:

> We have seldom felt more interested in any performance. The
> pictures are excellent; and this praise extends not only to those
> which have been borrowed from the painter, but to several
> [others]: Martin surrounded by his children, the Robber scene,
> Rachael fainting across her husband's knee, the broken chair,
> and the finale where the painter indeed may be indebted to
> the compositions of the stage manager.[42]

Wilkie wrote a letter to the scenic artist, Clarkson Stan-
field, in which he acknowledged with gratitude the "unpre-
cedented honor from the dramatic to the painter's art." The
play became so lucrative that the manager of the Haymarket appropriated the play to restore his theater's failing fi-
nances.

Less ambitious tableaux were employed to end acts and
to emphasize the mood of the scene—lest there be any
doubt about it. Thus, in G. D. Pitt's *Sweeney Todd*, as
Jonas Fogg and his men were about to seize Tobias and
carry him to the madhouse at Sweeney Todd's behest, the
window was shivered: *Jarvis Williams dashes through and,
protecting Tobias, confronts the others with his fists.
Picture.* This courageous act no doubt won the plaudits of
the gallery and symbolized to their sentimental hearts the
forces of good that ever favor the oppressed. Many other
moods could be visualized by pictures. A sense of despair
could be communicated to the audience. A case in point is
a tableau in *East Lynne* that was made into a poster. This
picture reveals the characters in several of the positions
illustrated in the books of rhetorical gesture. At the end of
act 2 of Clifton Tayleure's version of *East Lynne*, (Brooklyn
Academy of Music, 1862), the following picture is described
in the stage directions: *Archibald in chair, overcome by
deep grief; Joyce, appealing to heaven; Miss Cornelia*

42. *Theatrical Examiner* (5 February 1832), p. 85.

The "picture" end of Act 2 of *East Lynne* (CHEROKEE BOOKS)

bending over Archibald. A poster advertising the play shows a similar situation except for the addition of two extra characters. A male figure, presumably Lord Mount Severn, stands with his arms raised high above his head. Such a gesture appeared to be a literal enactment of "throwing one's hands up in despair." This gesture is, in fact, given by Siddons as symbolizing "Awe and Appeal." The other additional character is a young girl seen reaching toward her father in a gesture indicative of "supplication." Although the servant Joyce does not appear in this particular poster, she may be found in another poster entitled, *"East Lynne,"* in exactly the position described in Tayleure's stage directions.[43]

Frequently the word *tableau* was used in stage directions in place of *picture*. Essentially the two words mean the same thing. Tableau was taken from the French expression *tableaux vivants*, that is, living pictures. *Tableaux vivants* were also a form of entertainment in which scantily costumed actors assumed motionless poses for sustained periods of time. It seems, however, that the practice of tableaux was German in origin:

> Perhaps *The Theatrical Repertory* is right in tracing the tradition to the German plays where "all the characters are arranged in picturesque manner, and stand in fixed attitudes, like images on pedestals, when the curtain drops." By the twenties of the century the "images on pedestals" had become thoroughly English. . . . This tendency towards the tableau is itself part of the spectacular movement of the early nineteenth century and is connected, too, with the miming indulged in so freely by the makers and producers of the melodrama. These "pictures" were loved by the spectators almost as much as dialogue and dramatic action, and the more successful effects were loudly applauded.[44]

Tableaux were also popular because their dramatic and exciting nature was in direct contrast to the hard, drab exis-

43. *Specimens of Show Printing* (Hollywood, California: Cherokee Books, n.d.), p. 256.

44. Allardyce Nicoll, *A History of Early Nineteenth-century English Drama*, 2 vols. (Cambridge, England: Cambridge University Press, 1930), 1: 46–47.

tence led by most members of the audience. Some plays
were little more than a series of tableaux; others, such as
Leopold Lewis's *The Bells*, contained a series of tableaux,
several of which were indicated in the stage directions. One
occurred, for example, at Mathias's first entrance (accompanied by the inevitable chord on the piano):

> *Mathias passes the window then enters at C. door; he wears a*
> *long cloak covered with snow, a large cap made of otter's skin,*
> *gaiters and spurs, and carries a large riding-whip in his*
> *hand—chord—tableau.*

Throughout his career, and especially in his Shakespearean
productions, Irving never forgot the nature of his audience.
He continued to employ tableaux, all the time making them
more breathtaking and imaginative.

Tableaux were carefully rehearsed. If an actual picture
were to be copied, the original illustration was placed in a
prominent spot so that all participants could study their
positions and gestures. In production, the exact length of
time for which a tableau was held varied, but the overall
value of the tableau as a means of dramatic communication
lay in the fact that it emphasized a point and gave the audience time to reflect upon it. An ideal view of life as it
should be, or an illustration of fears about to be realized,
could be dramatically represented in a tableau. Most
domestic drama ended on a firm moral tableau, since this
was the lesson that the playwright wanted his audiences to
carry home with them. Frequently the final tableau emphasized the happy victory of tested virtue over vanquished
vice. G. D. Pitt's version of *Sweeney Todd* concluded with
a tableau revealing Mark Ingestrie standing over Sweeney
Todd, who had fainted at the appearance of his supposed
victim. The couple were surrounded by astonished witnesses and the Judge. Ingestrie voiced the dire moral of the
play, which was that the very dead will rise and return "to
confound the guilty and protect the innocent." The ending
of Fred Hazleton's version of the same play was equally
direct—informing the audience of the dreadful fate that

awaited all murderers. "Officers enter at every side and fire at Todd—at the same time the scene opens at back—the steps give way—Todd falls dead—the whole scene at back is enveloped in flames—tableau." The message of this tableau and others was very plain. Erle commented, "The moral of the piece is intended to be good, since the final tableau exhibits all the good characters with knives at the throats of all the bad ones, respectively."[45]

Several other forms of communication, some of them quite unintentional were restricted to certain theaters. One of the most unusual was found at the Adelphi Theatre, where a group of "supers" dressed as partygoers was enough to establish immediately the fact that someone was to meet his end at a function requiring evening dress. This group became known as the Adelphi Guests who

> grouped themselves according to fixed traditions, gazing with horror on the suicide or murdered man as the case might be, while the curtain descended slowly to Adelphi music.[46]

Other signals were found in the stage setting. Domestic drama, like Gothic melodrama, offered its auditors an escapist world, but the settings were vastly different. Dramatists seized upon the fact that their supporters lived for the most part in slum conditions within sight of a factory or workplace. Accordingly the city setting began to symbolize evil, while the countryside indicated domestic bliss and tranquility. The nostalgia that nineteenth-century audiences felt for the countryside will be examined in Chapter 4. Suffice it to say here that innocence and poverty went hand in hand. The sight of a sparsely furnished cottage was enough to tell the audience that its inhabitants were both virtuous and needy. A stage setting from a toy theater strip showed Dame Hatley's cottage in *Black Ey'd Susan*: virtually unfurnished, with cracks in the walls, this was the sure and certain home of virtue. Jerome K. Jerome commented:

45. Erle, 1: 72–73.
46. Fitzgerald, pp. 209–10. Leopold Wagner wrote in 1899 that the Adelphi Guests were finally ousted by "educated young men and women."

All the virtuous people in the play lived in cottages. I never saw such a run on cottages. . . . After one or two more appearances, the cottage became an established favourite of the gallery. So much so, indeed, that when two scenes passed without it being let down, there were many and anxious inquiries after it, and an earnest hope expressed that nothing serious had happened to it.[47]

The cottage was often presented in marked contrast to the tavern or country house, which were generally signals of idle luxuriance and immorality. Just as often a wretched garret or an elegant dining room in the city symbolized life at its worst. It was to the city, or tavern, or both, that the drunkard went, and it was in the city that the profligate or gamester would lose what remained of his self-respect.

Stage scenery at poorer minor theaters remained, on the whole, unrealistic. For the first half of the nineteenth century, the theaters made do with crude flats, backdrops, and stock sets. Such an arrangement made it possible for touring companies to perform anywhere without much difficulty. Special effects and costumes were the only extras needed. As the century progressed, authors began calling for more and more "practicables," which is to say, scenery that was functional. In the sixties, Tom Robertson's concern with "realistic scenery" became a legend.

When stages were lighted chiefly by oil, actors tended to stand in a straight line trying to get into what was called *the focus*. Gas lighting reached the English stage in 1817, and by 1827 most of the theaters were lighted by it. It is difficult to discover just how much improvement gas brought with it; frequent complaints were voiced that the stage was made too glaring and painful to the eyes. In fact the subtlety of facial impression possible with candles or oil may well have been lost. Nevertheless, attempts were made to employ lighting for effect. In Hazlewood's *The Mother's Dying Child; or, Woman's Fate*, (Britannia, 1864), the villain stabbed his wife to death; she fell into the water, and he fled by boat, but at that moment: "The form of Stella

47. Jerome, *On the Stage*, pp. 59–60.

floats on left, illuminated by the limelight, which also makes the waters appear transparent."

Since melodramatic vision was paranoid, all things living or dead seemed to combine to persecute the good. There was thus an extensive use of bad weather and natural calamity. Storms and thunder (the latter often accompanied a *snow* storm) were indispensable. The value of a thunderstorm could scarcely be overlooked by the author of *The Lear of Private Life*. Indeed, Moncrieff rose to the occasion by permitting the heroine to voice a dramatic comparison and a pious hope:

> AGNES. . . . What is this storm that rages now without to that which rages here? I left my father at midnight for Alvanley, and shall I shrink to leave at midnight that poor wretch for him? No, no; I will arise and go to my father's house and tell him I have sinned. When he sees his child—his penitent child—return worn and unprotected, through the horrors of a winter's night, to beg at once his pity and his pardon, surely he will—he must—forgive me! (act 2, scene 1).

There was a further signal from stage to audience found in many theaters, and this was a strip of green baize that was laid down whenever a scene of violence was scheduled. This strange convention was really a fossilized stage tradition. Originally green baize had symbolized tragedy, but its more mundane purpose had been to protect the lavish dresses from contact with a dirty stage when its wearer collapsed and died. Some theaters continued to utilize the green drugget to signal tragedy or excitement to come:

> Another convention was the green carpet (generally of baize) which was always laid on the stage when there was a tragedy to be enacted or some terrible scene to move spectators. It was supposed to be a good thing to prepare audiences for a thrill, and so when they saw the green drugget they knew for certain that their feelings were going to be harrowed.[48]

48. Errol Sherson, *London's Lost Theatres of the Nineteenth Century* (London: Bodley Head, 1925), pp. 44–45.

The green baize was gradually abandoned as a signal as sets became even more lavish. At first the carpet became a strip, but by Irving's time it had disappeared entirely.

Accompanying these visual signals were a number of aural signals. Aural communication consisted not only of what was spoken, but also of the way the lines were delivered and by whom. The other important aural signal lay at the very heart of domestic drama—in the music and the songs that had played such a prominent role in melodrama from its very inception at the end of the eighteenth century.

Melodramatic rhetoric, however, was not the invention of the nineteenth century:

> In England the postmedieval drama begins with the establishment of a melodramatic rhetoric in Marlowe's *Tamburlaine,* and melodramatic rhetoric subserved tragedy, or declined into bombast or banality, or merely served its natural purpose as the proper style of melodrama, until about 1850.[49]

An "elevated" rhetoric was the natural language of melodrama—a conversational, colloquial English would not suffice. Though it is a far cry from the language of domestic drama to that of the modern stage, it would be foolish to deny that the one developed into the other. At first domestic dramatists relied heavily upon action and stage direction for effects. It was easier to write stage directions than dialogue; it was easier to paint with directions than with words. The last scene of T. J. Dibdin's *Suil Dhuv, the Coiner,* (Sadler's Wells, 1828), is a case in point:

> (*Enter Paddy Moran with a small torch, or link, L. U. E.* [Left Upper Entrance])
> PADDY. I heard a drum a while since—the military are abroad, sure; but now all's quiet: on the top of every one of those pillars a train is laid, and must be lighted, to show our lads a clane way, for de red-coats are sometimes pleased to be in ambush. (*Faint shriek.*) They're coming ho! ho! dis way; 'tis

49. Eric Bentley, *The Life of the Drama* (New York: Atheneum, 1964), p. 207.

best not to light too soon, de inimy as well as friends may get de profit.

(*Enter Lilly and Kitty, who are brought on by the coiners, R., and are met by Robert Kumbra, L.*)

ROBERT. Hold, villains! (*Runs at the coiners.*)

(*Enter Suil Dhuv, L. U. E.*)

SUIL DHUV. Hold, you!

(*Enter O'Byrne, R.*)

O'BRYNE. Give me my child! (*Attacking Paddy who runs.*)

PADDY. Nay, then, it's time to see who's who.

(*Paddy touches each stone—they form a magnificent semicircular blaze.*

Enter Hogandorff, who runs from the circle and attacks Suil Dhuv at the moment he is striking down Robert. Enter Sarah, R.)

SARAH. Hold! father! husband!

(*Sarah rushes between them—a drum beats—soldiers rush from behind, surround the robbers, and form a grand tableau—Suil Dhuv dexterously escapes from two soldiers—he is met by Robert at the sword's point, and, as he turns from him he is met by Hogandorff—he beats down both their swords, and fights his way, pursued by soldiers, to the top of a precipice, from which he leaps to another, leaving his pursuers behind—he waves his cap triumphantly, while the soldiers on the rock and the group below present their pieces at him.*)

OFFICER. (*To Suil Dhuv.*) Surrender! or they fire!

SARAH. Oh, no—fire not! for mercy—for my child's sake!

(*She places herself before the soldiers who are on the stage—her father runs to take her from so dangerous a situation, but she resists—the child [she has been brought on by Minny] runs to her—she snatches it up—the officer gives a sign to the soldiers who recover their arms.*)

OFFICER. Once more, surrender, and accept of mercy.

SUIL DHUV. I am beyond the hope on't.

SARAH. Oh, yes! Mark, Mark! dear Mark!

SUIL DHUV. (*To soldiers.*) Make ready! (*They intuitively do so.*) Present!

(*The officer, waving his sword, commands them to obey—Suil Dhuv leaping from the rock into the lake below, and rising above the surface.*)

SUIL DHUV. Fire! ha, ha, ha!

(*He plunges beneath the water as they fire—Sarah screams, and falls into the arms of her father, who supports the child—Robert kneels to Lilly O'Byrne, whose father joins their hands—Remy embraces Kitty and his old mother by turns—the*

*coiners are guarded in groups by the soldiers, and the curtain
falls to a characteristic symphony* (act 2, scene 8).

Such a heavy preponderance of stage directions was by no
means unusual in the early melodramas, since it was the
very nature of melodrama to stress action and deed rather
than language and dialogue. The value of a musical direction "characteristic symphony" is best left to the imagination!

So many situations and characters were alike in domestic
drama that a type of verbal shorthand arose. For authors
turning out scores of plays, it became necessary to draw
characters as swiftly as possible with as little difficulty as
possible. Any moments in a drama that required skillful
handling could be avoided by a stage direction or by a
character describing his emotions rather than revealing
them through his actions. Romantic scenes were particularly badly handled, usually in the most unconvincing of
language and even, as in Edward Fitzball's *Jonathan
Bradford*, in weak blank verse:

> BRADFORD. (*R.*) Give me a kiss, wife; another!
> The wine is good that smacks upon the lips:
> How are the bantlings?
> ANN. (*L.*) Well, and both abed.
> BRADFORD. I've brought the lemons and the nutmegs,
> The sugar and the comforts for the children:
> I've brought besides—what think you this is, Ann?
> (*Showing small packet.*)
> ANN. What can it be?
> BRADFORD. I'll tell thee.
> It is a pair of buckles; though not diamonds,
> Glittering bright they shine, as stars at even;
> Not costly are they, save as love enriches,
> And turneth all things golden. Wear them, Ann,
> For my sake. (act 1, scene 1).

More important than the language and dialogue of
domestic drama, at least in the eyes of the minor-theater
manager and player, was its delivery. In chapter 1 it was
pointed out that the size of many theaters required that ac-

tors project their voices into an immense cavern. Young actors of "promise" were often assured by managers experienced in the profession that if they could learn to shout in the right places they would have little to fear. Old play books are mute testimony to the desired style of voice projection.[50] Passages can still be seen with underscorings that indicated "claptraps" (moments at which applause could be forced). Players were required to deliver these lines in such a way that the audience would be compelled to applaud. Kean's delivery of the line, "I am a Jew," in act 3, scene 1 of *The Merchant of Venice*, was such a powerful change from the declamatory to the conversational that it always produced a storm of applause. Kean was also a master in the use of the pause and produced some of his best effects by its use:

> One of his means of effect—sometimes one of his tricks—was to make long pauses between certain phrases. For instance, on quitting the scene, Sir Edward Mortimer [in Colman's *The Iron Chest*] has to say warningly, "Wilford, remember!" Kean used to pause after "Wilford," and during the pause his face underwent a rapid succession of expressions fluently melting into each other, and all tending to one climax of threat; and then the deep tones of "remember!" came like muttered thunder . . . sometimes the pauses were only tricks, but often they were subtle truths.[51]

As domestic drama developed, it could not be played in the style that Kean had popularized and that of Macready was found more suitable. The eminent tragedian's followers praised his "natural style" of playing, despite its frequent pauses and its intense syllabification. His critics, such as Fannie Kemble, were less kind:

> It may have been his consciousness of his imperfect declamation of blank verse that induced him to adopt what his

---

50. However, Antony Coleman's article "Mossop as Wolsey," *Theatre Notebook* 25, no. 1 (Autumn 1970): 11–14, shows how much effort some actors were prepared to make to get their voice projection correct.

51. George M. Lewes, *On Actors and the Art of Acting* (New York: Henry Holt and Co., 1880), p. 19.

admirers called *the natural style of speaking it*; which was simply chopping it up into prose—a method easily followed by speakers who have never learned the difference between the two, and that blank-verse demands the same care and method that music does, and when not uttered with due regard to its artificial construction, and rules of rhythm and measure, is precisely as faulty as music sung out of time.[52]

Whatever else may be said of Macready, he was the most frequently imitated of actors. His supers faithfully imitated his rolling gait, and it comes as no surprise to discover that his elocution was *de rigueur* among the actors of his day. It was undoubtedly Macready's stature in the profession that influenced lesser actors to deliver melodramatic lines with overly frequent pauses that often fell between the article, adjective, and substantive, and were followed by strong stress upon the initial words. The peculiar style of melodramatic pronunciation and delivery was humorously satirized by such writers as Dickens, Erle, Cook, and the American, H. J. Smith. The latter commented upon the pronunciation of the word "innocent":

> The heroine's name is Grace,—or it may be Gladys or Rose; that does not matter. "I swear to you that I am innocent," she declares, *molto tremoloso,* and with an appealing look that wings its way beyond the uttermost gallery-god. No one but an habitué of the Thalia or some other shrine of the popular melodrama knows the authoritative pronunciation of that word *in-no-cent.* It should be dwelt on syllable by syllable, and certain long-drawn prominence should be given to the n's. For gesture, one hand may be slightly extended and upraised, the other pressed timidly upon the breast; and at the close of the word the eyes should fall, the head droop forward with sweet submission. This position may be retained for several seconds. Then the gallery will clap,—tumultuously, sealing the truth of Grace's assertation. This is as much a foregone conclusion as the sentiment that calls it forth.[53]

It was, of course, only the extravagant nature of the drama and its broad style of playing that allowed actors to

52. Frances Ann Kemble, *Records of Later Life* (New York: Henry Holt and Co., 1883), p. 636.

53. H. J. Smith, "Melodrama," *Atlantic Monthly* 99 (March 1907): 321.

carry the day. Erle devoted considerable space to discussing the vernacular of the minor theaters. He quoted several examples:

> The walking gentleman is never so exulting as when his sweetheart's name is Susan, because then when he has to deliver the time-honoured speech of, "In the ole kee-yabinet of nature's gee-yems, there is none arruf so bee-yeau-tiful as the lovely Zoozan," the "Zoozan" affords him an opening for what may be called *intense syllabification,* which he lingers upon with infinite relish.[54]

The melodramatic elocution was not short-lived and existed in certain theaters until late in the century. Dutton Cook, H. Barton Baker, and William Archer all make reference to the continuance of this type of elocution in the final quarter of the century:

> There is said to be an actor on the English stage who can make four syllables of the word "blood," by pronouncing it "ber-a-lud-a." In no particular instance, perhaps, does Mr. Irving quite attain to this height, but his "transmogrification" of his mother tongue is as thoroughgoing as it well can be.[55]

Tone of voice was another important aspect of theatrical communication. Very little is written on this subject, but it is clear that tone was mated to character stereotype. Accordingly, accounts mentioning tone of voice generally stress the need for a bass voice for the villain. Erle informs us that "black" villains have a "basso profundo, or rather profundissimo" voice, while the voice of the "white-livered villain has no comfortable heartiness in it. . . .[56] Many years later, matters had not changed at the more lowly theaters:

> The villain of the stage must have a cold, clear, acid voice. A vein of sneerery must run through that voice—a kind of vitriolic thread, as it were. . . . A villain who cannot convey

54. Erle, 2: 57.
55. William Archer, *The Fashionable Tragedian: A Criticism* (Edinburgh: Thomas Gray and Co., 1877), p. 8.
56. Erle, 1: 97–98.

sneerery in his voice has no class, as they put it in the Old Kent Road.[57]

Accompanying the "sneerery" was often a diabolical laugh. The cold laugh of O. [Richard John] Smith became a conventional signal of villainy in domestic dramas:

> O. Smith had a formidable assortment of terrifying tricks in his bag; a half-crazed look and manner, a stealthy step, a hollow voice; and a piercing eye; and he was a master of gruesome makeup. His trump card, however, was his laugh, a taunting, deliberate basso-profundo effect in three syllables that never failed to start pleasant tremors down the not particularly sensitive spines of transpontine addicts of blood-and-thunder drama. That laugh was widely imitated in the profession and became a convention in the interpretation of villain roles.[58]

The base of the villain, the tenor of the hero, the *multo tremoloso* of the heroine, and the platitudinous drone of the old man, were all attempts to communicate with more than just the spoken word.

Almost as noticeable as the actor's use of language was the playwright's inclusion of "set" speeches. These speeches were of two basic types—those that were employed by the playwright for technical reasons and those that were always associated with the various character stereotypes in the plays. The best-known technical reason for a set speech was that of providing enough information to make the action comprehensible. It was considered more desirable to have speeches of this type so that the audience would not need to trouble itself seeking for motivation, logic, or clues to the action on the stage. Explanatory speeches were stereotyped forms of communication that audiences frequently greeted with humorous banter. J. H. Barnes referred to one such incident in Lord Newry's *Ecarté*:

> A sort of heavy father of the story sat down in an easy chair with his daughter on a footstool at his knee, and began what bade fair to be a good stereotyped explanatory speech . . .

57. Kennedy, p. 107.
58. Frank Rahill, *The World of Melodrama* (University Park, Pennsylvania: Pennsylvania State University Press, 1967), pp. 208–209.

" 'Tis many years ago my child, your mother died," when a fellow-countryman of Lord Newry's in the gallery observed in the sweetest brogue imaginable: "Och! now thin for the plot!"[59]

Soliloquies and asides were used for similar reasons. They were a great help in the problems of writing exposition that the episodic nature of domestic drama imposed upon the dramatist. They were also useful in the more traditional manner of revealing the nature, motivation, and inner feelings of the characters. A typical example was the soliloquy of William Corder as he bared his soul to the audience in *Maria Martin* [*sic*]; *or, The Murder in the Red Barn* (Star Theatre, Swansea, 1842), revealing his murderous intent toward Maria Marten, his supposed sweetheart:

CORDER. How well this pent-up soul assumes the garb of smiling love to give my fiendlike thoughts the prospect of success! In vain does nature, reason, conscience, all oppose it. The thought has got such firm possession of my heart, such despotic sway, that naught can turn me from my fixed resolve; and conscience, feeble guide to virtue, only shows us when we go astray, but wants the power to stop us in our course. The deed were bloody, sure; but, I will do it, and rid me of this hated plague. Her very shadow moves a scorpion in my path. I loathe the banquet I have fed upon. By heaven! Be still, my heart (act 1, scene 2).

One of the best-known forms of speech employed by domestic-drama characters was that of the British tar. Comic and singing sailors made their bows at theaters ranging from Drury Lane to Astley's Amphitheatre. As early as 1793, J. C. Cross's play *The Purse; or, The Benevolent Tar* was performed at the Little Theatre in the Haymarket. This "musical drama" was little more than a one-act melodrama, but its hero, Will Steady, ushered in a whole race of sailor heroes.

The nautical heroes, who flourished under such names as Harry Hawser, Harry Hallyard, Jack Gallant, and Union Jack developed considerable dexterity in manipulating their jargon in such a way that it sufficed for all occasions.

59. Barnes, p. 99.

Whether audiences could understand everything their sailor heroes said is improbable, but it was not so much the meaning of what was said but its forceful or melancholy delivery that counted most. Nautical language told an audience that the speaker could be believed and trusted, that his nature was honest and true, and that his sentiments were always of the noblest.

The most noticeable feature of nautical jargon was the recurring use of "sea metaphors," naval exclamations, and nautical terminology. The following are the words of William in *Black Ey'd Susan* after he has been condemned to death for striking an officer:

> Damn it, my top lights are rather misty! Your honours, I had been three years at sea, and had never looked upon or heard from my wife—as sweet a little craft as was ever launched. I had come ashore, and I was as lively as a petrel in a storm. I found Susan—that's my wife your honours—all her gilt taken by land sharks; but yet all taut, with a face as red and rosy as the King's head on the side of a fire bucket . . . (act 2, scene 2).

Nautical language was also notable for the patriotic and democratic sentiments that it voiced. These plays were often dramas of protest, but naval figures often gave the lion's roar or spoke as the conscience of the humble-but-honest man. Here are the words of Harry Hallyard when left in charge of a captured slave ship in John Haines's *My Poll and My Partner Joe,*

> HARRY. Follow me, my lad, we'll overhaul your log. And, do you hear, boys? Let the wounded be looked to—let the poor niggers go free upon deck. Dance, you black angels, no more captivity; the British flag flies over your head, and the very rustling of its folds knocks every fetter from the limbs of the poor slave (act 2, scene 2).

Land-based heroes had less jargon to work with but were equally adept at mouthing moral sentiments and circumlocutory avowals of love. Jerome K. Jerome satirized the convention, but his observation is not far removed from the truth:

The Stage hero never talks in a simple, straightforward way, like a mere ordinary mortal.

"You will write to me, when you are away, Dear won't you," says the heroine. A mere human being would reply: "Why, of course I shall, Ducky, every day." But the Stage hero is a superior creature. He says: "Dost see yonder star, Sweet?" She looks up, and owns that she does see yonder star; and then off he starts and drivels on about that star for five full minutes, and says that he will cease to write to her when that pale star has fallen from its place amidst the firmament of Heaven.[60]

Heroes, and often "old fathers," frequently had speeches that were strongly moral in tone. The language might be expressive of the hero's remorse or repentence, or it might refer to the hero's views on right and wrong. Temperance dramas contained some of the most obvious examples, but they are found throughout domestic drama. When in William Smith's *The Drunkard; or, The Fallen Saved*, (Boston Museum, 1844), Lawyer Cribbs tried to persuade Edward Middleton to forge Arden Rencelaw's name on a check, the air was filled with indignant moralizing:

EDWARD. What! forgery? and on whom? The princely merchant! the noble philanthropist! the poor man's friend! the orphan's benefactor! Out and out on you for a villain, and coward! I must be sunk indeed, when you dare propose such a business to my father's son. Wretch as I am, by the world despised, shunned and neglected by those who should save and succour me, I would sooner perish on the first dunghill— than that my child should blush for her father's crimes. Take back your base bribe, miscalled charity; the maddening drink that I should purchase with it, would be redolent of sin, and rendered still more poisonous by your foul hypocrisy. (*Throws down money.*) (act 3, scene 1).

Such language presented the actor with a chance to show what he could do. A point often mentioned by early commentators was that domestic drama did give actors a chance to *act*. It is also clear that this speech, like others of the type, is bristling with claptraps—many of which, underlined in the actor's text, would supply him with a series of oppor-

60. Jerome, *Stage Land*, p. 7.

tunities to urge the playwright's lesson home and to force the audience to applaud.

To some extent, attempts were made by dramatists to differentiate the language of heroes from that of heroines. However, the differences were relatively minor. Generally the method selected was to give heroines a language of the most stilted delicacy. Whatever might be said about the language of naval figures and even that of heroes, it was at times a lively and refreshing contrast to the sticky speech and cloying sentiments of many heroines. This exotic tongue descended in large measure from the works of eighteenth-century sentimentalists. It was only a short step from the language of the heroines (and heroes) of Steele, Lillo, Mrs. Inchbald, and Cumberland to that of Jerrold, Buckstone, and hundreds of others.

Since the heroine's primary function in a domestic drama was to lament piteously the blows of fate, it followed that her language was molded to fit situations of pity, suffering, and loss. Frequent mention and emphasis is found throughout "heroine-in-distress" speeches of "haplessness," "loneliness," "wretchedness," "friendlessness," and other terms of deprivation. Great stress was laid upon the enunciation of these words in performance so that the point could not be missed by any in the audience. No flinty heart could remain unmoved by this speech in *The Ticket of Leave Man* by May Edwards (who refers to herself as a "helpless and friendless girl"):

> MAY. Oh, if I could only get away from this weary work! if some kind lady would take me in. I'm quick at my needle; but who'd take me, a vagabond, without a friend to speak for me? I'm alone in the world now. It's strange how people's life is made for 'em. I see so many girls, nicely dressed, well off, with parents to love and care for 'em. I can't bear it sometimes, to see them, and think what I am, and what's before me. (*Puts her hand to her face.*) I'm a silly girl: it's all because I'm so weak from the fever (act 1, scene 1).

Arousing the audience's sympathies was only one of the verbal duties assigned to domestic-drama heroines. It was frequently their task to verbalize those sentiments that the audience held so dear. Since self-sacrifice, piety, and duty were the ennobling virtues of the poor, the message of the drama was that those who held true to their duty would reap the ultimate rewards. Scores of heroines echoed the same pious hopes as Laura, in Augustin Daly's *Under the Gaslight*:

> LAURA. Let the woman you look upon be wise or vain, beautiful or homely, rich or poor, she has but one thing she can really give or refuse—her heart! Her beauty, her wit, her accomplishments, she may sell to you—but her love is the treasure without money and without price (act 3, scene 1).

It often happened that the heroine's "treasure" was attempted by the villain and, as a result, no one suffered such verbal onslaughts as he did. Often his only "crime" was to offer to marry the heroine. For his pains, he received a verbal assault that seemed to be out of all proportion to its cause. The reason for the attack was clear enough in performance, however. Since the appearance of the villain told the audience what his character was, there was no need to wait until a specific moment in the story when his villainy was fully in evidence. Any moment would do for the heroine to launch her prepared attack on the evil that he symbolized. In rejecting his advances, heroines employed variations of a phrase first found in Cumberland— "Unhand me, sir!" This phrase, or one of the many variants—"Release me, ruffian," "Unloose me, wretches" —became one of the best-known verbal signals in later domestic drama.

Heroines were frequently inclined to voice lengthy comparisons between the villain and their true loves, always, it is unnecessary to add, in the latter's favor. When Lawyer Cribbs attempted to take advantage of Mary's poverty in *The Drunkard*, he was roundly denounced in typical, domestic-drama fashion:

> MARY. Wretch! (*Throws him off.*) Have you not now proved yourself a slanderer, and to effect your own vile purposes. But

know, despisable wretch, that my poor husband, clothed in rags, covered with mire, and lying drunk at my feet, is a being whose shoes you are not worthy to unloose (act 3, scene 5).

The villain's language was calculated to reveal his essential duplicity—at times fawning and hypocritical, and at others demoniac in nature. He employed the soliloquy and the aside a great deal. Serious villains explicitly rejected moral control in soliloquies giving themselves to the devil's work, as William Corder did while waiting to murder his pregnant mistress, Maria Marten:

> CORDER. Suspicious self will sleep, ay sleep for ever. Yet, twixt thought and action, how harrowed is the brain with wild conjecture. The burning fever round my temples gives to this livid cheek a pallid hue. Hark! By heavens she comes! Now all ye fiends of hell, spur me to the deed—teach me not to feel pity nor remorse; let me show the cause of quarrel for the act.
>
> "Hand, heart, be firm, my reputation save,
> And hurl my victim to an early grave" (act 1, scene 5).

Less dramatic, but equally sinister, threats could be made by use of the shorter aside:

> MARIA. William, you'll not be so long?
> CORDER. No, dearest. *(Aside.)* I'll be there *too soon for you* (act 1, scene 3).

The printing of passages in italics in plays or setting them off in inverted commas was a popular device. It indicated to the actor that a particular kind of intonation was required. Montagu Slater commented on this matter in a version of Maria Marten edited by himself:

> Some of the people have Wagnerian motifs. Tim's is, "Dosta say so?" Corder's is, "Curse the girl!" They are often written in the MS in inverted commas, and they are intended to be repeated with a variety of intonation and expression at any suitable pause in the action.[61]

61. Montagu Slater, *Maria Marten; or, The Murder in the Red Barn* (London: Gerald Howe, 1928), n.p.

One of the features of the villain's soliloquy was that it often permitted the actor to build it up to a climax. In this soliloquy from *The Drunkard*, Lawyer Cribbs laid his plans for the downfall of Edward Middleton in a rising crescendo of threats:

> CRIBBS. I will do him some unexpected favor, worm myself into his good graces, invite him to the village barroom, and if he falls, then, ha! ha! I shall see them begging their bread yet. The wife on her bended knees to me, praying for a morsel of food for her starving children—it will be revenge, revenge! (act 1, scene 4).

It was in the nature of villains to reveal their hubris by such premature gloatings at the anticipated success of their machinations. Dan Macraisey, the villain of *Jonathan Bradford*, is an example—"Not laugh!—Why not? Haven't I just doubled the gallows-hunters?—They won't think of hunting in here, I calculate." The unfortunate Luke of *Luke the Labourer* exulted in his anticipated revenge:

> LUKE. There be a light in the place where the farmer sleeps; I'll watch here till it be out. . . . Ah, he ha' put out the candle; now to make all ready for climbing—this shall do it—I'll take my aim steady and sure; then I'll snap the trigger; then there'll be a stunning sound, a cry of death, a flooding o' blood on the floor and Luke's revenge finished. Ha, ha! (act 2, scene 4).

Again the phrases build up to a climax allowing the actor great opportunities for the broad acting style that domestic drama demanded.

Villains seldom if ever succeeded in their nefarious schemes, and they greeted their defeats with a series of "oaths" and highsounding resignations to the fickleness of fate:

> "Death and furies!", "Foiled! Hell and Confusion," and "Foiled again!" gained currency from the frequency of their repetition. Villains usually died, sometimes reciting their own epitaph: "Betrayed, my schemes annihilated—myself undone, my enemies triumphant—lost—lost—all is destroyed—all—all

(falls)." Often the villain's death speech underlined the play's lesson: "Is all hope excluded? All, all! Slaves of guilt! Votaries of passion! See here the recompense that awaits you." If the villain failed to point out the moral, some other character would: "In this heaven speaks its doom with awful voice."[62]

Yet a surprising feature, in light of the stern morality found in melodrama, was the dignity with which villains faced their fates. Often they refused to repent, and even attempted in some plays, such as *The Rent Day*, to justify their villainy:

> GRANTLEY. What is this? . . . (*Reading bill.*) "Escaped from Newgate—John Harris!"—who can this mean?
> CRUMBS. The man your father robbed! Read and see what time and he have made of him. I took ten guineas from a rich usurer, and was condemned for Tyburn. Your father stole the wife of my bosom, and lived a wealthy, charitable gentleman—had the respect of all while on earth and a lying tombstone when under it. May I leave now? (act 3, scene 4).

Whatever else may be said about the true villain he knew how to make his final bow and win a last round of applause.

The last aural signals to be considered in this chapter are musical. Music was, of course, as significant as the drama itself in the earliest days of melodrama. Pixérécourt's plays were scored for an orchestra and only in opera did music play a more important role. These scores are fairly rare, though there are printed music cues in the stage directions of melodrama texts. In Holcroft's *A Tale of Mystery* there were directions to the orchestra for music to cover every eventuality. Music was required "to express chattering contention," "to express pain and disorder," "to express dejection." The music, of course, reflected the nature of the scene, too. At times it was "confused, loud, and discordant," "soft," "violent-distracted." John Coleman remem-

62. David Grimsted, *Melodrama Unveiled: American Theatre and Culture, 1800–1850* (Chicago: University of Chicago Press, 1968), p. 179.

bered playing a role in the play and the difficulties he encountered:

> I had the temerity—or shall I say the folly——to attempt, in an emergency at a few hours notice, Count Romaldi in *A Tale of Mystery*—a "villain of the deepest dye," who gives about two hundred music cues for a mysterious dumb man to pantomine to.[63]

The musical score of Holcroft's play was by Busby, and there seems reason to believe that many changes were made from the original score of the Paris production of Pixérécourt's *Coelina; ou, l'enfant du mystère*.

A copy of French's Acting Edition of Hazlewood's *Waiting for the Verdict* in the Enthoven Collection of the Victoria and Albert Museum contained marginal notes as musical cues that would both heighten the action on stage and allow the conductor to unite music and drama as closely as possible. These directions generally ranged no further than "slow," "lively," "hurry," "cautious," and "chord." Some were a little more descriptive "lively then slow," "slow then lively to change [of scene]." The dynamic markings, "pp" and "ff " for very loud or soft were used. Somewhat more exotic directions were often found in scripts. Hazlewood's *Taking the Veil; or, The Harsh Stepfather*, (Britannia, 1870), required "music descriptive of warbling birds."

A complete score of *Black Ey'd Susan* by J. Blewitt is located in volume 2 of the Thomas Potter Cooke material in the Enthoven Collection. The central idea for the play came, of course, from John Gay's ballad "Sweet William," but the majority of the music came from Charles Dibdin's naval airs. The music contained printing errors that are so typical of musical publications of the period. The score was not orchestrated and circulated with piano accompaniment, since the piano-vocal score was the more salable version. The melodies were simple and the vocal selections were either a two- or three-part song form.

63. John Coleman, *Fifty Years of an Actor's Life*, 2 vols. (London: Hutchinson and Co., 1904), 1: 111.

An excerpt from Jonathan Blewitt's score of *Black Ey'd Susan*
(VICTORIA AND ALBERT MUSEUM)

The overture resembled that of the opera overtures of the period and provided the audience with a preview of the important melodies in the work. It commenced with the "Black Ey'd Susan" melody, building tension by increasing the tempo from that of the opening, and by employing *fioratura* passages reminiscent of Rossini. It contained two songs not found in the body of the score, though "Cease Rude Boreas" was given to Crosstree in the text of the play (act 2, scene 3).

The main musical text was divided into twenty-six separate interludes. The majority of these were preceded by a music cue on the left and the stage directions on the right. Half of the selections were to be played "allegro," while the other half were assigned opposite markings for tempo —largo, adagio, andante, solemn. The majority of the pieces were employed to bring actors on and off the stage. Susan had her own tune derived from the song, "All in the Downs," though there was apparently no villain music as such at this time. A particularly significant use of music was to accompany the tableau that concluded each of the acts. Act 2 ended with William striking his captain:

> (*William turns away horror-struck. Susan falls on her knees, the sailors bend over the Captain. Slow music. Tableau.*)

Music accompanied fight scenes and moments of violent action. In these cases, as in all others, it was the tempo and rapid harmonic changes within the music that counted rather than anything else. Because of the particular requirements of melodrama, the quality and integrity of the music diminished very considerably. The composer, once as important as the dramatist, became a mere hack. This is not to say that music was ever entirely absent from domestic drama in one form or another. In working-class theaters, such as the Britannia or Astley's, music always played a significant role as an *adjunct* to melodrama. Jerome K. Jerome wrote of a production in the 1880s:

> The play was one of the regular old-fashioned melodramas, and the orchestra had all its work cut out to keep up with it.

Nearly all the performers had a bar of music to bring them on each time and another to take them off; a bar when they sat down, and a bar when they got up again; while it took a small overture to get them across the stage. As for the leading lady, every mortal thing she did or said, from remarking that the snow was cold in the first act, to fancying she saw her mother and then dying, in the last, was preceded by a regular concerto. I firmly believe that if . . . she had shown signs of wanting to sneeze, the band would have struck up quick music.[64]

When domestic drama transferred to film early in this century, it did not take theater managers long to realize that music was of great use in eliciting and heightening emotional response. Thus, drama and music never completely separated, but within a relatively short time since the inception of the genre, the role of music had become that of a poor relation. Music was given certain jobs to do. It was used to underline the emotional nature of the scenes and to direct and control the audience's responses. It was employed to bring characters on and off stage. Some characters had special themes to identify them, though these themes soon became standard signals, such as threatening music for a villain or pitiful strains for the heroine. It was crucial to many actors' greatest points that music should be employed to heighten the effect of them. Perhaps most important of all, music could cover up a multitude of sins—as the success today of many operas with inane plots and stereotyped characters but excellent music amply demonstrates. Songs (and dances) were frequently interpolated into domestic dramas. They were arranged in such a way that they could be lengthened or removed entirely depending on the actor's skill.

After the early days of domestic drama, the choice of music was left to the musical director. He had his standard repertoire that covered all eventualities. For sword fights, "round eights" were often employed. Combatants struck or parried in monotonous obedience to the orchestra, even taking a *minim rest* if dictated. The director also had his

64. Jerome, *On the Stage*, pp. 41–42.

"storm music," his "soft music," and his "hurry music." The latter was apparently successful, as Gordon Craig suggested:

> The slow, quiet talk which mumbled on—and above all, the queer "hurry music" as it is called, which was astonishingly dramatic; all these things led up to the first point to be made, and with decision, "Here is the man!" And now watch what he will do—better still, how he will do it—best of all, watch his face and figure and follow what it is these are hinting at.[65]

One service music always provided as long as it had any role to play in domestic drama was the heightening of mood. Loud chords emphasized dramatic tableaux or moments. Such an event occurred as Walter was telling the story of the apparent murder of the Polish Jew in *The Bells*:

> WALTER. . . . At eleven o'clock the Night Watchman came in. Everyone went his way, and the Jew was left alone.
> (*Chord of music—loud gust of wind—crash of glass off— hurry* [music]. *All start to their feet. Music continued.*)

This violent moment was turned into an anticlimax by the discovery that the kitchen windows had been left open and had smashed in the storm. The real reason for the inclusion of the sudden noise was, however, to leave the audience in an uneasy and agitated state—ready for Irving's first entrance as Mathias. Only a minute later, the audience was given the ominous information that Mathias's good fortune began shortly after the Jew's disappearance. Music again heightened the suspense.

> HANS. . . . everything has succeeded with Mathias for the last fifteen years. (*Music commences.*)

Within two lines of this musical warning, Mathias was seen passing the window and entered to a "chord—tableau."

> MATHIAS. It is I—It is I! (*Music ceases.*)

65. Edward Gordon Craig, *Henry Irving* (London: J. M. Dent and Sons, 1930), p. 56.

Even from the bare stage direction, something of the excitement and tempo of the scene is apparent, and from this point on Mathias was accompanied by theme music of a "mysterioso" nature.

The limited musical resources of many minor theaters resulted in certain incongruities. T. W. Erle reported on a performance at the Royal Britannia, Hoxton:

> The consummation of a tragical situation at the R. B. is usually intensified by the tune of "I loves a drop of good beer," played pensively. Objections might of course be made by tiresome rigorists to the adoption of so genial and festive an air as an accompaniment to proceedings partaking in no degree of a convivial spirit. But those who resort to a theatre in a mean and nasty spirit of petty captiousness are in no proper frame of mind for appreciating the pathetic and touching effects which the management has had an eye to.[66]

The presence of songs and duets in domestic drama had been, in part, a means of circumventing the monopoly that the patent theaters enjoyed on the production of the legitimate drama. It is not surprising to find that even after legal restrictions had ceased to be a consideration, songs were found throughout domestic drama. One could be fairly certain, for instance, that a domestic drama would commence with music—often a dance or a chorus of villagers or sailors. *The Lear of Private Life* opened to the strains of a duet and chorus celebrating the successful completion of the harvest. Similar types of choruses were used to bring plays to a joyous conclusion. *The Drunkard* ended upon a regular banquet of songs. Edward, purged of his alcoholism, played "Home Sweet Home" on the flute with Julia singing the first verse. She was accompanied by the solo flute. Gradually the villagers took up the song off-stage:

(Orchestral accompaniments, etc.—Gradually crescendo, forte.—Villagers enter from C. gradually grouping L. and C.—Action of recognition and good wishes, etc., while the

66. Erle, 2: 38.

melody is progressing—The melody is repeated quicker, and all retire, with the exception of Edward, Mary, Julia, William, and Agnes singing, and becoming gradually diminuendo:—Air repeated slowly.—Julia kneels to Edward, who is at table, R., seated in prayer.—Edward's hand on Bible, and pointing up. Mary standing, leaning upon his chair.—William and Agnes, L. C.—Music till curtain falls.—Picture (act 5, scene 3).

Thus, as was often the case, the moral lesson of the play was presented to the audience visually in the final tableau and aurally by the strains of the song, "There is no place like [a temperance] home."

Few demands were placed on heroes and villains as far as singing was concerned, though they might have been required to take part in a drinking song or two. Heroines were expected, on occasion, "to put over" a lyric piece that emphasized the refinement and delicacy of their natures. Sometimes these were adapted from songs already written, often they were the result of the author's overly sanguine estimate of his abilities to equal the Shakespeare of the romantic comedies. Agnes Fitzarden, the heroine of *The Lear of Private Life*, not only sang Handel's "Deborah" (adapted at her father's request), but also accompanied herself on the harp:

AGNES. Tears, such as tender fathers shed
    .Warm from my aged eyes descend,
  For joy, to think, when I am dead,
    My son will have mankind his friend.

FITZARDEN. No. No; you know I have altered the last line, "For joy, to think, when I am dead, Agnes will have mankind her friend" (act 1, scene 2).

Most songs, however, were given to the comic man and the soubrette. Often the songs and duets they sang had to do with their affection for each other or with unrequited love—often in a comic vein. The first verse of a song that Sally sang in *Jonathan Bradford* gives an idea of the quality of the songs found in domestic melodramas:

A kind old man came wooing to me,
  When my age it was scarce eighteen;
He ask'd with a sigh, if his bride I'd be,
  And he'd make me as rich as a queen.
No parents I had, no money I had,
  Nor sweetheart that ever prov'd true—
If young men won't, and old men will,
  Lawks, what can a poor maiden do?
    Heigho-heigho!
  Lawks, what can a poor maiden do? (act 1, scene 1).

The comic man had generally more songs than any other character. He had his share of unrequited love songs that had a "comic" tone to them. William Dowton of *The Drunkard* sang:

When I was a young and roving boy
  Where fancy led me I did wander,
Sweet Caroline was all my joy,
  But I missed the goose and hit the gander (act 1, scene 3).

while Myles-na-Coppaleen, comic man of *The Colleen Bawn*, mixed Irish airs and comic songs:

Brian O'Linn had no breeches to wear
So he brought him a sheepskin to make him a pair;
The skinny side out, and woolly side in,
"They are cool and convanient," said Brian O'Linn (act 2,
  scene 4).

Nautical melodramas contained many songs and dances. It was expected that a hornpipe or two would be danced and that several sea songs would be sung. As early as 1760, Isaac Bickerstaffe, himself an ex-marine, had written *Thomas and Sally; or, The Sailor's Return*, (Covent Garden, 1760), that was designed as a vehicle for Thomas's songs of the sea. Having sung his songs, Thomas proceeded to rescue Sally from the clutches of a libidinous squire. "Jolly Jack Tars" were regular performers at music houses around London, and the combination of the sailor, music, and domestic drama ensured the success of *Black Ey'd Susan*.

Surprisingly, the hero William has no songs, but he was expected to dance a hornpipe, and there is no reason to suppose that songs could not be interpolated as needed. Act 3 of that typical nautical drama, *My Poll and My Partner Joe*, opened with a veritable symphony of nautical effects:

(*The church bells ringing a joyful peal. A fiddler discovered on a high chair—another outside the window in the street, playing different nautical tunes—Sailors and Girls dancing.*)

CHORUS OF SAILORS

Sailors lead a jolly, jolly life,
   While roving on the ocean;
In every port they have a wife;
   Of every girl a notion.
      Tol de rol., etc. (act e, scene 1).

It was only to be expected that some themes became inalienably associated with particular plays. "Black Ey'd Susan" (originally a ballad by Gay) was sung first by Susan and later by Blue Peter. It was inevitably associated with Jerrold's play and, like "Green Bushes" in Buckstone's *The Green Bushes; or, A Hundred Years Ago*, (Adelphi, 1845), or "Kathleen Mavourneen" in William Traver's *Kathleen Mavourneen; or, St. Patrick's Eve*, (Pavilion, 1862), was what might be called a theme song of the type found in muscial comedies today. Other plays became associated with a particular song. At the end of the first act of T. A. Palmer's version of *East Lynne*, Lady Isabel sang "You'll Remember Me" from *The Bohemian Girl*. This piece was apparently repeated during the course of the play as Lady Isabel moved inexorably towards her doom. A contrast was set up having Barbara sing the same song to Archibald in the first scene of the fourth act. So associated did this particular song and play become that it was possible to identify what was playing in a theater simply by hearing the music. In *Town Hall Tonight*, Harlowe Hoyte recalled American productions of *East Lynne* acted to the strains of "Then You'll Remember Me." *East Lynne* was a favorite midweek matinee offering, and you could identify the play without entering the hall. The combination of feminine sniffles to an accompaniment of Balfe's music proclaimed *East Lynne* beyond a doubt.[67]

The using of music to heighten emotional effect was one reason for the inclusion of songs, but there was another more technical reason for including them brought about by the nature of staging plays in the nineteenth century. Elaborate sets were required for certain key scenes in productions. It was necessary that a short, preferably noisy scene should take place, to cover the sounds of the scene shifters. Dion Boucicault, who claimed to have introduced the idea of the spectacular scene into serious dramas, was a frequent user of what became called *carpenters' scenes* in the business. Before the famous water-cave scene in *The Colleen Bawn*, there was a short, singing scene by Myles-na-Coppaleen. The scene was played in the first grooves, that is, with as small a stage as it was possible to get. Myles sang "Brian O'Linn" and introduced the idea of the water cave. He exited singing:

> (*Exit Myles singing, R.—Music till Myles begins to speak next scene.*
> *Scene sixth. A Cave. Enter Myles singing, top of rock. R. U. E.* [Right Upper Entrance]) (act 2, scene 6).

This awkwardness of Myles's exit and entrance was produced by the fact that Boucicault did not want to put any other scenes between Myles's song and his entrance into the cave. The author attempted to cover his scene change by having Myles sing a song. It is also evident that carpenters' scenes were controlled from the wings. The stage manager could signal an actor to sing another chorus or cut it short depending on the expeditiousness of the stage

67. Harlowe Hoyt, *Town Hall Tonight* (Englewood Cliffs, New Jersey: Prentice-Hall, [1955]), p. 41.

hands. Audiences were quite used to these scenes and apparently accepted them as stage pauses unconnected with the main plot but giving the comic man (generally) a chance to show his mettle. In printed play texts, it is not unusual to see the stage direction *a comic song may be introduced here*.

Considerable latitude also existed in the interpolation of songs favored by actors or audiences. With little or no concern for period or setting, actors could demand the inclusion of certain songs that were their favorites or that were in their particular key. Even more imperious were the demands of the audience. Henry Mayhew discovered in his talks with costermongers that though "nigger music" had become stale, patriotic songs, even those translated from the French, were extremely popular. Patriotic songs could become the source of audience disturbances, and managers went to a great deal of trouble to accommodate various factions in their audiences. The manager of the Belfast Theatre in 1806 was forced to take a stand on the question of patriotic songs because of the particularly sensitive nature of the Belfast gallery. He decreed that patriotic songs would not be permitted except as he would stipulate. Between the first two acts of the play, the orchestra would play "Rule Britannia," after the fourth act "God Save the King," and before the farce "St. Patrick's Day." One of the attractions of these tunes was that the audience could join in and sing them. It is clear from contemporary accounts that audiences reveled in the opportunity to sing choruses with the actors:

> The grand hit of the evening is always when a song is sung to which the entire gallery can join in the chorus. Then a deep silence prevails through all the stanzas. Should any burst in before his time, a shout of "orda-a-r" is raised and the intruder put down by a thousand indignant cries.[68]

The domestic dramatist was always something of a moralist at heart. He realized that his message might slip

68. Henry Mayhew, *London Labour and London Poor* (C. Griffin and Co., 1861–62), 1: 19.

down more easily with a little sugarcoating. If a whole audience wished to sing, "There's no place like home," why
should he prevent them? Was not this his message and was
not music part of his medium? It is now the task, having
examined the sugarcoating, to analyze the pill.

4
THE WORLD OF
DOMESTIC DRAMA

It was the artist's first duty to communicate, and the substance of his message was necessarily of social, and, therefore, moral significance.

Buckley, *The Victorian Temper*[1]

THE NINETEENTH CENTURY IS still generally looked upon as a period of smug complacency, of hypocritical piety, a time when everyone knew his place, an era in which prudery and class consciousness ruled supreme. Nothing, of course, could be less true. At the turn of the century, society was urgently seeking a means to avoid the social upheaval that had terrorized France and was basing its faith upon the Industrial Revolution, on progress, and utilitarianism. The social unrest that accompanied the Chartist agitation and demands for Corn Law repeal did not lead to violent revolution but

1. Jerome Buckley, *The Victorian Temper: A Study in Literary Culture* (Cambridge, Massachusetts: Harvard University Press, 1951), p. 10.

to steady, if slow, political and social reforms. While revolution wracked Europe in the 1830s, Parliament finally passed the Reform Bill in 1832. Though this bill did nothing directly for the working-class franchise, it showed that peaceful change was possible. The "hungry forties" were weathered, and when England escaped not only the revolutions of 1848 but was able, in 1851, to display her industrial might in the Great Exhibition, worker and capitalist alike felt that England had been chosen for a special destiny. Though the poor still suffered injustices, even they never doubted that England was the best of all worlds. Confidence grew that any problems that existed would ultimately be taken care of by scientific and industrial advances.

It has become a platitude to say that an age is reflected in its literature. Whether this is true or not remains debatable, but there can be little objection to the statement that frequently what is most representative of an age is neither read nor, in the case of the stage, performed. An accurate picture of the late seventeenth century could not be constructed from Restoration drama any more than a picture of Georgian or Victorian England could be deduced from the domestic drama. It can, however, reveal a great deal about working-class life and ideals. As Richard Hoggart has pointed out, it is not easy to define the ways in which literature illuminates society.[2] Nevertheless, it is clear that literature provides in its own right a distinctive knowledge about a society. "Literature may help to keep open our sense of the richness of human experience, the virtually inexhaustible meanings in each gesture and word spoken if they are understood in their context."[3] The most that can be said is that in this chapter there can be shown something about a particular group within a certain society.

While there is a grave danger of regarding the domestic drama as monolithic, it is true that between the years 1820 (the date of the first domestic drama) and 1865 (the debut

2. Richard Hoggart, *Speaking to Each Other*, 2 vols. (London: Chatto and Windus, 1970), 2: 19.
3. Ibid., p. 270.

of Robertson's *Society*) certain concerns were felt by working-class audiences to be of vital import. These matters might reflect the prejudices of society in general, such as the predominance of subject over treatment, or morality over sensuality and aesthetics, for the British public, as Lady Eastlake wrote in 1863, "had scarcely advanced beyond the lowest step of the aesthetic ladder, the estimate of a subject."[4] Or they might involve subjects that were almost exclusively restricted to the working-class milieu—the press gang, game laws, nostalgia for a rural heritage.

A basic requirement for discovering what kind of gratification audiences expected from their drama is gleaned from examining the contents of representative plays, at which time it becomes clear that the staple fare is not so much escapist, as is generally assumed, but rather something that holds that life is intrinsically interesting. Domestic drama is flattering, for it purports to portray on the stage people like those who are watching it; however, it simultaneously and subtly romanticizes their world. Life is more exciting, people less complicated, the future (ultimately) bright. At the theater, members of the audience could break through the frustrations of daily life into a factitious world that endowed everyday living with meaning and significance. The domestic dramatist provided, in essence, a world view for those who either lacked one or who historically only saw it piecemeal.

A factitious world, by definition, cannot be the real world, and though social criticism could be introduced into domestic dramas, it had to be restricted both in range (some subjects were taboo) and depth.[5] Any social commentary could only be secondary to the story of domestic tranquility threatened by external forces. In several instances, too much realism resulted in the early termination of thea-

4. Quoted in G. M. Young, ed., *Early Victorian England, 1830–1865*, 2 vols. (London: Oxford University Press, 1934) 2: 140.

5. Michael Booth in "East End Melodrama," (paper delivered at The Conference on Nineteenth-century British Theatre, Amherst, Massachusetts, 11 May 1974), p. 13, discovered that "social protest . . . is mostly confined to a few plays set in the country in which the game laws are passionately denounced."

ter runs. Douglas Jerrold's *Sally in Our Alley*, (Surrey, 1830), was his most realistic drama, but it failed to hold the stage for long. His play *The Factory Girl*, (Drury Lane, 1832), was a satire on the industrial system that seems to have been too powerful for audience taste. Charles Reade's *It's Never Too Late to Mend*, (Leeds, 1864), besides marking an important advance in the history of nineteenth-century drama, protested the conditions in English prisons. His brutal exposé of those conditions—the silent system, the separate system, the treadmill, flogging, and the excesses of prison officials—said no more than the government Blue Books had, but loud protests greeted the realistic depiction of the inside of a prison. Its London performance was recorded in *The Era*:

> A storm of indignation . . . caused Mr. Vining . . . to address the audience . . . "It has been acknowledged that the book from which this play is taken has done a great deal of good. We are not here presenting a system, but the abuse of a system, and I may refer you to the Blue-Books"—
> (A voice from the pit here exclaimed: "We want no Blue-Books on the stage").[6]

Such audience reactions and the stress placed upon comedy, farce, extravaganza, burlesque, and melodrama encouraged the belief that nineteenth-century audiences sought purely escapist drama. This is not so; they looked for color where their lives were drab; they sought excitement where their lives were dull; they wanted richness to mitigate their poverty. They were, in short, no different from the vast majority of people in all ages and all countries. It would be wrong, however, to suggest that domestic dramatists were not permitted to touch on many of the social problems of the day. Domestic drama did reflect popular and even radical feelings, albeit crudely. It was the only dramatic form before the rise of the "problem" play to treat such matters as slavery, alcoholism, repressive laws,

6. Quoted in John Coleman, *Charles Reade as I Knew Him* (London: Treherne and Co., 1903), p. 209.

laissez-faire economics, the class system, industrialism, gambling, and contemporary social relationships.

Areas that remained largely unexplored were avoided because of their sensitive natures (religion, sex) or because they held little interest for the popular mind (psychology, philosophy). The reader looks in vain for any insights into the religious ferment of the century. It is not difficult to fathom the reasons why. Organized religion had made little impression on workers. A count taken on the last Sunday of March 1851 revealed that less than a third of the adults in England and Wales attended church. Social and religious workers in the poorer districts constantly reported that they encountered indifference and ignorance on all sides. This was a result that could have been predicted, since religion had steadily become associated with the Establishment. The continuing improvement of the legal and social status of dissenters, particularly after the repeal of the Test and Corporation Acts, had led them to lose touch with political radicalism and, thus, with those whose lot in society needed urgent amelioration, so none of these important issues found their way onto the popular stage. Neither will the reader find any mention of doctrinal debate, philosophical disputation, nor any of the spiritual agony of the age, nor of the brief return to authoritarian dogma encouraged by the Oxford Movement.

The lack of concern with religious questions was also due to the workers' attitude toward the clergy. They regarded clergymen as having a job to do, but not much else. They were not overtly hostile to the cloth—merely indifferent. None of the anticlericism of France developed in England. Naturally marriages, deaths, and christenings took place in church, but for daily life, the church seemed to have little to offer. Many clerics, even though they knew and even experienced the sufferings of their flocks, remained staunchly conservative. Bishops voted in the House of Lords and clergymen sat on boards of magistrates, directed local administration, and levied church rates. The clergy was closely associated with Toryism and the landed interest.

They at first greeted Robert Owen's socialistic and philanthropic schemes with praise, but after he began to attack certain aspects of religion, he lost their support totally, and the utopian New Lanark mills received no pulpit praise. Likewise the Church had supported the Corn Laws, opposed the Chartists, and, worst of all, had accepted social evils as divinely ordained. The urban masses found scant comfort in the belief that to be poor was to be good, simply because poverty removed its victim from temptation. Only Methodism had much to offer industrial workers, yet even it, despite enormous gains, was concentrating on the wrong things. Since Wesley had laid stress upon the urgent need to save souls for the next world, his followers had less time for the social ills of this one. Methodists offered fire and fervor, but they held out little hope of a social revolution. Plays of village life occasionally voiced nostalgia at the thought of a village Sunday sermon, but as far as the stage was concerned, the religious activity of the nineteenth century might never have existed.[7] The indifference of workers to religious matters did not mean that authors and audiences were unaffected by the Evangelical Movement. On the contrary:

> Lay Evangelicals were tireless in charitable organizations, in distributing edifying tracts, in visiting the poor and the sick. From their families came some of the most remarkable of the Victorians. The Brontë sisters, Macaulay, George Eliot, Samuel Butler, and Elizabeth Barrett [were] among [the] literary figures.[8]

The Evangelicals had grown out of those who, although touched by Wesleyanism, had remained in the Established Church; it was the Evangelicals who generated a social and political revolution that touched all classes. For the first

7. There was another strong reason for the lack of allusion to religious matters and that was the Examiner of Plays. When George Colman, the younger, was asked by the Select Committee what his attitude toward religious reference was, he stated: "I conceive all Scripture is much too sacred for the stage except in very solemn scenes indeed." *Report of the Select Committee*, para. 357.

8. J. B. Schneewind, *Backgrounds of English Victorian Literature* (New York: Random House, 1970), p. 58.

time a substantial part of the aristocracy and the workers shared the ideals and values of the middle class. Nothing else can explain the middle-class morality and idealism that permeates domestic drama. True, domestic drama expressed some exclusively working-class concerns, but the strong emphasis on middle-class values can only be explained in terms of a shared ethic. Thus, the bourgeois qualities —prudery, family life, materialism—became the virtues espoused by working-class drama.

Though the Evangelicals professed little interest in changing society, they are remembered best for a political achievement—the ending of slavery. William Wilberforce led the attack, and, though the taxpayer was called upon to finance a payment of twenty million pounds compensation to slave owners, there appears to have been little resentment. Later working-class support of the North in America's Civil War was strong, though the lack of raw cotton made suffering in England intense, especially in Lancashire. It is not surprising that feeling for the slave found its way onto the stage—after all, were not factory workers slaves themselves? A villain thus could be identified by his attitude to slaves, as Brandon is in J. T. Haines's *My Poll and My Partner Joe*, a play written two years after slavery was abolished in the British Empire:

BRANDON. Are all the black cattle safe aboard?
SEAMAN. Ay, Ay.
BRANDON. . . . Hark ye, ye nigger animals, if I hear the least noise, or see the least sign of grumbling among ye, I'll make sharks' meat of every devil of you (act 2, scene 2).

It was the same Evangelical reforming zeal that attacked other evils that plagued Victorian society. Alternately fascinated and repelled by man's self-destructive urge, zealots turned their attention to gambling and drinking. The period of cheap gin had been from 1720–1750. Gin had been a powerful factor in keeping the increase of population down, though its effects have often been exaggerated. In 1751 a high tax on spirits removed their excessive use from the hands of the poor, yet even at that time medical men attributed over ten percent of the adult deaths to alcohol. When gin became popular once more in the nineteenth century, Cruikshank's prints of *The Bottle* were sold by tens of thousands, and a play of the same name based on his drawings was written by T. P. Taylor. The cover page of the printed text depicted a bottle with a snake's head protruding from its neck.

The Temperance Movement, especially in America, received tremendous help from the authors of "temperance melodramas" and from the sensational posters that advertised them. Such dramas were, of course, domestic dramas in which the perils of alcohol were graphically displayed and were, in short, dramatized sermons. Temperance propaganda made a particularly powerful impact from the stage since the supporters of temperance movements used extremism as their basic technique, pointing dramatically to the awful consequences faced by those who indulged. Though not entirely honest in their selection of the word *temperance* for a movement that worked for total abstinence, the reformers took to their work with deadly earnestness:

> Nowhere is temperance propaganda more extreme or more violent than in nineteenth-century melodrama. In selecting the stage as a medium, temperance writers chose wisely, for melodrama itself is a form given over wholly to extremes of moral behavior and character delineation, violent emotionalism and physical incident, the rewarding of virtue and the punishment of vice. These characteristics could only be expressed by exaggerated acting techniques and inflated dialogue. As a means to an end, melodrama was ideally suited to moral admonition and horrifying displays of the consequences of drink. Sensationalism was an essential aspect of temperance appeal, and it was most powerfully expressed on the stage.[9]

Though a modern audience tends to regard temperance dramas as humorous in their sensationalism, there should

9. Michael Booth, "The Drunkard's Progress—Nineteenth Century Temperance Melodrama," *Dalhousie Review* 44 (Summer 1964): 206.

HOME OF SOBRIETY

MY FATHER KEEPS A TAVERN | **MY HUSBAND SPENDS HIS MONEY AT THE TAVERN**

Theater posters designed to accompany temperance dramas
(CHEROKEE BOOKS)

be no doubt as to the powerful effect the plays had on their audiences. Thousands of shaking hands signed pledges in the theater lobbies after seeing the fit of *delirium tremens* included in all such plays.

The evil of drink was a theme particularly suited to domestic drama and of especial relevance to audiences. The precarious economic status of most working-class families could not survive an onslaught of the "demon drink." Even moderate expenditures on drinking could lead to financial collapse, family quarrels, and loss of respect, position, and home. Drink is still regarded in England as the major threat to a working-class family's well-being. In a very real sense alcohol became a melodramatic villain; since alcoholism was little understood, it roused fears out of proportion to its danger. These irrational fears were at the heart of melodrama and were largely responsible for the terrors they raised in the audience as the stricken hero was slowly and methodically deprived of family, home, and sometimes life itself.

In the first English temperance-drama, Douglas Jerrold's *Fifteen Years of a Drunkard's Life* (1828), the warning was an awful one. Vernon slowly fell prey to alcohol, and in a drunken frenzy killed his wife and died by the villain Glanville's bullet. Other temperance plays followed. T. P. Taylor's *The Bottle* (1847) was written to Cruikshank's engravings of the same title. In order to support his drinking, Thornley took up gambling. His youngest son died of starvation, his second son was apprenticed to criminals, and he killed his wife in a drunken rage with "the Instrument of all their Grief" and ended, like Copeau in Charles Reade's *Drink*, (Princess's, 1879), chained in a madhouse.

English domestic dramas tended to show the evils of alcohol, but they were less forceful than their American counterparts. American versions were much more hysterical in tone, reflecting a social upheaval that has left some counties in the United States officially "dry" to this day. The lessons of the plays were made absolutely clear to the audience. At the conclusion of James McCloskey's *The Fatal Glass; or, The Curse of Drink*, (Brooklyn Park, 1872), the

Spirit of Temperance advanced with a glass of water dispensing with it the following advice:

> SPIRIT. Drink from this fount, a pure and crystal draught,
> The only beverage that man should quaff;
> No crime, nor bruised hearts in this be found:
> That poisoned distillation dash to ground!
> By this, long life and happiness the sum;
> Shame, death, here and hereinafter, you will find in rum!
> AMBROSE. (*Takes glass.*) From your lips, darling, let no harsh
>   word pass.
> MABEL. The lesson is a good one. Henceforth shun the fatal
>   glass!

(*Music. Chimes. Chorus repeated.*) (act 3, scene 7).

William Pratt's *Ten Nights in a Bar Room* (National, New York, 1858) went much further. A whole village was virtually destroyed by the opening of the "Sickle and Sheaf." Simon Slade was the landlord. Once a prosperous miller, he became lazy and good-for-nothing, and during the ten years of the play's action, he became "bloated and one eye gone, clothes much worn." His wife he drove into the madhouse; he was killed in a drunken brawl by his son, Frank. The Squire's son, Willie (class ranks were closed against a common enemy), was stabbed, and his father died in a pauper's grave. The drunkard was Joe Morgan, who was saved by the death of his daughter, Mary. Even the terrifying *delirium tremens* scene could not match the death of Mary for effect. She had come to fetch her father away from the tavern when she was struck down (off-stage) by a flying glass tankard. Even as Joe mourned over her dying body, he was attacked by *delirium tremens*. Exacting a promise from her father never to visit a bar again, Mary died with a pathetic quatrain on future hopes:

> We shall meet in the land where spring is eternal,
>   Where darkness ne'er cometh—no sorrow nor pain;
> Where the flowers never fade—in that clime ever vernal
>   We shall meet, and our parting be never again.

(*Mary dies; Morgan falls on the couch. Mrs. Morgan sobs over the body. Slow music. Tableau. Curtain.*) (act 4, scene 3).

Well might the audience agree with Joe Morgan that "a direful pestilence is in the air." If the message had escaped anyone, there was also a concluding passage (in couplets) where each character exhorted the audience to mend its ways and follow the lead of Bolton County by making the sale of liquor illegal. Such exhortations marked a crucial distinction between the American and British temperance dramas, for American plays suggested a possible line of social reform, but English plays were generally content to show the terrible havoc that alcohol could wreak upon society and individuals.

Gambling, while still a social problem, had less impact on the popular mind. For one thing, to gamble one had to have money, and the characters of domestic dramas and their audience spent a great deal of their time seeking the bare essentials of life. However, the innate puritanism of domestic drama, as we have seen, was firmly set against making easy money. The riches of life were granted only after three acts of suffering. A "romantic drama" of John Oxenford, *The Dice of Death!* (E. O. H, 1835), portrayed the suffering caused by gambling. Ernest Winter finally diced with Mephistopheles with predictable results. Ernest's fiancée died of a broken heart, and Ernest murdered Spiegelberg as he was suffering his own death throes. Many of the gambling domestic dramas ended with the protagonists' deaths. In *The Gambler's Fate; or, The Hut on the Red Mountain* by H. M. Milner, (Coburg, 1827), the protagonist stabbed himself, quitting life with an admonition:

> Shall I permit my virtuous son to be irremedially disgraced by my death upon a scaffold? No; there is yet a remedy for that. Unfortunate beings! whose existence I have cursed, do not pity me: I have merited this chastisement. My son, as you would avoid my crimes, my dismal fate, shun gaming (act 3, scene 2).

In gambling and temperance dramas, the hero could behave despicably and still be saved. Apart from selected criminal heroes, the bending of the strict moral code of domestic drama was reserved for those who overcame their destructive urge and reformed. These plays were the only ones where the hero's danger might be of spiritual rather than temporal concern. At all events, behavior that would have led to the indignant hissing of a villain was now excused by audiences. Their sympathies were with the fallen man, and they knew, perhaps from first hand, what husband, wife, and children were suffering. The tremendous effect that such domestic dramas had upon audiences was related to the fact that they had none of the usual guarantees that the play would end happily. The hero was Everyman; his sufferings could affect anyone in the audience, and, in many cases, the ravages of alcohol were well known from personal experience.

The domestic dramas of the nineteenth century lacked the revolutionary fervor found in many French dramas of the day. Very little of the intense political activity at home and abroad was represented on the stage. England had a-voided the bloodshed of the 1830 revolutions, and the Reform Bill, passed in 1832, had done much to dispel the belief that all reform would lead inevitably to civil disturbance on a massive scale. Nonetheless, the Reform Bill had done little, if anything, for the working-class franchise. Macauley could still proclaim in 1842 that granting a People's Charter would produce a new political power that would "plunder every man in the Kingdom who has a good coat on his back and a good roof over his head."[10] Others voiced many arguments, but what really governed them was the fear of enfranchising a largely illiterate mass of voters. John Stuart Mill proclaimed the common belief that the right to vote should be left to those with a "stake" in England's future. Workers who did not own property had no stake and therefore could not expect to vote. The opposition of laborers to the landed gentry in domestic dramas was in part a reflection of the rising class hatred of nineteenth-century England that attitudes like Mill's encouraged.

10. Quoted in Walter Houghton, *Victorian Frame of Mind, 1830–1870* (New Haven, Conn.: Yale University Press, 1957), p. 55.

However, one reform often leads to another. Agitation of workers was felt throughout the land. Factory conditions were attacked, and the workers' disappointment with the Reform Bill encouraged the Chartists. The thirties and forties saw this movement rise and fall. Chartism reflected the bitterness of its supporters with the treatment of the poor (a common domestic drama theme). Its proponents published a "People's Charter" in 1838 demanding six main points —all of which were designed to make Parliament the people's servant. The movement itself dragged on until it finally collapsed around 1848, but it undoubtedly played an important role in preparing a climate conducive to reforms. In this achievement, Chartism was probably helped by the rise of a new type of domestic drama—the factory play. Factory plays were no more than domestic dramas centered around factory life, and they constituted one of the strongest forms of protest to emerge in nineteenth-century theater.

The Industrial Revolution produced a new powerful capitalistic class, and domestic dramatists were correct in their assumption that the laborers' struggle was not so much against machinery as it was against the abuse of capital. The factory owner was singled out for opprobrium, while mechanization was only a secondary target. Factories could run at a handsome profit without the wholesale exploitation of the workers, but capitalism insisted on ever-increased profits at the expense of the life and health of factory employees. Consequently conditions in factories were a national disgrace and workers were constantly reminded of the inhumanity of those who put wealth before public welfare. Workmen and their families were summoned by a bell, an overseer enforced endless regulations, the workday might be fourteen hours long, and the machines never seemed to stop.[11] The sight of those mutilated by accidents caused by unsafe or ill-guarded machinery was constantly

11. In a Manchester mill there was a fine of six shillings "for steam" if a sick man could not find a substitute. J. L. Hammond, *The Town Labourer, 1760–1832* (London: Longmans, Green, and Co., 1917), p. 20.

before the eyes, and it is not impossible that factory dramas may have contributed to a climate that demanded such improvements as John Fielden's very important factory act, the Ten Hours Bill (1847).

The factory drama, as a subgenre of domestic drama, dealt with the threat to the tranquility of the home from such forces as mechanization, low wages, and unemployment. These forces were generally enshrined in the character of the factory owner—an industrial squire. R. B. Peake's *The Climbing Boy*, (Olympic, 1832), was probably the first of such plays. Hard on its heels came Jerrold's *The Factory Girl* at Drury Lane. Although a failure, one critic said of Jerrold that he "deserved our gratitude as well as our admiration, for [his] aim is not merely to amuse, but to plead . . . the cause of the poor and oppressed."[12] John Walker's important play *The Factory Lad* was so successful that it played at several theaters within the year. The popularity of this type of domestic drama was due in large measure to the common complaint it voiced that the law was on the side of the rich against the poor. The radical movement after Waterloo had had some success among factory workers, and the Peterloo massacre and the Six Acts had helped to spread the seeds of discontent among factory hands. Thus, it was natural that factory dramas should take the side of the workers, though there were occasions when this was not entirely the case.[13]

Walker's *The Factory Lad* contained a strong attack upon the differential treatment that the rich enjoyed compared to that of the poor under the law. The following exchange took place between Rushton, leader of the factory incendiaries, and a judge, significantly named Bias:

BIAS. The law is open to you, is it not?
RUSHTON. No; I am poor!

12. Quoted in Walter Jerrold, *Douglas Jerrold: Dramatist and Wit*, 2 vols. (London: Hodder and Stoughton, [1914]), 1: 212.

13. A very few, like G. F. Taylor's *The Factory Strike; or, Want, Crime and Retribution*, (Victoria, 1838), ended with their protagonists cursing the day they ever heard the word "strike," but they, too, concentrated on domestic matters.

BIAS. And what of that? The law is made alike for rich and poor.
RUSHTON. Is it? Why, then, does it so often lock the poor man in a gaol, while the rich goes free? (act 2, scene 5).

The legal profession was continually attacked in domestic dramas and not infrequently supplied the villain. Harrows of T. P. Taylor's *The Village Outcast*, (Olympic, 1846), told Muzzle (one of the Specials and the Magistrate's Headman) that he came from a place called "happy land, because there are no lawyers." Muzzle's hardhearted justification of the law's duties to Old Alice was clearly intended to rouse the audience to a fever pitch:

OLD ALICE. Surely they wouldn't thrust into the house of charity one so aged and infirm as I?
MUZZLE. But they do, though. What's the law to do with age? That's Nature's business. What's the law to do with infirmity? That's polticarriers [*sic*]. The law says this here wery building is to come down for improvements, consequently removal's the word.
OLD ALICE. And tomorrow I'm to be driven from the roof which so long has sheltered me—helpless and almost sinking into the grave—to die, perhaps in the fields.
MUZZLE. That's the law (act 1, scene 2).

It was traditional for the forces of law and order to commend the virtues of the workhouse to the poor, for to do so was certain to raise a violent outburst. Poorhouses had become hated symbols of an uncaring society, yet they had been begun with the most Christian of intentions. In 1795, the unfortunate Speenhamland system had come into being. Had the magistrates who devised the scheme insisted on a minimum wage all would have been well, but they decided instead that wages would be supplemented out of parish rates. Thus, no pressure existed for employers to pay a living wage. The Poor Law (Amendment) Act of 1834 only made matters incomparably worse. Mainly the work of Edwin Chadwick, the Act showed Benthamism at its worst. Chadwick's reasoning was that if the conditions of poorhouses were appalling, no one in his right mind could choose to be a pauper.[14] Chadwick was not inhuman, he simply could not believe, as many today can not, that anyone who looked for work could not find it. Thus, any attack on a poorhouse was an attack upon the harsh economic system of the country and was recognized as such. Rushton's outburst in *The Factory Lad* was a strong condemnation of the whole concept of parish charity:

> Aye, or a pauper, to go with your hat in your hand, and, after begging and telling them what they know to be the truth—that you have a wife and five, six, or eight children, one, perhaps, just born, another mayhap just dying—they'll give you eighteen pence to support them all for the week; and if you dare to complain, not a farthing; but place you in the stocks, or scourge you through the town as a vagabond! This is parish charity! I have known what it is. My back is still scored with the marks of their power. The slave abroad, the poor black, whom they affect to pity, is not so trampled on, hunted or ill-used as the peasant or hard-working fellow like yourselves (act 1, scene 2).

Another burning issue was mechanization. The Luddite riots had led to random destruction of machines. Similar riots had taken place before. (Taylor's *Arkwright's Wife* was set in the 1760s and its entire plot hinged on inventions and the workers' fears of what machinery might do to their livelihoods.) In *The Factory Lad*, Squire Westwood, the new owner of the factory, propounded laissez-faire economics and Benthamism:

> WESTWOOD. Times are now altered.
> ALLEN. They are indeed, sir. A poor man has now less wages for more work.
> WESTWOOD. The master having less money, resulting from there being less demand for the commodity manufactured.
> ALLEN. Less demand!

14. "The workhouse has been turned into as truly repulsive an abode as the perverted ingenuity of the Malthusians can devise. The food is worse than that enjoyed by the poorest labourer in employment." Friedrich Engels, *The Condition of the Working Class in England*, trans. W. O. Henderson (Oxford: Basil Blackwell, 1958), p. 324.

WESTWOOD. Hear me! If not less demand, a greater quantity is thrown into the markets at a cheaper rate. . . . Don't you buy where you please, at the cheapest place? Would you have bought that jerkin of one man more than another if he had charged you twice the sum for it, or even sixpence more? (act 1, scene 1).

Shortly after this encounter, Westwood departed into the factory "sneeringly."

Factory dramas were not intended as revolutionary theater. They treated the really serious contemporary issues as a backcloth against which a familiar domestic story was acted out. Protests against social conditions were gestures, but they were not organic to the factory drama. No factory drama made much of trade unionism, although unions were political issues of the day—particularly after the depression of 1828. No factory drama took up the important issues that the reformer Robert Owen had raised in his utopian community at New Lanark. His socialistic mills could have provided material for a series of factory dramas, but such plays were neither demanded nor produced. For an in-depth study of factory conditions and their debilitating effect on the human psyche, the reader must turn to the novel. What was popular on the stage were plays along the lines of *The Factory Strike* (*see* footnote 13 above), where Warner ended in prison to be visited by his grieving wife and children and where a last minute reprieve saved him from the gallows.

The excitement generated by factory legislation was paralleled by the struggle in the country and towns over the price of corn. During the Napoleonic Wars it had been necessary to produce a great deal of corn to prevent the country from being starved into submission. Even the much reviled policy of enclosure became an economic necessity in that critical period. Unfortunately, as is always the case, it was the poor farmer who was penalized and the rich one who prospered. For those small farmers who were not swallowed up by the large, the high price of corn (it had tripled during the Wars) had encouraged them to plant extensively.

After the Wars, prices plunged, ruining many farmers who had unwisely adapted to higher prices. Lockwood cried out in *The Farmer's Story*, (Lyceum, 1836), "Look at the change which has come about since the war was over! the poor are everywhere despised and driven into crime! the rich—be they black as mire with their offences—are encouraged in them" (act 1, scene 2). Even the Corn Laws passed in 1815 did not seem to help the small farmer, and they heavily penalized the industrial consumer. These Laws were always controversial and became a symbol of upper-class oppression. They added to the growing cleavage between city and country and, as the poor flocked to the cities, the rural skills they possessed were lost forever.

Almost as hated as the Corn Laws were the Game Laws. These laws were mentioned in several plays. They were selfish restrictions that directly affected the lives of the rural inhabitants of England. It was illegal for anyone who was not a squire or a squire's eldest son to kill game. Consequently the needy poor never had an opportunity to add to their larders with a partridge or a hare. To the poor, hunting game could mean a great deal, but to the squirearchy it was mainly sport. After 1816, any villager caught with nets or traps could legally be transported for seven years. More unpleasant was the device of hiding huge man-traps that maimed or killed poachers and even innocent wanderers. Although this practice was banned in 1827, it was referred to in Douglas Jerrold's *Sally in Our Alley* (1830):

> HARRY. The world is rich, well stocked—
> OLD FRANK. As my lord's garden. But there is a wall, a huge spiked wall, around it; and on every twentieth tree is written, "Spring-guns and man-traps set in these grounds" (act 1, scene 2).

The connection between Game Laws and the misery of the poor was sometimes made explicit, as, for example, by Lieutenant Florville in Colin Hazlewood's *Waiting for the Verdict*:

FLORVILLE. I am also aware that as much, if not more, misery
has been caused by the game laws of this country which protects the wild creatures of the earth with more regard in some
instances than it protects and educates the children of the poor
and needy; for, while the animals of the woods feed from every
man's land, many a human being wanders from door to door
hungry and uncared for (act 2, scene 2).

Distaste for the Game Laws led to the rise of a new type
of hero in domestic drama—the poacher. The classic drama
on the theme of poaching is George Dibdin Pitt's *Simon
Lee; or, The Murder of the Five-Fields Copse* (City of London, 1839). Simon lost his property on a legal technicality
(common enough in domestic melodrama) and turned
poacher. Todd went to warn him of an ambush, ("Though a
lawyer, I can't help feeling for this unfortunate couple"),
and to admonish him:

TODD. Poaching is forbidden by the laws—
SIMON. By the laws of a man but not of nature—the wild inhabitants of the forest and the field were intended for the subsistence of man and the property of all equally.
TODD. Think of the penalty.
SIMON. I am willing to labour; if work is denied me and a hare
or pheasant is to be had, my family shall not starve (act 2,
scene 1).

Despite the lawyer's warning and the even more ominous
dream of his wife, Grace, Simon went poaching. He killed a
gamekeeper and was sentenced to death with the comfort-
ing assurance that:

The judges have been too hasty. Had the jury conceived the
sentence could have been so severe, they never would have
yielded to the verdict. The prejudice of the rich against
poachers has doubtless increased the severity of Simon's case
(act 3, scene 4).

The audience was warned to expect a reprieve. It duly arrived, but too late to save Grace, who took poison. The
Game Laws had done their work well, and another type of
hero joined the pantheon of domestic drama.

It would seem at first that such criminal heroes are a reversal of the strict morality of domestic drama. In a sense, however, certain criminals became folk heroes, opponents of a system that the audience could neither join nor beat. A traditional release of the oppressed in dealing with authority has been to deflate it by poking fun at it and by revering those who have outwitted it in all its awful majesty. In the early Victorian era Jack Sheppard, Dick Turpin, and Claude Duval came to symbolize human freedom in opposition to authority and respectability—latter-day Robin Hoods. Jack and the others were seen as victims of an old social order and as rebels against it. It is clear that in the thirties Methodism had still not taken a strong enough hold on the popular mind to prevent the audience having a great deal of sympathy for the criminal in his fight against the forces of law and order:[15]

> The stage policemen were getting very much the worst of a free fight to the unbounded delight of pit and gallery. The sympathies of the audience, however, were kindly. They leaned to the starveling and the victim of fate; for four out of five understood only too well what hard life in Whitechapel meant, and had spent nights with the stars upon the stones of London.[16]

The spread of criminal heroes should not be overemphasized. They remained mainly historical—Dick Turpin, Claude Duval, Jack Sheppard, Paul Clifford. Less frequently they were contemporary figures, easy to sympathize with, but unlikely to win the audience's outright admiration. A whole genre of sensational melodramas treated criminal events, but their heroes, such as Sweeney Todd or William Corder, were not conceived to win the sympathies of audiences, but to serve as warnings to the potential evil-doer.

Nautical dramas were also a source of social criticism. The nautical aspects of the play were often kept in the

15. The Metropolitan police force had been founded by Robert Peel in 1829. Though incomparably better than previous law enforcers, "peelers" were nevertheless regarded with suspicion by working-class audiences.

16. Gustave Doré and Blanchard Jerrold, *London: A Pilgrimage* (New York: Harper & Brothers, 1890), p. 165.

background of a domestic story that was generally concerned with the lives of a sailor and his sweetheart or wife. Though the naval aspects of the hero's career were generally not the play's chief emphasis, Ernest Reynolds has said of these plays:

> In defense of the nautical melodrama, we have to realize that it was fulfilling a function which the legitimate stage neglected. However crude its form, it was giving far more expression to the spirit of the age (an age, we must remember, to which Nelson and Trafalgar were living names) than the decorous neo-Elizabethan and pseudo-classic dramas of men like Horne, Marston, and Talfourd.[17]

The Navy played a great role in British history and had no more glorious a period than that at the turn of the century when it had defeated Napoleon's forces at the Nile and at Trafalgar. The merchant navy had helped defeat Napoleon, too, and was the largest in the world (in George IV's reign, tonnage approached two and a half million). The popularity of naval stories was encouraged by the tales of sailors who were genuine heroes, the conquerors of Napoleon. As the Wars became more of a distant memory, tales about them became more colorful and romantic. The domestic drama, however, combined the romantic with the darker side of naval life. Conditions on board ship were far from pleasant, as was proved by the alarming mutinies at Spithead and the Nore in 1797. The seamen's claims were just, and their promise to defend the nation if trouble arose was a genuine one. (It was largely the same mutinous seamen who saved their nation at St. Vincent, Camperdown, and the Battle of the Nile.)

The spirit of mutiny, and widespread knowledge of conditions aboard ship, caused the nautical drama to take up cudgels against oppression. Thus, nautical melodramas voiced democratic sentiments and protests against injustice. Attacks were made, for instance, upon the system of "press-

17. Ernest Reynolds, *Early Victorian Drama, 1830–1870* (Cambridge, England: W. Heffer and Sons, Ltd., 1936), p. 132.

ing" men into naval service. Bands of men, armed with cutlasses, roamed the villages and taverns looking for likely lads to serve the nation. This system caused widespread misery, since families were broken up and breadwinners carried off. Better recruits could be found aboard merchant ships, but the results were equally disastrous for a victim and his family. For the individual pressed, life was hard, food unbelievably bad, and pay insufficient. In Haines's *My Poll and My Partner Joe*, Harry Hallyard spoke his mind on the subject of the press gang that snatched him from his bride of an hour, Mary Rosebud. (Such cases were known to occur; often part of the congregation was taken, too.) His sentiments must have stirred many a heart in the audience:

> Fiends incapable of pity first gave birth to the idea, and by fiends only is it advocated. What! Force a man from his happy home, to defend a country whose laws deprive him of his liberty? But I must submit; yet, oh, proud lordlings and rulers of the land, do ye think my arm will fall as heavily on the foe as though I were a volunteer? No!—I shall strike for the hearts I leave weeping for my absence without one thought of the green hills or the flowing rivers of a country that treats me as a slave! (act 1, scene 3).

As Bowse, the leader of the press gang, himself pointed out, "Pity aren't among the articles of the press service."

Jerrold's William was no "radical" but he was followed by Richard Parker, a real-life mutineer and the hero of *Mutiny at the Nore*, (Pavilion, 1830). The dramatic core of the play was still domestic; the cruel Captain Arlington had been Parker's rival for the hand of Mary. Interspersed throughout the play were various protests. Adams pointed to the terrible injuries sustained by seamen during battles:

> Dick is a fine, strong, healthy, fellow; the first broadside's poured in—where's Dick?—sprawling a cripple for life upon the deck (act 1, scene 1).

Parker, himself sentenced to five hundred lashes, attacked the system of flogging:

I have seen old men, husbands and fathers, men with venerable gray hairs, tied up, exposed, and lashed like basest beasts: scourged, whilest every stroke of the blood-bringing cat may have cut upon a scar received in an honourable fight (act 1, scene 2).

A similar outburst occurred in C. A. Somerset's *The Sea*, (Olympic, 1842), where the hero, Harry Helm said to his captain:

I trust the day is not far distant, when so foul a stain to our national character as the laceration of a fellow-creature's flesh, will be blotted from old England's naval and military code forever (act 2, scene 5).

Both Parker and Helm are executed—history and naval discipline would admit of no other conclusion. Jerrold and Somerset both backed away from continuing to examine the general issues and turned to melodrama. *The Mutiny at the Nore* became a personal contest between Parker and Arlington with the former shooting the latter rather than surrender after the mutiny. Nevertheless, it must be said on behalf of these plays that they raised issues and voiced protests, which is more than the legitimate stage did for over three quarters of the century.

The Irish situation gave rise to a series of protest plays written by Dion Boucicault. Ireland was a constant problem to the English, and the economic conditions of the country had worsened during the early Victorian period. By 1830, cattle maiming, farm burning, and other protests had drawn attention to the miserable plight of the Irish peasants. (The situation became much worse when the Fenians were organized in 1858.) No positive measures were put through in London until 1835, and no major British political figure showed much sympathy for Ireland's woes before Gladstone, who managed, in 1869, to push through a measure disestablishing the Church of England in Ireland.

Dion Boucicault, whose affection for the Old Sod did not extend to living on it, wrote a series of plays set in Ireland. In them, the Saxon oppressor generally came off second best. Though he continued to write plays with stage Irishmen in them, Boucicault changed them into wise fools, and the comic butt of the play then became an absurd Anglo-Irishman, who was a fool among the Irish wits. However, even Boucicault was no true rebel; he did what he did in the cause of Irish patriotism rather than of protest.

Perhaps Boucicault's most outspoken play was *Arrah-Na-Pogue; or, The Wicklow Wedding*, (Dublin, 1864). The background and spirit of the play was the historical rising against British rule in 1789. Boucicault so rewrote the words of his original source, "The Wearing of the Green," that the song was banned after the first London performance. The song ended as follows:

> I've heard a whisper of a country that lies beyond the sea
> Where rich and poor stand equal in the light of freedom's day.
> O Erin, must we leave you, driven by a tyrant's hand?
> Must we ask a mother's blessing from a strange and distant
>   land?
> Where the cruel cross of England shall never more be seen
> And where, please God, we'll live and die still wearing of the
>   green (act 1, scene 4).

The dignity of British justice was eroded in the court scene, where Shaun was on trial:

> MAJOR. Shaun *(writing)*, that's the Irish for John. I suppose.
> SHAUN. No, sir; John is the English for Shaun. . . .
> MAJOR. Now, prisoner, are you guilty or not guilty?
> SHAUN. Sure, Major, I thought that was what we'd all come here to find out (act 2, scene 4).

Boucicault's comic heroes were, in a sense, instruments to preserve the self-respect of an exploited people. As David Krause points out:

> For the long-suffering Irish peasant had been forced to assume a cheerful sense of anarchy which amused and protected him

from his careless and indifferent masters, who underestimated him and seldom realized how slyly and outrageously he fooled them. People who live as slaves often fight back with their only weapons, ironic attitudes and loaded words.[18]

Because Boucicault's plays were written in the cause of patriotism, he was typical in his generation of writers. He was no radical, as he proved when writing *The Octoroon*, (Winter Garden, New York, 1859), within a week of John Brown's execution. So defused was the racial bombshell in the play that there was scarcely a ripple of protest.

Foreign wars and military expeditions to Europe were largely ignored, though there were some plays that used settings made famous by contemporary events. J. E. Carpenter's *Love and Honour; or, Soldiers at Home, Heroes Abroad*, (Surrey, 1855), treated the Crimean War distantly. There was a spectacular tableau of the fall of Sebastopol at the end of the play, but the war remained incidental to the real concerns of the play. These remain solidly domestic, and the Crimean War was merely a backcloth against which domestic struggles took place. Occasionally serious mentions of European affairs are found, but only as by-products of concern with something else. When Old Frank mentioned the sufferings of the poor in Douglas Jerrold's *Sally in Our Alley*, he shied away from making his point explicit:

Oh, master, when I heard of great battles—of towns burnt—I have often thought that if the pains and sufferings of the poor man's fireside were registered, they would show more dismally than the "Gazette" of Trafalgar or Waterloo! But you have almost trapped me into a sermon (act 1, scene 1).

However vague allusions to foreign wars and nations might be, there was never any doubt but that all opportunities for patriotic and nationalistic fervor would be seized wholeheartedly by dramatists and players alike. No Victorian would have echoed Dr. Johnson's immortal stric-

18. David Krause, "The Theatre of Dion Boucicault," Introduction to *The Dolmen Boucicault* (Dublin: Dolmen Press, [1964]), p. 40.

tures on patriotism, for patriotic fervor on the stage was a true indicator of a man's virtue. All stage-patriots were virtuous by definition. The stress domestic drama placed on an Englishman's duty was an accurate reflection of the general public attitude that had become increasingly jingoistic. Throughout the century, an increasing number of foreign wars, coupled with better communications, had made the people of Britain more aware of their nation's position in Europe. Even the workers, appalling though their conditions were, became militantly patriotic. They had traditional liberties and could influence the affairs of the nation. Though generally unable to vote in the first part of the century, they were still able to influence factory acts, trade unions, and finally to gain the franchise for themselves. The absence of armed rebellion in 1830 and 1848 was evidence to the English that they were set apart from others. Any intervention by the British government in foreign affairs in support of liberty was popular in England. The failure of republicanism and the heartfelt love of the people for their queen culminated in the feeling of *civis Britannicus sum* (I am a citizen of Britain). By the time Victoria had ruled for fifty years, the English were convinced that manifest destiny had marked them down for special glories. The Great Exhibition in 1851 and the Jubilee celebrations of 1887 were public expressions of a nation's pride in its achievements and its hopes for the future.

Patriotism in domestic drama was the only indication, indirect as it was, that the priorities of Europe were being reshaped. England was becoming the most wealthy nation on earth. Many a patriotic sentiment was expressed by that lover of nautical dramas, James C. Cross. As early as 1798, he had written an entertainment called *The Genoese Pirate; or, Black Beard*, (Covent Garden, 1798), in which the desperate pirate quailed before a scroll bearing the noble inscription "the Enemy is British and will Conquer." In *Love and Honour*, the final scene of the play contained a spectacular patriotic tableau. (The favored treatment of France—extremely rare in domestic drama—was caused by the alliance of the two nations against Russia.)

GEORGE. The proudest distinction a British soldier can boast of is that he did his duty, and was present on the day on which he could exclaim "Sebastopol is won!"

(The walls of the battery explode, and fall with a crash, discovering the Town of Sebastopol in flames—The Russian troops are seen crossing the bridge of rafts in the distance—The forts blow up—Ships are seen burning in the harbour—Characters form on either side with the flags of England and France, and huzza!—The Band plays "God Save the Queen," and "Partant pour la Syrie" as the curtain falls.) (act 3, scene 5).

The nautical hero was ennobled by patriotism. Traditionally the Jolly Jack Tar was a comic fellow, but his love of country changed all that. Into his mouth were put the sentiments found in the hearts of all true Englishmen. In J. C. Cross's *The Purse; or, The Benevolent Tar*, the following exchange took place between the hero, Will Steady, and Edmund after their captivity by Algerians:

WILL. Cut me to the heart, d'ye! A British sailor loves native freedom too well, ever willingly to let a foreigner interfere with it.
EDMUND. True, William; and—
WILL. Had but a few score of our countrymen been on board, she'd ne'er ha' yielded; for an Englishman never strikes his colours, while he's able to strike another stroke.
EDMUND. But the Algerine force was superior.
WILL. What then? There's but little honour in drubbing an equal (scene 2).

Serious study of the great social struggles of the period had been taken up by novelists with considerable zeal.[19] Dickens was busily exploiting the exploiters, and Charlotte Brontë took up the question of the Luddite machine wreckers in *Shirley*. Mrs. Trollope and Mrs. Gaskell, among others, wrote novels in which they attacked the effects of industrialism, and it is interesting to examine, as Richard Altick has done, the difference between one of the novels of protest and the translation of that novel to the stage.

19. The stage, of course, was more censorable. The Select Committee asked the Examiner of Plays what he considered "politically wrong." He replied, "anything that may be so allusive to the times as to be applied to the existing moment, and which is likely to be inflamatory." *(Report of Select Committee,* para. 965)

Mary Barton is a novel dominated by the author's concern about the dehumanizing process that industrialism brings in its wake, and Dion Boucicault adapted the novel to the stage as *The Long Strike*, (Lyceum, 1866):

> Boucicault, who had no social conscience to speak of, and who knew that his audiences, if they had any, left it at the door as they entered the theatre, threw out the didactic content of the novel without a qualm . . . the antagonism between millown-ers and workmen serves only as a convenient trigger for the plot . . . as soon as the Jane-Jem-Radley triangle is established with the ensuing murder, the strikers go back to work and we hear no more about such dull sociological subjects. *The Long Strike* could not possibly be viewed as a *pièce à thèse*; it is melodrama.[20]

The dehumanizing process that the Industrial Revolution fostered was a major cause of the fear that a way of life with which generations were familiar was dying out and leaving in its place the unknown. Village communities were broken up for ever. The dispossessed were driven to the towns where they swelled the ranks of unskilled laborers. Even in the towns at the turn of the century, there had been a cer-tain unity, but in the 1820s a second generation of em-ployers was taking over—a generation that had no contact with the social life of its workers. The rural, lower-class cul-ture that expressed itself in ballads, broadsheets, and chap-books was fragmented when the farm laborer moved into the towns. His style of living was radically changed; he could no longer eke out his living by growing his own food. The close ties of village life had been replaced by the anonymity of cities. Social forces over which workers had no control were of paramount significance. Hence, the domestic drama stressed certain crucial themes—class hatred, democracy, economics, and, most noticeable of all, nostalgia. The audiences of the minor theaters wanted to have their fears raised and then assuaged. The inevitable result was that domestic drama became a defense against the cruel realities of the world outside.

20. Richard Altick, "Dion Boucicault Stages *Mary Barton*," *Nineteenth-century Fiction* 14, no. 1 (June 1959): 136–37.

As the conditions of farming worsened, laborers left for the city or were forced to emigrate. The English villagers during the first fifty years of the nineteenth century were excellent pioneer stock, well able to hold their own in an expanding Empire. Many English farm workers did not emigrate, however, except to the cities, and their drama looked upon emigration as yet another result of the selfishness and lack of foresight of the landowners. This was the theme of Mary's argument when the virtues of the new squire were extolled to her in W. Bayle Bernard's *The Farmer's Story,*

MARY. He hasn't done one thing properly—raising poor Mark Ryland's rent because his lease was out, and compelling him to give up the farm and go to Canada.
VAILS. The landed interest, Mrs. L., must be protected.
MARY. Yes, Mr. Vails—but if all the gentry go to London, and all the farmers go abroad, who'll be left to protect it?
VAILS. Well it's a bad thing, certainly, when farmers plough the ocean (act 1, scene 1).

The landed aristocracy became a natural target for a democratically oriented drama. In the previous century relationships between landlord and tenant had generally been close. Gentlemen acknowledged an obligation to be generous and no one was more despised than a skinflint. As the Industrial Revolution progressed, however, the relationship between master and men became vitiated. A man who had once worked with his hands now became a machine-minder, forced to leave the *relatively* healthy atmosphere of his cottage to sweat in a closed factory. Hereditary skill counted less and less as machinery took the place of craft:

Phrases like the "lower orders," the "swinish multitude," "the rabble," became habitual to men and women who felt themselves to be a different species from the poor toilers whose grandfathers and fathers had been equals of their own.[21]

Landowners had favored enclosure and supported the Corn and Game Laws at a time when poor farmers and in-

21. Arthur Bryant, *The Age of Elegance* (New York: Harper and Row, 1950), p. 340.

dustrial workers were starving. They had been frightened by the French Revolution and Tom Paine's *The Rights of Man*, but there was no widespread support for political revolution in England. Revolution was not only dangerous, it was also treasonable. What domestic dramatists demanded was that the upper classes live up to their duties and responsibilities. This was the tenor of Hatfield's complaint in *The Factory Lad*:

> HATFIELD. Squire Westwood! Squire Hard-heart! No man, no feeling! Call a man like that a squire! An English gentleman—a true English gentleman is he who feels for another, who relieves the distressed and not turns out the honest, hardworking man to beg or starve, because he forsooth, may keep his hunters and drink his foreign wines.
> SIMS. Aye; and go to foreign parts. Englishmen were happy when they knew naught but Englishmen (act 1, scene 5).

Hatred of the aristocracy was in part an importation from abroad, but it never had the fervor that the romantic dramas of Goethe and Schiller gave it. Neither was hatred of nobility as strong as it was in the melodramas of Pixérécourt and his school. Part of the reason for the difference was historical. The class system of France was far more rigid than it was in England where:

> Common interest in the village traditions, in the seasons and the weather, in the crops and animals, and a shared knowledge of certain crafts and skills, with a resulting common interest in their details, served to make contacts between men of different degrees easier at every level. Various rural festivals and sports provided yet another link between manor and cottage . . . fox hunting was a sport in which everyone could join. Even those who did not own a horse would come to see off the huntsmen and the pack and would follow as best they could the course of the chase. Despite the damage done to fields as hunters careered across them, the institution of the hunt—where proprieties could be less strictly observed, and where high and low worked together—did much to foster solidarity in the countryside.[22]

22. Schneewind, p. 105.

Another reason for use of the squirearchy as the source of villains was the obvious fact that the local aristocracy was the only human power that could significantly affect men's lives. The idea of a libidinous squire ran throughout domestic drama even before *Luke the Labourer* firmly established the pattern; however, the lascivious squire was far less a product of the real world than he was a symbol of those social forces at whose mercy the workers found themselves. In factory dramas, the owner was an obvious symbol of evil forces, and in the country the squire had to serve the same function. It was true that landlords had considerable power, but it was also a fact that they often protected the poor from too much exploitation and, while life was certainly hard for poor people, it was not desperate. When workers migrated to the cities they lost the beauty of nature, they gave up customs of centuries, and all the humane background of country living was gone. Minor audiences saw contemporary society as unfeeling and exploitive. In their drama, they asked for a nostalgic picture of a world where the old traditions were still maintained, where life was simple and uncomplicated.

Allied to the domestic drama's hatred of the aristocracy was the lip service it paid to the age-old literary convention of egalitarianism:

> Every cliché about virtue being the only just claim to superiority and love destroying the barriers of rank was emphasized. Differences in wealth and social position meant nothing, the melodrama argued to the play's end, when some occurrence or disclosure was introduced to make them nonexistent. The peasant in love with a princess, for example, learned that his supposed mother was actually only a nurse who had taken him at birth from his noble parents. Sometimes the melodrama allowed the prince to marry the peasant; but when a princess was inclined toward one of humble station, he invariably had to be proved in the end the aristocracy's as well as nature's nobleman.[23]

23. David Grimsted, *Melodrama Unveiled: American Theater and Culture, 1800–1850* (Chicago: University of Chicago Press, 1968), p. 208.

Characters in domestic dramas frequently voiced the opinion that the poor were as good as the rich. The villain of Thomas Wilks's *Michael Earle, the Maniac Lover*, (Surrey, 1839), was a lord and rival for Mary's hand. Mary was already betrothed to a young shopkeeper, "who in virtue and honour is fit to be a lord." The alliance of lowly birth and virtue became a stock cliché of the domestic drama. As Baldwin of the Burn put it in T. E. Wilks's *Woman's Love; or, Kate Wynsley, The Cottage Girl*, (Victoria, 1841):

> She might have done worse. To be the wife of a well-to-do young farmer, is a precious deal better than being the what-do-you-call-'em of a man who gets his money nobody knows how (act 1, scene 1).

The poor also have their pride. Attacks by unfeeling aristocrats upon the birth of those "beneath" them are commonly rebutted, as in this example from the same play:

> CLITHEROE. How dare you speak disrespectfully of my first wife, sirrah?
> HOLLYHOCK. Beg pardon, sir, never did nothing of the kind.
> CLITHEROE. You have told my daughter, Lady Jessy, that her mother was a cottage girl.
> HOLLYHOCK. Beg pardon, my lord, but there's nothing disrespectful in that. A cottage girl, if she be an honest girl, is as respectable as a queen, and I am quite sure your lordship must agree with me (act 2, scene 1).

When the ties that had bound men to their country neighbors and their village were severed by the exodus to the city, the sense of community was gone forever. Relationships that had lasted for generations were permanently lost, and the worker found that he had no time to concern himself with the affairs of others. Thus is found a prominant feature of domestic drama: a sense of isolation that was coupled with a belief that modern life had fragmented society.

> The feeling of isolation and loneliness, so characteristic of modern man, first appeared in the nineteenth century. With

the breakup of a long-established order and the resulting frag-
mentation of both society and thought, the old ties were
snapped, and men became acutely conscious of separation. They
felt isolated by dividing barriers; lonely for a lost companion-
ship, human and divine; nostalgic for an earlier world of country peace and unifying belief.[24]

What was called the *industrial society* was seldom a society
at all in the nineteenth century. The early machines had
been driven by water power. Situated in the country, the
early "factories" employed local inhabitants who knew each
other and their employer. Perfection of steam-power
changed all that, for a man could close down his factory for
a week and put a thousand men out of work without know-
ing more than a few of them or their problems. Carlyle's
Teufelsdröckh described the results: "Call ye that a Society
where there is no longer any Social Idea extant; not so
much as the Idea of a common Home, but only of a common overcrowded Lodging-house?"[25]
The persistent longing for a return to rural ways is a reminder that almost all the labor force in the first half of the
century had been born in the country. The longing for a
rural way of life was reactionary, illusory, and sentimental,
but its persistence is incontrovertible evidence of a continuing discontent and a homesickness for an idealized but not
completely imaginary past. The country became a symbol
not of escape but of saving the "spiritual" values that increasing industrialism was destroying. For those who could
not physically return to the village home, the theater provided the only contact with a better world where
utilitarianism, greed, and inhumanity were banished.
While it is undoubtedly true that country cottages were
never the healthiest places to live, they were incomparably
better than the industrial slums that were growing apace.[26]
Inevitably the imagination conjured up visions of

24. Houghton, p. 77.
25. Ibid.
26. At Victoria's accession, life expectancy in the city was less than thirty years.
See Schneewind, p. 38.

honeysuckle-covered cottages with thatched roofs. In the villages of domestic drama, suffering and poverty were temporary, in marked contrast to life in the cities where they seemed endless. The idealization of the village was at the heart of Payne's *Clari; or, The Maid of Milan,* with its famous song "Home Sweet Home":

'Mid pleasures and palaces, though we may roam,
Be it ever so humble, there's no place like home.
A charm from the sky seems to hallow us there,
Which, seek through the world, is ne'er met with elsewhere.

Home, sweet home!
There's no place like home!

An exile from home, splendour dazzles in vain!
Oh, give me my lowly thatch'd cottage again!
The birds singing gayly, that came at my call,—
Give me them, with the peace of mind dearer than all!

Home, sweet home!
There's no place like home! (act 1, scene1).

This song, with its rejection of palaces in favor of humble thatched cottages, later became standard in other domestic dramas.

Some dramatists found it useful to bring the city onstage for the sake of contrast. The comparison of life in town and country is an old theme in Western literature and the idealizing of country life is as old as Theocritus. Whenever the city was mentioned in domestic dramas, it was never to its credit. The drunkard's dissipation, though it might begin in his village, generally accelerated when he moved to the city. The city had what William called a "baneful atmosphere" in *Susan Hopley*. The city is a painted lady—all show and no substance. No kindness could be expected from the city, nor could anyone expect to be happy there, as Mary Lockwood told her husband in *The Farmer's Story*:

MARY. Well, I don't believe it's as good a club as the one you belonged to in Littleburn, at the Cow and Compasses, where you always broke up at half-past ten, and in order to prevent excess, every gentleman paid for his own ale.

LOCKWOOD. Ha! ha! ha! what a hint for the Cocoa Tree, or Brook's. "N. B.—To prevent excess, every gentleman will pay for his own ale!". . . .

MARY. But I am not convinced that you are happy—of course the world says so, because you have got a fine house and equipage, and servants; but these are only leaves, which are always thick when the fruit is wanting—your face tells a different story! (act 2, scene 1).

Economic considerations were profoundly important in domestic drama. In the country, the farmer and his men had eaten and worked together but industrialism finished all this in the cities and the country was not unaffected. As Mary complained in *The Farmer's Story*:

In the old times—before Sir John Ashton sold the manor—we always went up to the Hall at Christmas and Whitsuntide to play at blindman's buff and hunt the slipper; but that's all over now, because they say the times are so improved—so they've shut up the Hall, and built a new workhouse (act 1, scene 1).

For those farmers who gave up the plow entirely, the prospects in the city were less than inviting. City economics long favored a policy of laissez-faire. Almost everything was left to individual enterprise. Even Benthamism, which technically supported state intervention if it brought about the greatest happiness for the greatest number, seemed allied against the workers. As if this were not enough, Malthusian economics held that the poor should be suppressed, and works such as Samuel Smiles's *Self-Help; with Illustrations of Character Conduct, and Perseverance* (1859), were interpreted as meaning that the miseries of the poor were due more to character defects than external causes. In opposition to this callous disregard of working-class needs, the domestic drama constantly urged the theme that the laborer was willing to work hard. A clergyman disagreed: "It may be questioned whether any labourer, or artisan, who is honest, industrious, frugal, and sober, need ever resort to alms or to the workhouse. Abject want is almost always the result of grievous error, or of gross misconduct."[27]

The most common device for bringing villain and heroine together was unpaid rent and the shame it brought with it. Eileen lamented her fate in *Eileen Oge; or, Dark's the Hour Before the Dawn*, a play by Edmund Falconer first produced at the Princess's Theatre in 1871:

> Notice of distraint! Seizure for rent! My poor father, at his time of life—after always having held his head so high among his neighbours—to be subjected to such a disgrace; for alas, alas! though it be none to the honest man, poverty brings that penalty along with it in this world (act 2, scene 1).

Other plays selected particular economic abuses to attack. Tom Taylor's *Still Waters Run Deep* had a vein of criticism of laissez-faire economics and the manipulations of stocks and shares, but the majority of plays attacked social attitudes. Such was the case with Buckstone's *Luke the Labourer*. Although Luke's fall was caused by his own intemperance, society showed him no mercy once he was discharged. His revenge was presented in such a way that it almost seemed justified. Each member of the gallery knew that Luke's fate might well await him, so that the drama excited pity and fear, and the theme of the play was a veiled threat to the wealthy:

> LUKE. You turned me away, and I had no character, because you said I was a drunkard. I was out o' work week after week, till I had not a penny in the world, nor a bit o' bread to put in mine nor my wife's mouth. I then had a wife, but she sicken'd and died—yes, died—all—all—along o' you . . . she laid hold o' this hand, and putting her long thin fingers around it she said, "Luke, would na' the farmer give you sixpence if he thought I were dying o' want?" I said I'd try once more—I got up, to put her in a chair, when she fell, stone dead, down at my feet (act 1, scene 2).

The important point Buckstone was making is that all that Luke had suffered was not his fault. Without a reference,

27. Quoted in Schneewind, p. 29.

he was totally unable to act on his own behalf. He was at the mercy of an unfeeling economic system. A similar theme is found in Jerrold's *The Rent Day*. Here the focus turns to absentee landlords and the problems that they cause. The basic conflict was between Heywood's necessities and Grantley's pleasures. Grantley wanted money for pleasure; Heywood needed it to exist. Although an honest, hardworking fellow, Heywood could not survive. The causes of his poverty were totally beyond his control:

> Harvest after harvest's failed;—flock after flock has died; yet have I smiled upon't, and gone whistling 'bout the fields. I have been hunted by landlord—threatened by the taxman—yet I've put a stout heart upon't, and never drooped. . . .I may sit down and see my little ones pine by day; I may feel their wasting limbs, and hear them scream for bread; and I may stare in their white faces, and tell them to be patient (act 1, scene 3).

Heywood was saved by a typically melodramatic discovery of hidden gold, but the play was not without sociological significance. Another interesting feature of the play was that neither Crumbs, the steward, nor Bullfrog, the bailiff, were utterly despicable, but they *were* totally businesslike. They lacked, as Victorian economics did, a sense of humanity, a sense of compassion for their fellow men. Bullfrog and society were ruthless in their functioning. Nothing made this clearer than Bullfrog's calm listing of Heywood's personal effects: "one toasting fork, one bird-cage, one baby's rattle." Heywood's misery was symbolic of the inhumanity of Victorian society.[28]

The home was particularly idealized since it stood as a retreat from the inhumane society that existed outside its

28. Interestingly enough, Richard Hoggart in *The Uses of Literacy* (London: Chatto and Windus, 1957), p. 68, quotes a similar experience from his own childhood. "Our area was shocked by the clumsiness of a Board of Guardians visitor who suggested to an old woman that, since she was living on charity, she ought to sell a fine teapot she never used but had on show. 'Just fancy,' people went around saying, and no further analysis was needed. Everyone knew that the man had been guilty of an insensitive affront to human dignity."

sheltering walls. In the previous century the coffee house had often been the center of man's social life. If only because of the large size of Victorian families, life became more domestic, yet the increased amount of family life would not account for the almost mystical regard with which the very concept of family was enshrined. That regard could only come from the belief that the home was the storehouse of moral and spiritual_ values that were an answer to grasping capitalism and declining religious beliefs. The very essence of domestic drama was the selection of the right mate and the protection of the home against the incursions of outside forces.[29] The home was all; a happy home gave a character the strength to face anything. As Mary sang in *The Farmer's Story*:

> I sigh for home, for that sweet spot,
>   Where earth was all earth to me;
> Where with the wind, the storm came not,
>   And with the light the fruit would be.
> Where winter made the hearth more bright,
>   And summer but unclosed the door,
> Dear home—could'st thou have known a blight
>   It would have made me love thee more (act 2, scene 1).

Both playwrights (who were predominantly middle class in outlook) and audiences recognized the wife's role to be of paramount importance in the successful running of a home. In domestic dramas, it was generally the heroine-wife who suffered most until the happy reunion of the family. Indeed, so central was the idea of domestic bliss that *The Drunkard* ended to the strains of "Home Sweet Home" rather than something more overtly religious. The "lower orders" could return home to their fortress against the anxiety and work that society produced. Once the door was closed, an honest man and woman could laugh at fickle fortune. This was a sentiment expressed by Martha Roseblade in *Waiting for the Verdict*:

29. Richard Hoggart in *Speaking to Each Other*, 1: 51, states that the working class still assumes "that home and family life are the most important things in life."

HYLTON. You married his son, then, with the prospect of a much better lot than you have experienced, I am afraid?

MARTHA. Alas! yes sir; but that has only drawn the bonds of love closer between us, and taught us the lesson, that an honest man and wife joined hand and heart together, may live content and happy despising fickle fortune and all false friends; for, though little be their store, still, if it be blessed with love and hope, the cottage may still be happier than the mansion! (act 1, scene 1).

The home was of great significance to the majority of Victorian women, since it was there they spent most of their time—supervising the smooth running of domestic affairs. It was their world. As Margaret said in Tom Taylor's *Arkwright's Wife*, (Leeds, 1873):

And be mine the woman's royalty—the ruling of a well-ordered home! Oh, I dreamed not of such happiness! Friends, do not call me back to a waking less happy than my dream! (act 3, scene 1).

It was in the home, under the supervision of the mother, that the children received much of their training. The unfortunate heroine of *Mary Price; or, The Adventures of a Servant Girl* by C. Hazlewood, (Queens, 1853), having been abducted by the rapacious Lord Clavering, believed she saw her mother and called to her deliriously:

See the clouds expand, and from heaven descends an angel from—it hovers o'er my head—joy! it is my mother! She comes to guard her child! Oh bliss unutterable (act 2, scene 4).

Mary's abduction served only to highlight the bestial side of man's nature, and made female innocence, virtue, piety, and love, all the more precious. And, of all the rewards that the drama held out, none was greater than love.

Love in both Victorian society and domestic drama was seen as a spiritually uplifting experience. It was a gift of God. The motivation was obvious. If men were to be saved from the sensuality that threatened to undermine society, then love must be pure and free from sexuality. The literature of love found throughout the century was not necessarily related to the actual experience of the majority of men and women, but there does appear to be evidence that love was regarded in an exalted manner by a large segment of nineteenth-century society. When Edward was refused by Agnes in Buckstone's *Agnes de Vere*, (Adelphi, 1834), he said simply, "then happiness and I must part for ever." Undoubtedly part of this emphasis on love came as a psychological reaction against marriages that were generally arranged for other reasons and from the romantic tradition familiar to all readers of literature:

> But in the best fiction—notably in Thackeray, George Eliot, Trollope, and Charlotte Brontë—it was not a daydream, people found but a passionate insistence that those feelings should be a reality, and a bitter arraignment of the system that ignored them. In a society so permeated by the commercial spirit, love could be blatantly thrust aside if it interfered with more important values. "It would not signify about her being in love," says Mrs. Davilow in *Daniel Deronda*, speaking of her daughter, "if she would only accept the right person."[30]

Love became regarded as a powerful force for the betterment of men. It would keep them from the baseness of lust and would purify the moral will. The playbill to Wilks's *Woman's Love*, called love "the bright oasis in the Desert of Life—cheering in Prosperity, soothing in Adversity, and faithful to the last." Walter Houghton comments:

> "The Angel in the House"—there in the title of Coventry Patmore's famous poem is the essential character of Victorian love (though not its only form in the period): the passion that was very much tempered by reverence and confined to the home—that is, to potential or actual marriage—and the object that was scarcely mortal. Otherwise love was not love but lust. This conception looks like a curious blending of Protestant earnestness and Romantic enthusiasm, with a strong assist from chivalric literature (as ready a source for woman worship as for hero worship). But seeds explain nothing apart from the receptive soil. The circumstances of Victorian society made bliss

30. Houghton, p. 381.

connubial; and, indeed, even apart from love, decreed the exaltation of family life and feminine character.[31]

Love was the great leveler. All classes from prince to pauper could experience it, and nineteenth-century playwrights generally substituted love for all other passions:

> The central characters in most plays were in quest of their proper mates. The thin period of sexual adventure and danger sandwiched between the domesticity of childhood and married life was the meat of both the melodrama and the romantic novel. Plays concentrated on the adventures of the heroine and romances on those of the hero, but the theme was almost exactly the same; the victory of the forces of morality, social restraint and domesticity over what was dark, passionate, and anti-social.[32]

This love was, of course, the love of Aphrodite not Eros. Any form of concession to the passionate, any example of moral laxity, was always severely punished in domestic dramas, which contained little or no serious examination of sexual problems or passions. In a society that placed a premium upon girls who were innocent—not to say—ignorant, this was to be expected. It was true that the audience received a certain vicarious pleasure at the thought of meeting the ideal embodiment of the opposite sex, but there was nothing remotely erotic or salacious in melodrama. Though the lust of the villain was frequently a motivating force, the very purity of his victim made it unlikely that anything would come of his passionate pursuit. If a villain as much as touched a heroine, it was a remarkable achievement. All too often he was indignantly rebuffed and, resorting to physical attack, often met his nemesis in the shape of the hero, comic man, or a passing sailor. Few domestic dramas dealt with wife murderers. No would-be seducer killed his mistress, except in *Maria Marten*, which, perhaps because it dealt with a sex crime, no author would claim. Relations between the sexes had to be kept "clean."

31. Ibid., p. 341.
32. Grimsted, p. 220.

Augustin Filon pointed out that, "A secret marriage is always introduced in English plays wherever a seduction is to be found in [French dramas]."[33] Conservatism toward displaying sex on stage ran so high that when Stirling's *Seven Castles of the Passions* was produced at the Lyceum, the *Illustrated London News* of 26 October 1844 commented, "It was necessary to make several alterations in this spectacle consistent with English notions of propriety before it could be produced on our stage." One of the seven passions had to be changed from Lust to Love! Even thirty years later when Merritt and Conquest wrote *Seven Sins*, (Grecian, 1874), they were obliged to omit Lust and substitute a new deadly sin in the person of one Boozey, the incarnation of Intemperance. Fear of unfavorable reactions perhaps caused Tom Taylor to neglect the heart of *Still Waters Run Deep*, (Olympic, 1855). The French original had made the older woman the mother of the wife. Taylor made the relationship aunt and niece. He shifted his attention to the action of the play and took less heed of the interplay of character and passions that the play could have examined.

M. R. Lacy's *The Two Friends*, (Haymarket, 1828), was condemned in the *Dramatic Magazine* as "one of the most immoral and dangerous dramas" ever written.[34] What caused the furor was that Herbert and Elinor had believed themselves to be brother and sister, and, upon discovering that they were not, had confessed their love for each other. The play's severe condemnation by the public well bore out the opinion of those before the Select Committee who had assured the members that the public was the strongest guardian of public decency.

Naturally any themes that might be called immoral were turned into admonitory discourses in dialogue. A fearful dread of seduction or elopement pervaded the domestic drama as it did Victorian society in general. There were

33. Augustin Filon, *The English Stage: Being an Account of the Victorian Drama*, trans. Frederic Whyte (London: John Milne, 1897), pp. 59–60.
34. *The Dramatic Magazine* (1829), p. 194.

dreadful fates awaiting those who eloped or married against the wishes of parents. When Agnes Gordon married Albert de Vere (an early example of the return to aristocratic characters), it killed her father, Sir Gordon, and Agnes herself died of a broken heart after she had murdered her husband. In Henry Holl's *Grace Huntley*, (Adelphi, 1833), the heroine, who had married against her father's wishes, paid the penalty. She watched by helplessly

> while her husband trained their son to be a thief. When she remonstrated, the father threatened to bring their son to the gallows. "At this horrible threat," comments a contemporary critic, "an universal shudder ran through the audience; and the perfect amazement that spellbound every bosom was succeeded by loud sobs and tears that showed how many fathers and mothers sympathized with the scene." After Grace reluctantly denounced her husband to the police, he repented and tearfully pleaded with her to wean their son from further criminal courses.[35]

Attempted seduction of working-class girls is a common theme of domestic drama, and it reflected a state of affairs that caused considerable alarm. In 1851, over forty-two thousand illegitimate babies were born, which showed that nearly eight percent of girls above puberty were unmarried mothers. It is surprising, perhaps, that Agnes Fitzarden, the seduced daughter in *The Lear of Private Life*, emerged as the heroine of the piece. Although she had a child, she was restored to quasi-respectability by the expedient of a marriage to her seducer. The reason this play did not cause an outcry was clear, however. Even by 1820, seduced daughters had become such clearly established stereotypes that the gallery gods accepted them without undue alarm. The introductory remarks to the play make it clear that the author's intention was to show "a fond father driven to despair and madness by the seduction of his only child."[36]

35. J. P. Stoakes, "English Melodrama: Forerunner of Modern Social Drama," *Florida State University Studies*, no. 3 (1951), p. 58.

36. Quoted in Gary Scrimgeour, "Drama and Theatre in the Early Nineteenth Century" (unpublished Ph.D. dissertation, Princeton University, 1968), pp. 435–36.

Morality does not enter into Agnes's case. She herself accepted the official line of condemnation without question:

> I am a wretched, guilty creature; nor should I dare intrude myself on your goodness, and solicit you to let me remain under your roof, were I not severely punished for my crime, and resolved to spend the remainder of my days in solitude and labour[37] (act 3, scene 1).

Seduction, because it could lead subsequently to total rejection of a woman, was a factor in the number of prostitutes that had increased alarmingly by the middle of the century. Other causes are not hard to find. The low factory wages paid women, the secrecy that cities made possible, and the postponement of marriage by ambitious young men helped swell the ranks of prostitution. By the middle of the century, London had at least eight thousand known prostitutes. "Learned" articles appeared claiming that the availability of prostitutes made a contribution to social stability. *The Westminster Review* of July 1864 complained bitterly of this: "Anonyma is to a certain extent the pet of the age and is openly pleaded for by many practical moralists as a present necessity to the convenience and harmony of the world." It was undoubtedly the ready availability of prostitutes that led to a strong protective movement in morals and the effort, carried onto the stage, to idealize love and women. J. B. Schneewind points out that "the Victorian insistence on female purity, hysterical as it sounds at times, is in part a reaction against the masculine impurity imposed by the economics of middle-class sexuality."[38] And, perhaps, behind it all was the fear that the life of the demimonde was more alluring than that of the home and hearth.

The temptations of "another woman" are thus occasionally found in domestic dramas—with predictable results. Bernard made the hero of *The Farmer's Story* find Lady Melville far more exciting than his wife, but John T. Haines went further. He based an entire play on six of

37. It is interesting to note a further value of work—as atonement.
38. Schneewind, p. 115.

Hogarth's drawings entitled *The Harlot's Progress*. Haines's play was called *The Life of a Woman; or, The Curate's Daughter*, (Surrey, 1840). It followed the relentless fall of Fanny Rosemary from curate's daughter to cast-off mistress. Fanny's straying from the path of virtue cost her her life and emphasized the stern moral, "A deviation from virtue is a departure from happiness." Fanny Rosemary is an example of a type of fallen woman whose fall was the result of inner weakness or an inability to resist temptation. There were many female figures of this type and they were considered suitable characters for the domestic drama. The "courtesan drama" was never popular in England, for the professional magdalene was not emotionally involved enough and not enough tears flowed. Additionally an unchaste heroine was considered an affront to morality:

> "STOP! You that have wives or mothers or daughters, remember there is a lady on the stage." This appeal quelled a riot at the Princess's in 1875. The audience which had come to see *Heartsease*, by James Mortimer, strongly objected to the nature of the story. It had been taken from *La Dame aux Camélias* and the heroine was unchaste.[39]

Other French writers were involved in what was referred to in England as "the literature of prostitution." All through the period Balzac, Eugene Sue, and George Sand were savagely attacked by English critics in such a way that it was clear that more than puritanism was involved. The violent responses were evidence of a very real fear that the seducer and seduced were being portrayed too attractively in literature:

> The potential perils of such literature were felt and analyzed as early as 1819 in Hannah More's *Moral Sketches*: "Such fascinating qualities are lavished on the seducer, and such attractive graces on the seduced, that the images indulged with delight by fancy carry the reader imperceptibly to a point which is not so far from their indulgence in the act as some imagine.[40]

39. M. Willson Disher, *Melodrama: Plots that Thrilled* (London: Rockcliff and Co., [1954]), p. 102.

40. Houghton, pp. 359–60.

The Victorian ethic and an almost paranoid fear of immorality made the domestic drama prize marital fidelity, especially for women, above all else. Writers, such as Francis Newman writing in *Fraser's Magazine*, were fearful of "libertinism of the most demoralizing character," which is his assessment of what he considered the dangerous spread of "free-love."[41]

Whatever the cause for the severity of the sentence, one thing was certain—a fallen woman had little hope of rising once she had sinned. Adultery was the commonest sin found in heroines of domestic dramas. Kotzebue raised the fundamental question in *The Stranger* (1798) of what happens if society is not willing to forgive after a fallen woman's repentance. Mrs. Haller's actions after her sin show that she had only the tiniest flaw in her makeup. Kotzebue did seem to hint that a happy ending was possible, but English authors were inexorable. The classic example of a story of adultery is, of course, T. A. Palmer's *East Lynne*. The initial adultery was caused by a misinterpretation by Isabel of her husband's behavior toward another woman. Her fears were encouraged by Sir Francis Levinson, and she left her husband, was divorced, and became Levinson's mistress. He soon cast her off. Then Isabel realized the full extent of her loss:

> Oh, would that I had died when I might have heard kind loving voices as my spirit passed away from earth to heaven! My husband, my children!—Oh, never again to hear *him* say, "Isabel, my wife!" Never again to hear *their* infant tongues murmer the *holy* name of *"mother!"* Lost, degraded, friendless, abandoned, and alone! Alone—utterly alone—for ever-more!
> (*Sinks on her knees despairingly as The Curtain Falls: Music "Home Sweet Home."*) (act 2, scene 2).[42]

When Mrs. Wood first wrote the novel, divorce was sufficiently in the air (the Matrimonial Causes Act was passed in 1857) for her to make her erring heroine not only an adultress, but a divorcée. Be that as it may, few

41. Ibid., p. 365.
42. Quoted from T. A. Palmer's version, (Nottingham, 1874).

heroines have suffered as much as Lady Isabel as she attempted to redeem herself by suffering, humility, and poverty. Plays such as *East Lynne* ended with the death or insanity of the adultress. It was the latter that Clitheroe feared for his wife, Lady Adeline, in *Woman's Love,* when he discovered his first wife was still alive:

> The shock would be worse than death; the idea that, however unintentionally, she had been living in adultery with a married man, would so jar her sensitive nature, that reason would take refuge in insanity, and the gloom of the mad-house would await her (act 2, scene 3).

By the fortuitous circumstance of Lady Adeline's drowning, Clitheroe was saved from having to reveal the truth to her. Female villains were severely punished—frequently more harshly than their male counterparts. The end of a villainess was usually exile, imprisonment, madness, or death brought on by excessive guilt feelings. Lady Audley committed suicide:

> Yes. Your threat—the madhouse. I have taken poison—death is on me even now (*sinking to the ground*). If I had delayed but a few minutes only! But this torture heaven has reserved for the supreme moment (act 3, scene 3).

No discussion of woman's place in society would be complete without a brief consideration of a phenomenon of social and dramatic life—the "rebellion" of women against a society dominated by men. The submissive role of women had been laid down by the Princess's father in Tennyson's remarkable poem "The Princess," written in 1847:

> Man for the field, and woman for the hearth;
> Man for the sword, and for the needle she;
> Man with the head, and woman with the heart;
> Man to command, and woman to obey;
> All else confusion (part 5, lines 437–41).

This was certainly the view of most Victorian men and domestic-drama authors, and many Victorian women. It implied, however, that men had a duty and responsibility toward women, especially wives. When Baldwin of the Burn had his suit rejected by Kate Wynsley in *Woman's Love*, he sought evidence to expose her shame. (She is, of course, secretly married.) Kate congratulated Baldwin on his success:

> But what a victory it is! Man delights to protect and not to injure woman, the latter is the act not of a man but a ruffian! It is but a poor triumph at any time to conquer a woman, and I do not envy the heart of that man who desires to expose a female to the sneers of the world, even though she should be really faulty and unworthy (act 1, scene 2).

Just because a woman *had* to be utterly faithful, she was completely lost if her man were faithless to her. The problems of women, faced with their dependent status, were examined in *Victorine; or, I'll Sleep On It* by J. B. Buckstone, (Adelphi, 1831), but mawkish sentimentality prevented serious study in this and similar plays.

Gary Scrimgeour has developed an interesting theory in his unpublished dissertation that certain "she melodramas" provided women with vicarious gratification at their own powerlessness. Isabelle's concluding speech in *Isabelle; or, A Woman's Life* by J. B. Buckstone, (Adelphi, 1834), is:

> Dear girls, may your bright hopes never be shadowed by disappointment. And when you become wives and mothers, then think sometimes of Isabelle; and let her story teach you the best of all life's lessons—patience, fortitude, and a strong trust in all that is good.

Scrimgeour says that Isabelle's reward was the "power over her husband" she has won.[43] However, it seems much more probable that Isabelle's speech is a reiteration of the very common and approved nineteenth-century point of view that even though men do stray, a woman's life consists of patient waiting until he reforms. This "double standard" was attacked only on very rare occasions, such as the moment in *Woman's Love* when Kate said:

43. Quoted in Scrimgeour, p. 529.

There is where your sex has so unjust an advantage over ours. Man does that with impunity, nay, with smiling approval, of which, if a woman be guilty, she is lost for ever—yes, so lost, that while her own sex turn from her with contempt and scorn, men deem her the fitting butt for contumely and insult (act 1, scene 1).

J. B. Buckstone's *Ellen Wareham, The Wife of Two Husbands*, (Haymarket, 1833), was another admonitory drama on the high standards expected of a woman. These are such high standards, indeed, that this play may be regarded as a problem drama. The plot was based on the fact that Ellen, believing that her husband Cresford died in the French wars, had married Captain Wareham. It transpired that Cresford had, in fact, survived and engineered a brilliant escape from France. A letter telling of his plans had miscarried and Ellen was brought to trial by Cresford, whose principal reason for wanting revenge was his discovery that Ellen had never loved him. Though Cresford conveniently died in the last act, the drama did confront a real issue. Unfortunately that was as far as the play went, and no solution nor serious comment upon Ellen's fate was forthcoming.

In *Agnes de Vere*, Buckstone confronted yet another serious issue; again he backed away into a melodramatic solution. Agnes wrongly believed that her husband Alfred was having an affair with Lydia. Alfred was a libertine and Agnes was driven to fury by her helplessness:

What would turn a wife burning with jealousy and suspense, from her fixed resolve? I think I could endure every torment—every affliction of poverty and disgrace, without a murmur—were—he—were Alfred faithful to me; but to know that he abandons me, will be a knowledge that must bring with it madness and death (act 2, scene 2).

Complete agreement with Scrimgeour's conclusion that "she melodramas worked to gratify their audiences' desires under the guise of official morality"[44] is difficult, but this play did seek to sway the audience's sympathies in favor of

44. Scrimgeour, p. 530.

a woman wronged. Buckstone was very careful to make sure that Agnes's solutions to her problems were not considered as the right ones. Agnes, it was repeatedly stressed, had foreign origins; and she possessed "strong passions" inherited from her Italian mother. Though a sympathetic figure, Agnes suffered the fate of all women who attempted to go against conventional morality and upset the cosmic order. After killing her husband with his own deadly poisons, she died of a broken heart.

Even such "outspoken" plays as the "she melodramas" followed the established pattern of domestic dramas. Protests were permitted throughout domestic drama —something of a catharsis resulted—but conventional moral standards had to be reasserted by the play's conclusion. Firm official control of the stage via the licensing powers of the Lord Chamberlain's Office was certainly to blame for much of the failure of the domestic drama to take upon itself any reforming zeal—though the very retention of a liberal sentiment was in itself no mean achievement. Since, as George Colman himself admitted, no one checked to see if his "suggestions" had been carried out, it was possible that uncut versions were performed.

It was not the actions of the Examiner of Plays alone that were recognized by writers and managers. The audience, too, was looked upon as a censor to be reckoned with. As Charles Kemble told the Select Committee:

> I have frequently seen things, for instance, that have suffered to pass by the licenser which have not been suffered to pass by the audience, which is very strong proof that they are perhaps better guardians of their own moral and religious sentiments than anybody can be for them.[45]

The gallery at the Haymarket was no different. In 1844, Charles Mathews uttered Goldsmith's line, I "came to scoff, [but I] remained to pray." Mistaking this for a Biblical line, the audience loudly hissed what they felt to be flippant and

45. *Select Committee*, para. 708.

blasphemous. A reviewer in *Actors by Gaslight* took to task
C. P. Thompson, the author of *Poachers and Petticoats*,
(Strand, 1836), because "two ladies are made to doff their
own habiliments for those of the opposite sex. . . . The
thing is altogether an unredeemable piece of obscenity."[46]
The situation had apparently changed little when later in
the century Jerome K. Jerome commented ironically, "The
early Christian martyrs were sinful and worldly, compared
with an Adelphi gallery."[47]

Under such pressures as those mentioned above, it is
hardly surprising that domestic drama was frankly conservative in many of its beliefs. The prescriptive morality of the
domestic drama was of the type that did not threaten the
social structure and that idealized the concepts of home,
family, duty, and obedience.

Surprisingly, the attempts to make the theater a force for
moral good had little official backing. Since the theater, in a
very real sense, provided the only "education" that most
workers received, there should have been stronger official
support for the drama. Not all people agreed, of course.
Some, like George Vandenhoff, attacked the theory of the
theater as pulpit, but they were in a decided minority:

> We have no more right to expect the stage to be either a pul-
> pit, or a school of morals, than we are entitled to demand of it
> theological discourses, or lessons in political science. The stage
> is simply a picture of human life in action, in which man may
> see himself "as in a glass;" both "his better and his worser
> part" fairly exhibited; and if the exhibition be a true one, it is
> the fault of the looker-on himself if he be not moved by self-
> contemplation to self-correction and improvement. The moral
> must be left to be inferred by the conscience of the
> audience.[48]

A much more typical view was that of P. J. Cooke. The fact
that he felt compelled to defend the moral value of dramas

46. *Actors by Gaslight*, 1 (23 June 1838): 77.

47. Jerome K. Jerome, *Stage Land: Curious Habits and Customs of Its
Inhabitants* (London: Chatto & Windus, 1889), p. 5.

48. George Vandenhoff, *Leaves from an Actor's Note-Book* (New York: D. Appleton and Co., 1860), pp. 339–40.

as late as 1895 shows that the theater was still considered injurious to public morality. The opponents of drama, he claimed:

> Forget the many useful lessons, both social and moral, which have been, and which continue to be, taught from the footlights and from the pages of dramatic literature. They forget that the object of the drama was originally intended as a popular medium by which great sacred truths were disseminated among the people. . . . The object of the drama has not changed to any great extent since then.[49]

Much of the argument in favor of Cooke's point of view lay in the very clear line of demarcation that was drawn between good and evil in the domestic dramas. The villain was always placed in such a despicable contrast to the hero and heroine that domestic drama seemed to be employed "to give a correct representation of the human passions in the manner most consistent with the refinement of the people."[50]

Though she wrote no domestic dramas as such, Joanna Baillie epitomized the desire of those who wished to see the stage as the inculcator of morality. She wrote a series of "plays of the passions," which were nothing more than dramatized sermons upon such passions as love, hate, and ambition. It is not necessary, however, to go outside domestic drama to find sermons on correct behavior. In Tom Taylor's *The Ticket of Leave Man*, there was a typical example aimed against the erratic Sam Willoughby (and, by extension, all young men like him):

> Sam, my lad, listen to me, if you won't harken to her. A bad beginning makes a bad end, and you're beginning badly; the road you're on leads downwards, and once in the slough at the bottom o't—oh! trust one who knows it—there's no working clear again. You may hold out your hand—you may cry for help—you may struggle hard—but the quicksands are under

49. P. J. Cooke, *A Handbook of the Drama. Its Philosophy and Teaching* (London: Roxburghe Press, [1895]), p. 93.
50. Ibid., p. 96.

your foot—and you sink down, down, till they close over
your head (act 4, scene 1).

When drama was not didactic in tone, it was frequently
condemned for having failed in its primary task. Authors
may or may not have shared the audience's concern with
didacticism, but they knew better than to ignore it. If their
audiences demanded unequivocal statements on what was
right and what was wrong, authors obliged them.

Domestic dramas, therefore, espoused the ideals of the
society for which they were designed. The belief that hard
work would lead to rich rewards was vigorously supported.
Part of the reason for the squirearchy's supplying the villains of melodrama was the "puritan" feeling that the aristocracy spent its time permanently in the pleasures of the
hunt, and, later, of the opera. The only other employment
squires were permitted involved the pursuing of young village girls. It is only fair to point out that agricultural workers were little affected by the middle-class work ethic. In
the first years of factory work, an extra day of rest was by
no means uncommon. Factory workers did not have to turn
to work as Carlyle did to keep doubts from preying on
them. They were also freed of a great deal of the terror of
failure that haunted the bourgeoisie, and they did not share
the latter's ambition for a life of gracious living as the
crowning success of a lifetime of work. The direction of
domestic drama was, nevertheless, toward material rewards
for hard work and a virtuous life. These rewards must also
have been earned, if by nothing else, at least by suffering.
The Farmer's Story was a cautionary tale on the dangers of
easy money (wealth comes to the hero by chance), and the
three acts are captioned to explain the portent of each:

Act 1—The Village, Labour and its Lesson
Act 2—The Metropolis, Wealth and its Temptations
Act 3—The Heath, Want and its Consequences.

Lockwood's character followed a similar course:

Stephen Lockwood, a Young Farmer
Lockwood, a Man of Fashion
Lockwood, a Reduced Gamester.

The hero, after showing his innately moral character, was saved from poverty by the fortuitous return of an ex-villager who had been forced to emigrate. Now rich, he had come seeking Lockwood to share the work (and wealth) of a life in Canada.

Just as hard work had its ultimate reward, so, too, did virtue. In domestic drama, no idea was promulgated more assiduously than the belief that virtue would triumph in the end. No casuistry, no complexities, no alteration of strict moral codes was permitted. In a society that was itself governed by a severe moral code, an audience could enjoy the sight of villainy without feelings of guilt, for justice would ultimately triumph. This inevitable victory of virtue was satirized by many, including Charles Dickens:

> The Pantomine was succeeded by a Melo-Drama. Throughout the evening I was pleased to observe Virtue quite as triumphant as she usually is out of doors, and indeed I thought rather more so. We all agreed (for the time) that honesty was the best policy, and we were as hard as iron upon Vice, and we wouldn't hear of Villainy getting on in the world—no, not on any consideration whatever.[51]

The great majority of earlier domestic dramas ended happily, which in nineteenth-century terms meant the right mate, love, a happy home, and freedom from want. Vice and virtue were viewed in terms of profit and loss. Domestic dramatists generally promised immediate dividends rather than future prospects, and great efforts were made to engineer such endings. Edward Fitzball took the story of "Jonathan Bradford" and made it a domestic drama. In the original the hero was hanged, but in the play there was a happy ending. Gary Scrimgeour comments:

> The happy endings of melodrama may be more sophisticated than we think. They may be no more than the necessary

51. Charles Dickens, *The Uncommercial Traveller and Reprinted Pieces* (London: Oxford University Press, 1958), p. 33.

psychological compromise with stability, the gesture that ena-
bles society and the individual to tolerate the gruesome display
of terror and injustice in the body of the play. Both the material in the body of the play and the happy ending have serious
purposes to serve and work together in harmony.[52]

The belief in a happy ending, which is to say the conviction
that virtue would always triumph, was deeply rooted in Victorian consciousness.[53] Carlyle had produced the argument
that "might is right" because in a universe created by God
only that which was right had been given strength to succeed. He admitted that right might take time to gain the
upper hand, but failed to specify how long this might be.
Any playwright could have told him that it was precisely
the length of a domestic drama.

In the final analysis, what counted was the skill with
which the playwright aroused the deep-rooted fears in his
audience's mind and then set them at rest. Strong anxiety
followed by a fittingly happy conclusion lay at the heart of
domestic drama. Often the ingenuity of man was incapable
of settling matters so that virtue and right did triumph.
Fortunately for characters (and their creators) there was always Divine Providence, which, though it might move in
mysterious ways, always came to the aid of the innocently
oppressed. As the Reverend Owen Hylton put it in
Waiting for the Verdict:

> HYLTON. It is impossible for me to say, my good girl, appear-
> ances are strongly against him; but what of that if he be truly
> innocent, he has nothing to fear, for Providence will never
> permit the innocent to suffer for the guilty, so let us trust in
> that Providence to deliver him from danger.
> BLINKEY. Yes, sir, let us trust to Providence as you say.
> There's nothing like it (act 2, scene 3).

The time arrived, however, when a divine solution to all
life's problems became unacceptable to the more discerning

---

52. Scrimgeour, pp. 533–34.
53. As domestic drama developed, it grew in complexity. Plays such as *East
Lynne* that ended in the tearful death of one of the characters became increasingly
common. Even so, the redemption (and death) of a sinner was a cause for celebra-
tion.

members of theater audiences. New forces were abroad that exerted continuing pressures upon the stage to play a less passive role in intellectual matters. The novels of George Eliot, George Meredith, Thomas Hardy, and the revolutionary theories of Charles Darwin, T. H. Huxley, and Auguste Comte encouraged the spread of intellectual discussion. In drama, the pioneer work of Tom Robertson bore fruit. As early as 1865, in cooperation with the Bancrofts, Robertson had striven to produce plays that dealt with serious issues in as lifelike a manner as possible. He was permitted by the Bancrofts to produce his own plays and, thus, to control both their staging and interpretation:

> Here were the first manifestations of the social drama, with recognizable English characters, recognizable English backgrounds, and recognizable human motives. Instead of the pale languishings of a Claude Melnotte or the lurid machinations of a Lady Audley, here were Tom Stylus shouting for the education of the masses, the chronically unemployed Eccles shouting for the rights of the working man, the aristocratic Hawtree upholding the "inexorable law of caste," and all with a definite social thesis behind it.[54]

Lesser known playwrights such as James Albery and Sidney Grundy had followed Robertson's lead, but it fell to W. S. Gilbert and Arthur Wing Pinero to supply themes that would stimulate intellectual debate among their audiences. A new breed of theater critics gave the aspiring problem play and its authors vigorous support, and one of them, William Archer, worked hard to get the plays of Ibsen accepted by London theatergoers.

The new dramatists differed from their predecessors and many of their contemporaries in several significant ways. For one thing, they made a serious effort to write dramatic *literature* that improved copyright laws and royalty payments encouraged. Conventional morality was questioned

---

54. Marjorie Northend, "Henry Arthur Jones and the Development of the Modern English Drama," *Review of English Studies* 18 (October 1942): 450. Bulwer-Lytton's *Money* (Haymarket, 1840) was a serious comedy that foreshadowed Robertson.

rather than prescribed, and the old stereotypes began to disappear as did the stock system under which they had flourished. Clear-cut confrontations between right and wrong were replaced by struggles between those who, because of differing standards of conduct, could *both* be in the right. Often the conflict was internalized so that the old tradition of a battle between villain, heroine, and hero was discarded. Instead, a conflict between warring inclinations within the mind of one character who was neither all good nor all bad was presented. Most of all, the endings of the plays were regarded as the *inevitable* outcome of the action of the drama. Divine providence and *dei ex machinis* were not permitted to resolve matters in favor of a conventionally acceptable moral statement.

The new drama did not replace the old overnight. Despite the efforts of Robertson and his supporters, domestic drama continued to exert its attraction and had a large following. A sizable audience still preferred to hear its moral philosophy expounded unchallenged from the stage. Characters, familiar from a hundred other plays, continued to tell the same story in one of its endless variations. However, by the end of last century, the drama of Robertson and his successors had virtually superseded domestic drama. The concerns of dramatists and their audiences could no longer be expressed in a theater of broad emotional appeals, rigid morality, stereotyping, and total predictability. Yet many of the elements of domestic drama have survived and flourished in film and television where stock figures—hero, heroine, villain, comic man—still act out their roles to a musical accompaniment. Virtue is unfailingly rewarded and triumphs though sorely tried, and spectacular effects abound.

Revivals of nineteenth-century plays have been attempted. Boucicault's comedy, *London Assurance*, recently played to full houses in London and New York, but generally directors have preferred to "send up" domestic dramas. Yet, amidst the laughter at the harrowing events onstage, may be seen, here and there, a tear.

A penny gaff performance is interrupted by an apple seller
(SOCIETY FOR THEATRE RESEARCH)

APPENDIX:
PENNY GAFF AND BLOOD
TUB

Part of the reason for the unruly behavior of Victorian audiences undoubtedly lay in the "training" that they received as youths in the penny theaters located in London's working-class districts. These theaters, familiarly referred to as "penny gaffs," were improvised theaters that specialized in performing the crudest of melodramas for their youthful clientele. Certain gaffs concentrated on particularly bloodthirsty pieces and were known as *blood-tubs*.[1]

Before the Theatre Regulation Act of 1843, there must have been well over a hundred penny theaters situated in the poorer sections of London. The areas that boasted the greatest number of gaffs were the East End and the Surrey side. Conditions at the theaters reflected those of their geo-

1. I am indebted to Phyllis Hartnoll, ed., *The Oxford Companion to the Theatre*, 3rd ed. (London: Oxford University Press, 1967, p. 296) for this term, which I have not encountered elsewhere. In Scotland, the gaffs were called *geggies*.

graphical locations. A gaff near the docks in Ratcliff Highway, for example, was simply dug into the ground, and the audience sat in imminent danger of contracting pneumonia.

The legal status of the gaffs was as murky as their settings. Technically, before 1843, the utterance of even a single word constituted an illegal act—just as it did in the minor theaters. However, the patent theaters and their informers were more concerned with protecting themselves against the incursions of the minors than those of the gaffs. Legal action against the gaffs generally came from well-meaning individuals who saw them as dens of iniquity, or from residents who deplored the proximity of gaffs and their shady followers. Arrests of actors were exceedingly common—the whole troupe left shivering on a bench in pitiful costume awaiting the arrival of a magistrate. Sometimes even the audience was taken in charge. That the law against dialogue was broken is not in doubt, for Henry Mayhew was told that a typical show would include:

> A variety of singing and dancing and ballets, from one hour and a half to two hours. There are no penny theatres where speaking is allowed, though they do it to a great extent, and at all of 'em at Christmas a pantomine is played at which Clown and Pantaloon speaks.[2]

The laws still allowed magistrates to treat actors at unlicensed theaters as "rogues and vagabonds." A fine could be levied as high as one hundred pounds, but in general fines were much less than this. In 1840, for instance, a magistrate contented himself by fining members of a company one shilling each. Considering the salaries of gaff actors, this was a severe enough blow, especially when coupled with the closing of the gaff itself.

The average size of a gaff permitted audiences of around two hundred to be packed together for each show. Some gaffs were considerably larger; one reportedly held two thousand; several held more than five hundred. When it is

2. Henry Mayhew, *London Labour and the London Poor*, 4 vols. (London: C. Griffin and Co., 1861–62), 3: 121.

considered that many penny theaters held four or more performances, an average gaff might sell over a thousand tickets nightly, six times a week. At Christmas time, when the penny theaters put on pantomimes, attendance at the London gaffs must certainly have topped fifty thousand.

A gaff's "quality" could be taken on trust, but a certain amount of crude advertising did take place. Newspaper puffing was too expensive a business for most gaffs, but placards were often used. These were frequently hand-lettered signs in which bright colors and large print were notable features. Though most of the audience was largely illiterate, the impact of the placard could scarcely be mistaken. Some printed announcements were also employed—a typical example came from the Vine Yard Theatre in 1837. It announced a week:

> To commence with the
> Spectre King
> To conclude every evening with a
> SONG AND FARCE!
> The following week, will be produced
> Jane Shore
> Jim Crow
> Fiend of the Flood
> Fatal Cataract
> John Overy [the Miser]
> Open at 5, begin at half past. One penny

Some theaters even sold pictures of their "artistes" for sixpence or ninepence. As a further inducement to enter a gaff, an "orchestra" played. Consisting of at least one fiddler, the orchestra could be relied on to assail the ears of the passers-by:

> An old grand-piano, whose canvas-covered top extended the entire length of the stage, sent forth its wiry notes under the be-ringed fingers of a "professor Wilkinsini," while another professional, with his head resting on his violin, played vigorously, as he stared unconcernedly at the noisy audience.[3]

3. Mayhew, 1: 41.

The smallness of the gaff stage should be no surprise when it is considered that no theaters were specially built as gaffs. Converted shops and warehouses were favorite locations for penny theaters. Often some form of anteroom was found. This anteroom had a dual function. It was both a waiting room for those who arrived during a prior performance and also a place to sell liquor and refreshments. Little decoration was felt necessary in the "auditorium," but should any accidentally remain after conversion it was left:

> To form the theatre, the first floor had been removed; the whitewashed beams however still stretched from wall to wall. The lower room had evidently been the warehouse while the upper apartment had been the sitting room, for the paper was still on the walls.[4]

Those gaffs that used tickets sold them on the premises or (as in the case of certain minor theaters) at a local shop. The North London Concert Room hired a local police constable to take their money for them. A police officer, working for the other side, told a magistrate that he had procured a ticket of admission inscribed, *"Domine dirige nos,"* [God direct us] which he took to mean "admit the bearer immediately." Other tickets were merely pieces of cardboard with the price crudely scrawled on them. Of course there were only two prices at most gaffs—the pit at twopence and the gallery at a penny (a penny was seldom refused for a pit seat if a house was less than packed). Most of those admitted paid a penny to sit in what was usually a singularly unsafe gallery. The ascent to the gallery was often by means of a ladder. Those who would not, or could not, make the precarious upward journey paid twopence and occasionally sat on a planed bench or even had seats on the stage. At one theater, unlike most, the sexes in the gallery were separated:

> The separation of the sexes is owing to a great refinement of feeling. The gentlemen, chiefly labourers and apprentices, luxuriate during the representation in the aroma of their "pick-

4. Ibid.

wicks," a weed of which we can assure the reader that it is not
to be found in the Havana; but they are gallant enough to
keep the only window in the house wide open.[5]

The stage itself was usually of the most miniscule
proportions—so much so that the "broad" acting style be-
loved of the Victorian audience had to be severely curtailed. A few planks formed a raised platform upon which
the actors performed and lighting was by candle or gas jet.
The latter form of illumination generally flared dangerously
by the side of the stage. A single jet had virtually no power
of illumination, and it served better as a means of lighting
pipes. Scenery, when used, consisted of three or four
crudely painted pieces of cloth, and, in the best tradition of
the minor theaters, one backcloth served for many scenes.

The audiences of penny theaters consisted almost exclusively of young people between the ages of eight and sixteen. This was just as well, since only the agility and
foolhardiness of youth would risk climbing and sitting on
the rickety galleries found in the typical gaff. Occasionally
younger children and old people were to be found, but the
main bulk of the audience consisted of youths. Boys patronized gaffs more than girls, but both sexes were found in
eager attendance. The audiences of the gaffs came in for a
great deal of criticism:

> Our attention was then engaged with the company who fre-
> quent here, which are for the most part prostitutes, pick-
> pockets, cracksmen from St. Giles', linen drapers' shop boys,
> milliners' girls. . . . Many of the fair sex may be seen sitting in
> the drapers' laps.[6]

The dramatic taste of the budding costermonger despised
equivocation. Like his parents, he would tolerate nothing
static or introspective, and "real life" had to be macabre
and violent. A local crime was a godsend to the penny gaffs:

5. Max Schlesinger, *Saunterings In and About London* (London: Nathaniel
Cooke, 1853), p. 273.

6. Frederick Burgess, *Penny Theatres: Illustrated with Views, Bills, Advertisements, etc.* (an unpublished collection of press cuttings on penny gaffs—no
page numbers—Harvard Theater Collection, Cambridge, Mass.).

> The recent atrocity known by the name of the Edgeware murder, was quite a windfall to many of the Penny Theatres. Pieces founded on the most frightful of the circumstances connected with it were forthwith got up, and acted to crowded houses, amidst great applause.[7]

It is not totally impossible that one of the youngsters sitting entranced at a lurid Whitechapel gaff would later become Whitechapel's most notorious son—Jack the Ripper.

A performance generally lasted an hour and a half and began as soon as the manager felt he had a reasonably full house. Some managers tried to cram in six performances an evening, and some gaffs actually ran all day. A man was employed at some theaters to "keep order" and to ring a bell at the end of each show. Those who did not wish to leave could stay on production of another penny. The type of performance varied, but it seems that at least two pieces, liberally interspersed with song, were de rigueur. Songs were extremely popular and, of course, the 1737 Licensing Act did not prohibit either songs or pantomime.

James Greenwood described at some length the ill-fated attempts of one gaff to produce a highwayman drama. The laws against the use of dialogue made it necessary for the highwayman to explain his motivations via an extended song. Despite the bold announcement on the placard promising a horse and carriage on the stage, the animal refused to oblige:

> Gentleman Jack spurred him, but though the bold rider sawed at its bit until the animal's toothless gums were visible, and spurred it until the rowels were completely clogged with the yielding hair of its flanks, it only wagged its tail languidly and snorted.[8]

Few of the actors took much time to memorize parts. The plays changed too frequently, and it was easier to im-

7. James Grant, *Penny Theatres* (London: Society for Theatre Research Pamphlet Series, no. 1, 1952), p. 24.

8. James Greenwood, *The Wilds of London* (London: Chatto and Windus, 1874), p. 17.

provise an ending than to try to remember business and moves. Comments on the ability of the players varied, but it was clear that the audience kept them on their mettle. An actor who could succeed in a gaff might well move up to a minor theater; less fortunate actors moved the other way. On 7 January 1840 a famous Drury Lane harlequin was brought before a magistrate for playing in a gaff. Many actors suffered similar fates—a sorry end to a theatrical career.

A correspondent writing in the London *Times* recalled that the favorite pieces at the penny theaters were those that were similarly popular at the minor theaters. Such sure-fire hits as *Maria Marten, Sweeney Todd,* and *Uncle Tom's Cabin* were adapted for the small stages. As the minor theater audiences demanded their "spectacular" scene, so the gaff audiences demanded theirs. They were less grandiose but effective:

> The grand finale of *Maria Marten* was intensely popular, especially when the murderer Corder was shown in the condemned cell with a vision of the body of Maria. At this moment, a sepulchral voice intoned: "Will—iam Corrder, behold your miserable victim and ponder on your inevitable doom!"[9]

Many plays were "abridged" for gaff production, for many penny theaters put on a dozen new pieces a week. Shakespeare's plays were shortened, often to twenty minutes. *Othello* was often acted because the actor's make-up was easy to assume with soot. The same was true of *Uncle Tom's Cabin*:

> The part is acted by no less distinguished a person than the director himself. His face is blackened, he has a woolly wig on his head, and heavy chains on his wrists and ankles; and to prevent all misunderstandings, there is pinned to his waistcoat an enormous placard, with the magic words of "UNCLE TOM."[10]

9. *The [London] Times,* 2 January 1953, p. 10.
10. Schlesinger, p. 275.

The only concern in adapting a piece was time. The manager often gauged the audience's response and behaved accordingly. If a fresh house were available, the curtain fell with astonishing rapidity, and if a performance was lagging, important transitions were simply cut. Those who wrote originals or adaptations would even leave out an ending so that the conclusion could be hastened or delayed according to audience or managerial taste. Since the actors generally had no sense of pace, having seldom seen the complete manuscript (if indeed one existed), they took their timing from the manager.

The themes of gaff pieces echoed those of the minor theaters. Nationalistic and patriotic fervor pervaded the air. Attacks on privilege were loudly applauded. Naturally crime and excitement had to prevail, but they were strongly buttressed by appeals to "Liber-r-rty" and the impassioned singing of "God Save the Queen." That favorite figure of domestic drama, the British seaman, played his usual role—the vanquisher of tyrants:

> The monster [Napoleon] bawls out "INVASION!" while, to the great delight of the ladies and gentlemen, he bumps his head several times against the chalky cliffs of Britain, which on the present emergency, are represented by the wooden planks of the stage. The very sailor-boy, still dancing his hornpipe, shows his contempt for so much ferocity and dullness. He greets the invader with a scornful—"Parli-vow Frenchi?" . . . but just as the invader has gained the edge of the stage, he is attacked by the sailor, who, applying his foot to a part of the Frenchman's body which shall be nameless, kicks that warrior back into the pit. The public cheer, Britannia and the Lord Mayor dance a polka, and the sailor sings "God Save the Queen!"[11]

Even Thackeray attended gaffs and once pointed out that, "Popular fun is always kind: it is the champion of the humble against the great . . . it is little Jack that conquers."[12]

11. Ibid., p. 276.
12. Quoted in Maurice W. Disher, *Blood and Thunder: Mid-Victorian Melodrama and Its Origins* (London: Frederick Muller, 1949), p. 138.

The fate of dramatic authors in Victorian England is well known. Writers at gaffs suffered even more. Dramatists were either hacks pressed into service or members of the company who, like Nicholas Nickleby, could translate a French piece. The resulting fare was thus of the crudest type, mingling tubs of blood with the worst forms of sentimentality.

Virtually no features of the penny theaters worked in favor of the performance. It was not uncommon for the audience to eat during a performance and, as a gracious tribute, food might be thrown onto the stage in the midst of a performance; such delicacies as a pig's trotter (foot) were not to be scorned. A grateful actress "bowed her thanks to our box and carried it off with as much grace as a leading lady at the West End would have carried off a bouquet."[13] The sale of food was a profitable side line at all London theaters. A plate of oysters could be purchased for twopence at a gaff, and fruit was always available. Foodsellers were notorious for their obliviousness to the drama in progress. James Grant recalls a moment in a production when the audience was wrapt in horror at a double murder and a suicide. At that moment, a ragged boy "stepping over the bodies of the dying trio, as careless-like as if he had been walking on the Waterloo-road, sang out "Apples!—six a penny."[14]

The costumes of gaff actors were the products of long usage and low income. Since actors traditionally supplied their own costumes, it is not at all surprising that contemporary accounts talked of costumes being held together by shreds and patches. Indeed, on occasions, the patches had totally replaced the original garment. Such a state of affairs is easily understood when considering the financial status of the profession. A gaff clown told Henry Mayhew that when he was the highest paid member of a company, he received

13. Quoted in Albert E. Wilson, *East End Entertainment* (London: Arthur Barker, [1954]), p. 53.
14. Grant p. 22.

eighteen shillings a week. Other clowns might expect to re-
ceive much less—though more was possible around the
Christmas pantomime season. Lesser lights might average
only five shillings a week, a totally inadequate amount for a
man with a family. In order to increase the earnings of his
players, it was not uncommon for the manager to toss a
penny on the stage in hopes others would follow suit. As
often as not the production ceased in order to allow the actors to locate and seize the solitary coin. When actors
genuinely pleased their audiences, they were gratified to
hear the cry, "Chuck 'em on!"

> Besides shouts of "Hencore!" and stamping and whistling,
> there was a cry of "Chuck 'em on!" followed by a casting of
> halfpence on to the stage. Not many, however; not more than
> amounted to sixpence; but the dashing highwayman seemed
> very grateful, and looking after the rolling coins with an avidity
> that showed how ill he could afford to forego the smallest of
> them.[15]

Numerous accounts are found of actors who refused to perform without receiving some tangible return for their previous histrionic endeavors. Many times a manager's greed
caused him to withhold salaries, but often

> the proprietors of Penny Theatres are as poor as the
> players . . . and it does sometimes happen that in imitation of
> the conduct which has of late been once or twice pursued at
> some of the larger theatrical establishments, the actors unani-
> mously refuse to play until their arrears or at least an install-
> ment of them, are paid up.[16]

Certain gaffs specialized in animal acts. The actors came
slightly more cheaply this way and "dog dramas" and other
animal shows were popular. The size of a gaff stage tended
to limit the scope of animal acts, but dog dramas were
common enough, and an occasional bear was not unknown.
Playbills would proudly announce such promises as "the

15. Greenwood, *Wilds*, p. 16.
16. Grant, p. 13.

Celebrated DOG Neptune will likewise add to the amusement."

The gaffs, as was to be expected, came in for strong criticism from almost all educated men who visited them. The common complaint was that the penny theaters encouraged theft and immorality. Henry Mayhew believed that the gaffs were the schoolrooms where the young would pick up their moral precepts. He further thought that no chance was missed to pass on an obscene thought and that gaffs appealed to the most brutal instincts. Contemporary newspaper accounts were no less damning. They spoke of the penny theaters as "abominable nuisances" and "the haunts of juvenile offenders." James Greenwood visited a gaff in Shoreditch and waited with the young people for the previous show to conclude:

> There was a stench of tobacco smoke, and an uproar of mingled youthful voices—swearing, chaffing, in boisterious mirth. . . . A few romping about—"larking" as it is termed —but the majority, girls and boys, were squatted on the floor, telling and listening to stories, the quality of which might but too truly [be] guessed from the sort of applause they elicited.[17]

Attention was frequently drawn to the number of "Cyprians" who were present at gaffs and to the coarse behavior of the young costermongers. Nevertheless, at least one attempt was made to turn public attention to the need to reform the gaffs into forces for good. After all, gaffs were less unwholesome than dice, cards, and liquor:

> The point we have in view is to show the eagerness with which this sort of *education* is taken advantage of, and that it is in truth the only sort of instruction to which many can attend . . . we are inclined to think that the penny theatres, as now managed, do more harm than good, and that they might be very greatly improved, not only with advantages to the owners of them, but also to the visitors.[18]

17. James Greenwood, *The Seven Curses of London* (London: Stanley Rivers and Co., [1868]), p. 74.
18. *The Builder* (5 June 1858), p. 386.

A penny theater audience in London (*The Builder*)

Though nothing came of this initiative, the penny gaffs lingered on until the end of Victoria's reign, but their popularity declined rapidly after the 1870s. However, Elizabeth Pennell wrote of a gaff version of *Faust* in 1887,[19] but by the turn of the century the gaff was virtually dead. By that time, moreover, all the thrill had gone. Increased prosperity, rising costs, growth of theaters, and, most of all, a growing sophistication, killed the gallery-apprenticeship system. No longer would youths hang precariously from wooden galleries shouting "hencore" and pitching their greasy halfpence to the eager, if inadequate, toilers beneath.

19. Elizabeth Pennell, "Decline and Fall of Dr. Faustus," *Contemporary Review*, n.s. 51 (March 1887): 401–404.

BIBLIOGRAPHY

Plays

Bernard, Bayle. *The Farmer's Story*. 1836.

Bickerstaffe, Isaac. *Thomas and Sally; or, The Sailor's Return*. 1760.

Bolton, G. *Civil War of Poetry*. 1846.

Boucicault, Dion. *After Dark: A Tale of London Life*. 1868; *Arrah-na-Pogue; or, The Wicklow Wedding*. 1864; *The Colleen Bawn; or, The Brides of Garryowen*. 1860; *London Assurance*. 1841; *The Long Strike*. 1866; and *The Octoroon; or, Life in Louisiana*. 1859.

Brougham, J. *Jane Eyre; or, The Secrets of Thornfield Manor House*. 1848.

Browning, Robert. *A Blot in the 'Scutcheon*. 1843; and *Strafford*. 1837.

Buckstone, J. B. *Agnes de Vere; or, The Broken Heart*. 1834; *The Dream at Sea*. 1835; *Ellen Wareham, the Wife of Two Husbands*. 1833; *The Green Bushes; or, A Hundred Years*

Ago. 1845; *Isabelle; or, A Woman's Life.* 1834; *Last Days of Pompeii.* 1834; *Luke the Labourer; or, The Lost Son.* 1826; *Victorine; or, I'll Sleep On It.* 1831; and *The Wreck Ashore.* 1830.

Byron, H. J. *The Lancashire Lass; or, Tempted, Tried, and True.* 1867.

Carpenter, J. E. *Love and Honour; or, Soldiers at Home—Heroes Abroad.* 1855.

Coleridge, S. T. *Remorse.* 1813.

Colman, George. *The Iron Chest.* 1796.

Cross, J. C. *The Purse; or, The Benevolent Tar.* 1794.

Daly, Augustin. *Under the Gaslight; or, Life and Love in These Times.* 1867.

Dibdin, T. J. *Suil Dhuv the Coiner.* 1828.

Falconer, Edmund. *Eileen Oge; or, Dark's the Hour Before the Dawn.* 1871.

Fatal Cataract. [1837?].

Fiend of the Flood. [1837?].

Fitzball, Edward. *Hans of Iceland.* 1841; *Jonathan Bradford; or, The Murder at the Roadside Inn.* 1833; and *The Red Rover; or, The Mutiny of the Dolphin.* 1829.

Gilbert, W. S. *Engaged.* 1877.

Goethe, Johann. *Faust.* 1808.

Haines, J. T. *The Life of a Woman; or, A Curate's Daughter.* 1840; and *My Poll and My Partner Joe.* 1835.

Hazlewood, Colin. *Mary Price; or, The Adventures of a Servant Girl.* 1853; *Taking the Veil.* 1870; *Waiting for the Verdict; or, Falsely Accused.* 1859.

Holl, Henry. *Grace Huntley.* 1833.

Jerrold, Douglas. *Black Ey'd Susan; or, "All in the Downs."* 1829; *The Factory Girl.* 1832; *Fifteen Years of a Drunkard's Life.* 1828; *John Overy the Miser; or, The Southwark Ferry.* 1829. *Mutiny at the Nore; or, British Sailors in 1797.* 1830; *The Rent Day.* 1832; and *Sally in Our Alley.* 1830.

Jim Crow. [1837?].

Jones, Henry. *The Silver King.* 1882.

Kenney, James. *Ella Rosenberg.* 1807; and *Masaniello.* 1829.

Knowles, J. S. *Brian Boroihme; or, The Maid of Erin.* 1812; *Virginius; or, The Liberation of Rome.* 1820.

Kotzebue, A. F. *The Stranger.* 1798.

Lacy, M. R. *The Two Friends.* 1828.

Lewis, Leopold. *The Bells.* 1871.

Lytton, Lord. *Lady of Lyons; or, Love-and Pride.* 1838; *Money.* 1840; and *Richelieu; or, The Conspiracy.* 1839.

Maria Marten; or, The Murder in the Red Barn. 1842.

Marston, J. W. *The Patrician's Daughter.* 1842.

McCloskey, James. *The Fatal Glass; or, The Curse of Drink.* 1872.

Merritt, P. and Conquest, G. *Seven Sins; or, Passion's Paradise.* 1874.

Milner, H. *The Hut on the Red Mountains; or, Thirty Years a Gambler's Life.* 1827.

Moncrieff, W. T. *The Lear of Private Life; or, Father and Daughter.* 1820; *The Somnambulist; or, The Phantom of the Village.* 1828; and *Tom and Jerry; or, Life in London.* 1821.

Newry, Lord. *Ecarté.* 1870.

Oxenford, John. *The Dice of Death.* 1835.

Palmer, T. A. *East Lynne.* 1874.

Payne, J. H. *Clari; or, The Maid of Milan.* 1823.

Peake, R. B. *The Climbing Boy.* 1832; and *Presumption; or, The Fate of Frankenstein.* 1823.

Pitt, George D. *Simon Lee; or, The Murder of the Five Fields Copse.* 1839; *A String of Pearls; or, The Fiend of Fleet Street.* 1847; and *Susan Hopley; or, The Vicissitudes of a Servant Girl.* 1841.

Pratt, William. *Ten Nights in a Bar-room.* 1867.

Rayner, Alfred. *The Foundling of the Sea; or, The Outcast Son.* 1859.

Rayner, Barnabas. *The Factory Assassin; or, The Dumb Man of Manchester.* 1837.

Reade, Charles. *Drink.* 1879; and *It's Never Too Late to Mend.*
1864.

Robertson, Tom. *Caste.* 1867; *Ours.* 1866; and *Society.* 1865.

Rowe, Nicholas. *Jane Shaw.* 1714.

Smith, William. *The Drunkard; or, The Fallen Saved.* 1844.
Spectre King. [1837?].

Somerset, C. A. *The Sea.* 1842.

Stirling, Edward. *Seven Castles of the Passions.* 1844.

Talfourd, Thomas. *Ion.* 1836.

Taylor, G. F. *The Factory Strike; or, Want, Crime, and
Retribution.* 1838.

Taylor, Tom. *Arkwright's Wife.* 1873; *Still Waters Run Deep.*
1855; and *Ticket of Leave Man.* 1863.

Taylor, T. P. *The Bottle.* 1847; and *The Village Outcast.* 1846.

Thompson, C. P. *Poachers and Petticoats.* 1836.

Travers, William. *Kathleen Mavourneen; or, Saint Patrick's Eve.*
1862.

Walker, John. *The Factory Lad.* 1832.

Wilkins, John. *Civilization.* 1852.

Wilks, Thomas E. *The Dream Spectre.* 1843; *Michael Earle, The
Maniac Lover.* 1839; and *Woman's Love; or, Kate Wynsley, the Cottage Girl.* 1845.

Books

Amerongen, Juda. *The Actor in Dickens.* London: Cecil Palmer,
1926.

Archer, William. *About the Theatre.* London: T. F. Unwin, 1886.

———. *English Dramatists of Today.* London: Sampson Low,
1882.

———. *The Fashionable Tragedian: A Criticism.* Edinburgh:
Thomas Gray and Co., 1877.

———. *The Old Drama and the New.* Boston: Small, Maynard,
and Co., [1923].

Arliss, George. *On the Stage: An Autobiography.* London: John

Murray, [1928].

Ashley, Leonard. *Nineteenth-century British Drama*. Glenview, Illinois: Scott, Foresman, and Co., 1967.

Bailey, J. O. *British Plays of the Nineteenth Century*. New York: Odyssey Press, 1966.

Baker, Henry Barton. *A History of the London Stage and Its Famous Players (1576–1903)*. London: Routledge and Sons, 1904.

————. *The London Stage: Its History and Tradition, 1576–1888*. 2 vols. London: W. H. Allen and Co., 1889.

————. *Our Old Actors*. London: Richard Bentley and Son, 1878.

Bancroft, Sir Squire and Lady. *Mr. and Mrs. Bancroft On and Off the Stage, Written by Themselves*. 2 vols. London: Richard Bentley and Son, 1888.

Barnes, John H. *Forty Years on the Stage; Others (Principally) and Myself*. London: Chapman and Hall, 1914.

Bedford, Paul. *Recollections and Wanderings of Paul Bedford*. London: Routledge, Warne, and Routledge, 1864.

Bell, Aldon D. *London in the Age of Dickens*. Norman, Oklahoma: University of Oklahoma Press, 1967.

Bentley, Eric. *The Life of the Drama*. New York: Atheneum, 1964.

Bernard, John. *Retrospections of the Stage*. 2 vols. London: Henry Colburn and Richard Bentley, 1830.

Bertram, James. *Glimpses of Real Life as Seen in the Theatrical World and in Bohemia*. Edinburgh: William Nimmo, 1864.

Besant, Sir Walter. *East London*. New York: Century Co., 1901.

————. *London in the Nineteenth Century*. London: Adam and Charles Black, 1909.

Best, Thomas. *Sermons on the Amusements of the Stage*. Sheffield, Yorkshire: George Ridge, 1831.

Birdoff, Harry. *The World's Greatest Hit: Uncle Tom's Cabin*. New York: S. F. Vanni, [1947].

Boaden, James. *Memoirs of Mrs. Inchbald* London: Richard Bentley, 1833.

————. *Memoirs of the Life of John Philip Kemble, Esq.* 2 vols. London: Longman, Hurst, and Co., 1825.

Longman, Hurst, and Co., 1825.

Booth, John. *A Century of Theatre History. 1816–1916: The "Old Vic."* London: Stead's Publishing House, 1917.

Booth, Michael. "East End Melodrama." Paper delivered at the Conference on Nineteenth-century British Theatre, Amherst, Massachusetts, 11 May 1974.

———. *English Melodrama.* London: Herbert Jenkins, [1965].

———. *English Plays of the Nineteenth Century.* 5 vols. Oxford: Clarendon Press, 1969–76.

———. *Hiss the Villain: Six English and American Melodramas.* London: Eyre and Spottiswoode, 1964.

Boucicault, Dion. *The Art of Acting.* Publications of the Dramatic Museum of Columbia University, Fifth Series. New York: Dramatic Museum of Columbia University, 1926.

Boulton, William. *The Amusements of Old London.* 2 vols. London: John Nimmo, 1901.

Brereton, Austin. *The Lyceum and Henry Irving.* London: Lawrence and Bullen, 1903.

Broadbent, R. J. *Stage Whispers.* London: Simpkin Marshall and Co., [1901].

Brockett, Oscar. *The Theatre: An Introduction.* New York: Holt, Rinehart, and Winston, 1966.

Bryant, Arthur. *The Age of Elegance.* New York: Harper and Row, 1950.

Buckley, Jerome. *The Victorian Temper: A Study in Literary Culture.* Cambridge, Massachusetts: Harvard University Press, 1951.

Bunn, Alfred. *Old England and New England.* 2 vols. London: Richard Bentley, 1853.

———. *The Stage: Both Before and Behind the Curtain from "Observations Taken on the Spot."* 3 vols. London: Richard Bentley, 1840.

Burgess, Frederick. *Penny Theatres: Illustrated with Views, Bills, Advertisements, Etc.* Unpublished collection of press cuttings in the Harvard Theater Collection, Cambridge, Massachusetts.

Burton, J. G. *The Critic's Budget; or, A Peep into the Amateur

Green Room. London: J. Onwhyn, [1819].

Byron, Henry J. *The Lancashire Lass.* New York: DeWitt Publishing House, [1868?].

Chandler, E. Beresford. *Annals of Covent Garden and Its Neighbourhood.* London: Hutchinson and Co., [1930].

——. *The Pleasure Haunts of London during Four Centuries.* London: Constable and Co., 1925.

Chandler, Frank W. *Aspects of Modern Drama.* New York: Macmillan and Co., 1914.

Clinton-Baddeley, V. C. *The Burlesque Tradition in the English Theatre after 1660.* London: Methuen and Co., [1952].

Coad, Oral S. *William Dunlap: A Study of His Life and Works and of His Place in Contemporary Culture.* New York: Dunlap Society, 1917.

Cole, John William. *The Life and Theatrical Times of Charles Kean F. S. A.* London: Richard Bentley, 1859.

Coleman, John. *Charles Reade as I Knew Him.* London: Treherne and Co., 1903.

——. *Fifty Years of an Actor's Life.* 2 vols. London: Hutchinson and Co., 1904.

Cook, Dutton. *A Book of the Play.* 2nd ed. 2 vols. London: Sampson Low and Co., 1876.

——. *Hours with the Players.* 2 vols. London: Chatto and Windus, 1881.

——. *Nights at the Play.* London: Chatto and Windus, 1883.

——. *On the Stage: Studies of Theatrical History and the Actor's Art.* 2 vols. London: Sampson Low and Co., 1883.

Cooke, P. J. *A Handbook of the Drama. Its Philosophy and Teaching.* London: Roxburghe Press, [1895?].

Cordell, Richard A. *Henry Arthur Jones and Modern Drama.* New York: R. Long and Smith, 1932.

Corrigan, Robert W. *Laurel British Drama: The Nineteenth Century.* New York: Dell Publishing Co., 1967.

[Corry, John.] *The English Metropolis; or, London in the Year 1820.* London: Barnard and Farley, 1820.

Courtneidge, Robert. *I Was an Actor Once.* London: Hutchinson and Co., [1930].

Craig, Edward Gordon. *Henry Irving*. London: J. M. Dent and Sons, 1930.

Cumberland, John. *Cumberland's British Theatre*. London: John Cumberland, 1826–.

Cunliffe, John W. *Modern English Playwrights: A Short History of English Drama from 1825*. New York: Harper and Brothers, 1927.

Darbyshire, Alfred. *The Art of the Victorian Stage: Notes and Recollections*. London: Sherratt and Hughes, 1907.

Davis, Owen. *I'd Like to Do It Again*. New York: Farrar and Rinehart, Inc., [1931].

———. *My First Fifty Years in the Theatre*. Boston: W. H. Baker and Co., [1950].

Decastro, Jacob. *The Memoirs of J. Decastro, Comedian*. London: Sherwood, Jones, and Co., 1824.

Dibdin, Charles. *Professional and Literary Memoirs of Charles Dibdin, the Younger*. Edited by George Speaight. London: Society for Theatre Research, 1956.

Dibdin, Thomas. *The Reminiscences of Thomas Dibdin*. 2 vols. London: H. Colburn, 1837.

Dickens, Charles. *Life and Adventures of Nicholas Nickelby*. London: Oxford University Press, 1950.

———. *Sketches of Young Gentlemen*. London: Chapman and Hall, 1838.

———. *The Uncommercial Traveller and Reprinted Pieces, Etc.* London: Oxford University Press, 1958.

Dicks, John. *Dicks's Standard Plays*. 16 vols. London: J. Dicks, [1875–1908].

Diprose, John. *Diprose's Book of the Stage and the Players*. London: Diprose and Bateman, 1877.

Disher, Maurice Willson. *Blood and Thunder: Mid-Victorian Melodrama and Its Origins*. London: Frederick Muller, 1949.

———. *Mad Genius: A Biography of Edmund Kean*. London: Hutchinson and Co., 1950.

———. *Melodrama: Plots That Thrilled*. London: Rockliff and

Company, [1954].

———. *Pleasures of London.* London: Robert Hale, [1950].

Donaldson, Walter. *Recollections of an Actor.* London: John Maxwell and Co., 1865.

———. *Theatrical Portraits.* London: Varnham and Co., 1870.

Donohue, Joseph. *Dramatic Character in the English Romantic Age.* Princeton, New Jersey: Princeton University Press, 1970.

Doran, John. *In and About Drury Lane.* London: Richard Bentley and Son, 1881.

———. *Their Majesties' Servants: Annals of the English Stage, From Thomas Betterton to Edmund Kean.* New York: W. J. Widdleton, 1865.

Doré, Gustave and Jerrold, Blanchard. *London: A Pilgrimage.* New York: Harper and Brothers, 1890.

Downer, Alan. *The Eminent Tragedian: William Charles Macready.* Cambridge, Massachusetts: Harvard University Press, 1966.

Egan, Pierce. *Life in London.* London: Sherwood, Neely, and Jones, 1821.

———. *Life of an Actor.* London: C. S. Arnold, 1825.

Elliot, W. G. *Amateur Clubs and Actors.* London: Edward Arnold, 1898.

Engels, Friedrich. *The Condition of the Working Class in England.* Translated by W. O. Henderson. Oxford: Basil Blackwell, 1958.

Erle, Twynihoe W. *Letters from a Theatrical Scene-painter.* 2 vols. London: privately published, 1859–62.

Evans, Bertrand. *Gothic Drama from Walpole to Shelley.* Berkeley, California: University of California Press, 1947.

Filon, P. M. Augustin. *The English Stage: Being an Account of the Victorian Drama.* Translated by Frederic Whyte. London: John Milne, 1897.

Fitzball, Edward. *Thirty-five Years of a Dramatic Author's Life.* 2 vols. London: T. C. Newby, 1859.

Fitzgerald, Percy. *The Art of Acting: In Connection with the Study of Character, the Spirit of Comedy, and Stage*

Illusion. London: Swan Sonnenschein and Co., 1892.

———. *A Book of Theatrical Anecdotes*. London: George Routledge and Sons, 1874.

———. *Henry Irving: A Record of Twenty Years at the Lyceum*.
London: Chapman and Hall, 1893.

———. *A New History of the English Stage*. 2 vols. London:
Tinsley Brothers, 1882.

———. *The World Behind the Scenes*. London: Chatto and Windus, 1881.

Fletcher, Robert. *English Romantic Drama, 1793–1843*. New
York: Exposition Press, 1966.

Forbes-Robertson, Sir Johnston. *A Player Under Three Reigns*.
Boston: Little, Brown, and Co., 1925.

[Genest, Rev. John.] *Some Account of the English Stage From the
Restoration in 1660 to 1830*. 10 vols. Bath, England: H.
E. Carrington, 1832.

Gomme, George L. *London in the Reign of Victoria, 1837–1897*.
London: Blackie and Sons, 1898.

Grant, James. *Penny Theatres*. Society for Theatre Research
Pamphlet Series, No. 1. London: Society for Theatre Research, 1952.

Greenwood, James. *The Seven Curses of London*. London: Stanley Rivers and Co., [1869].

———. *The Wilds of London*. London: Chatto and Windus,
1874.

Grimsted, David. *Melodrama Unveiled; American Theatre and
Culture, 1800–1850*. Chicago: University of Chicago
Press, 1968.

Hamilton, Clayton. *Studies in Stagecraft*. New York: Henry Holt
and Co., 1914.

Hammerton, John A. *The Actor's Art*. London: George Redway,
1897.

Hammond, J. L. *The Town Labourer, 1760–1832*. London:
Longmans, Green, and Co., 1917.

Harbage, Alfred. *Thomas Killigrew, Cavalier Dramatist,
1612–1683*. Lancaster, Pennsylvania: University of Pennsylvania Press, 1930.

Hartnoll, Phyllis, editor. *The Oxford Companion to the Theatre.* 3rd. ed. London: Oxford University Press, 1967.

Hatlen, Theodore. *Orientation to the Theatre.* New York: Appleton-Century-Crofts, [1962].

Hayward, Arthur. *The Days of Dickens.* New York: E. P. Dutton and Co., 1926.

Hazlitt, William. *Hazlitt on Theatre.* New York: Hill and Wang, [1957].

Hewitt, Barnard. *History of the Theatre from 1800 to the Present.* New York: Random House, [1970].

Hibbert, Henry G. *A Playgoer's Memories.* London: Grant Richards, Ltd., 1920.

Hill, Benson E. *Playing About; or, Theatrical Anecdotes and Adventures.* 2 vols. London: W. Sams, 1840.

Hoggart, Richard. *Speaking to Each Other.* 2 vols. London: Chatto and Windus, 1970.

———. *The Uses of Literacy.* London: Chatto and Windus, 1957.

Hollingshead, John. *My Lifetime.* 2 vols. London: Sampson Low and Co., 1895.

Holmes, Martin R. *Stage Costume and Accessories in the London Museum.* London: H. M. S. O., 1968.

Houghton, Walter. *Victorian Frame of Mind, 1830–1870.* New Haven, Connecticut: Yale University Press, 1957.

Hoyt, Harlowe. *Town Hall Tonight.* Englewood Cliffs, New Jersey: Prentice-Hall, [1955].

Hudson, Lynton. *The English Stage, 1850–1950.* London: Harrap and Co., [1951].

Irving, Henry. *The Art of Acting.* Chicago: Dramatic Publishing Company, [1887].

Jefferson, Joseph. *The Autobiography of Joseph Jefferson.* New York: Century Company, [1890].

James, Louis. *Fiction for the Working Man, 1830–1850.* London: Oxford University Press, 1963.

Jerome, Jerome K. *On the Stage—and Off: The Brief Career of a Would-be Actor.* New York: Henry Holt and Co., 1891.

———. *Stage Land: Curious Habits and Customs of Its*

Inhabitants. London: Chatto and Windus, 1889.

Jerrold, Blanchard. *The Life and Remains of Douglas Jerrold*. Boston: Ticknor and Fields, 1859.

Jerrold, Walter. *Douglas Jerrold: Dramatist and Wit*. 2 vols. London: Hodder and Stoughton, [1914?].

Johnson, Edgar, and Johnson, Eleanor, editors. *The Dickens Theatrical Reader*. Boston: Little, Brown, and Co., 1964.

Jones, Henry Arthur. *The Renascence of English Drama*. London: Macmillan and Co., 1895.

――――. *Representative Plays*. 4 vols. Boston: Little, Brown, and Co., 1925.

Joseph, Stephen. *The Story of the Playhouse in England*. London: Barrie and Rockliff, [1963].

Kemble, Frances Ann. *Records of Later Life*. New York: Henry Holt and Co., 1883.

Kennedy, Bart. *Footlights*. London: Henry Walker, 1928.

Kingsley, Charles. *Alton Locke* London: Cassell, 1967.

Knight, Charles. *London*. 6 vols. London: Henry G. Bohn, 1851.

Korg, Jacob. *London in Dickens's Day*. Englewood Cliffs, New Jersey: Prentice-Hall, 1960.

Krause, David. *The Dolmen Boucicault*. Dublin: Dolmen Press, [1964].

Lacy, Alexander. *Pixérécourt and the French Romantic Drama*. Toronto: University of Toronto Press, 1928.

Lacy, Thomas H. *The Amateur's Handbook*. London: Samuel French, [1866?].

――――. *Lacy's Acting Editions of Plays*. 165 vols. London: T. H. Lacy, [1849–1917].

Lawrence, William John. *Old Theatre Days and Ways*. London: Harrap and Co., [1935].

Lennox, William Pitt. *Plays, Playhouses at Home and Abroad with Anecdotes of the Drama and the Stage*. 2 vols. London: Hurst, Blackett, 1881.

Lewes, George H. *On Actors and the Art of Acting*. New York: Henry Holt and Co., 1880.

McCormick, Donald. *The Red Barn Mystery*. London: John Lang,

1967.

Macqueen-Pope, W. J. *Theatre Royal Drury Lane*. London: W. H. Allen, c. 1945.

Macready, William. *Macready's Reminiscences and Selections from His Diaries and Letters*. 2 vols. Edited by Sir Frederick Pollock. London: Macmillan and Co., 1875.

Mander, Raymond. *British Music Hall*. London: Studio Vista, 1965.

———. *Lost Theatres of London*. London: Rupert Hart-Davis, 1968.

———. *A Picture History of the British Theatre*. New York: Macmillan Co., [1957].

———. *The Theatres of London*. London: Rupert Hart-Davis, 1961.

Marshall, Norman. *The Producer and the Play*. London: Macdonald, [1957].

Marston, John Westland. *Our Recent Actors*. 2 vols. London: Sampson Low, Ltd., 1888.

Mayhew, Henry. *London Labour and the London Poor*. 4 vols. London: C. Griffin and Co., 1861–62.

Meeks, Leslie. *Sheridan Knowles and the Theatre of His Time*. Bloomington, Indiana: Principia Press, 1933.

Meisel, Martin. *Shaw and the Nineteenth-century Theatre*. Princeton, New Jersey: Princeton University Press, 1963.

Moses, Montrose. *The American Dramatist*. Boston: Little, Brown, and Co., 1925.

———. *Representative British Dramas: Victorian and Modern*. Boston: Little, Brown, and Co., 1918.

Nagler, Alois M. *Sources of Theatrical History*. New York: Theatre Annual, [1952].

Nathan, Archie. *Costumes by Nathan*. London: Newnes and Co., 1960.

Nelson, Alfred L. and Cross, Gilbert B. editors. *Drury Lane Journal: Selections from the Diaries of James Winston, 1819–1827*. London: Society for Theatre Research, 1974.

Nicholson, Watson. *The Struggle for a Free Stage in London*. Boston: Houghton Mifflin, 1906.

Nicoll, Allardyce. *The Development of the Theatre.* New York: Harcourt, Brace, and Co., 1927.

———. *A History of Early Nineteenth Century Drama, 1800–1850.* 2 vols. Cambridge, England: Cambridge University Press, 1930.

Old Stager [pseud.]. *A Practical Guide to Private Theatricals.* London: Thomas Scott, 1875.

Otten, Terry. *The Deserted Stage.* Athens, Ohio: Ohio University Press, 1972.

Pedicord, Harry W. *The Theatrical Public in the Time of Garrick.* New York: King's Crown Press, 1954.

Pemberton, Thomas. *Charles Dickens and the Stage.* London: George Redway, 1888.

Planché, James R. *The Recollections and Reflections of J. R. Planché: A Professional Autobiography.* London: Tinsley Bros., 1872.

[Pückler-Muskau, Hermann]. *Tour in England, Ireland, and France in the Years 1826, 1827, 1828, and 1829.* Translated by Sarah Austin. Zurich: Massie Publishing Co., 1940.

Purnell, Thomas. *Dramatists of the Present Day.* London: Chapman and Hall, 1871.

Rahill, Frank. *The World of Melodrama.* University Park, Pennsylvania: Pennsylvania State University Press, 1967.

Raymond, George. *Memoirs of Robert William Elliston.* 2nd. ed. London: John Ollivier, 1846.

Rede, Leman T. *The Road to the Stage: Contains Clear and Ample Instructions for Obtaining Theatrical Engagements.* rev. ed. London: J. Onwhyn, 1835.

Report from the Select Committee on Dramatic Literature. London: 1832.

Reynolds, Ernest R. *Early Victorian Drama (1830–1870).* Cambridge, England: W. Heffer and Sons, Ltd., 1936.

Rice, Charles. *The London Theatres in the Eighteen-thirties.* London: Society for Theatre Research, 1950.

Richardson's New Minor Drama. 4 vols. London: Richardson and Co., 1829–31.

Ritchie, Anna C. *Mimic Life; or, Before and Behind the Curtain.* Boston: Ticknor and Fields, 1856.

Robinson, Henry Crabb. *The London Theatre, 1811–1866*. Edited by Eluned Brown. London: Society for Theatre Research, 1966.

Rose, Millicent. *The East End of London*. London: Cresset Press, 1951.

Rowell, George, editor. *Nineteenth-century Plays*. London: Oxford University Press, [1953].

———. *The Victorian Theatre*. London: Oxford University Press, 1956.

Schlesinger, Max. *Saunterings In and About London*. London: Nathaniel Cooke, 1853.

Schneewind, J. B. *Backgrounds of English Victorian Literature*. New York: Random House, 1970.

Scott, Clement. *The Drama of Yesterday and Today*. 2 vols. London: Macmillan and Co., 1899.

———. *From "The Bells" to "King Arthur," a Critical Record*. London: J. Macqueen, 1896.

Scott, Constance. *Old Days in Bohemian London*. London: Hutchinson and Co., [1919].

Scrimgeour, Gary. "Drama and Theatre in the Early Nineteenth Century." Ph.D. dissertation, Princeton University, 1968.

Sharp, Robert Farquharson. *Short History of the English Stage*. London: Walter Scott Publishing Co., 1909.

Shattuck, Charles H. *Bulwer and Macready: A Chronicle of the Early Victorian Theatre*. Urbana, Illinois: University of Illinois Press, 1958.

Sherson, Errol. *London's Lost Theatres of the Nineteenth Century*. London: John Lane, The Bodley Head, 1925.

Siddons, Henry. *Practical Illustrations of Rhetorical Gesture and Action Adapted to the English Drama*. 2 ed. London: Sherwood, Neely, and Jones, 1822.

Slater, Montagu. *Maria Marten; or, The Murder in the Red Barn*. London: Gerald Howe, 1928.

Smiles, Samuel. *Self Help; with Illustrations of Character Conduct and Perseverance*. London: John Murray, 1859.

Southern, Richard. *The Victorian Theatre: A Pictorial Survey*. Newton Abbot, Devon: David and Charles, 1970.

Speaight, George. *History of the English Toy Theatre*. London: Studio Vista, Ltd., 1969.

———. *Juvenile Drama: The History of the English Toy Theatre*. London: Macdonald and Co., [1946].

Specimens of Show Printing. Hollywood, California: Cherokee Books, n.d.

Spence, Edward F. *Our Stage and Its Critics by "E. F. S."* London: Methuen and Co., [1910].

Stirling, Edward. *Old Drury Lane: Fifty Years' Recollections of Author, Actor, Manager*. 2 vols. London: Chatto and Windus, 1881.

Stone, Harry. *Uncollected Writings from "Household Words," 1850–1859*. London: Alan Lane, 1969.

Strauss, Ivard. *Paint, Powder, and Make-up*. New Haven, Connecticut: Sweet and Son, 1936.

Taylor, John R. *Rise and Fall of the Well-Made Play*. New York: Hill and Wang, 1967.

Thespian Preceptor. Boston: Joshua Belcher, 1810.

Tolles, Winton. *Tom Taylor and Victorian Drama*. New York: Columbia University Press, 1940.

Tomlins, Frederick G. *A Brief View of the English Drama*. London: C. Mitchell, 1840.

———. *Major and Minor Theatres*. London: W. Strange, F. Tomlins, 1832.

———. *The Nature and State of the English Drama*. London: C. Mitchell, 1841.

Trewin, John C. *Mr. Macready—A Nineteenth-century Tragedian and His Theatre*. London: George Harrap and Co., [1955].

———. *The Night Has Been Unruly*. London: Robert Hale, [1957].

———. *The Pomping Folk in the Nineteenth Century*. London: J. M. Dent, 1968.

Vandenhoff, George. *Leaves from An Actor's Note-Book*. New York: D. Appleton and Co., 1860.

Vardac, A. N. *Stage to Screen: Theatrical Methods from Garrick to Griffith*. Cambridge, Massachusetts: Harvard University Press, 1949.

Wagenknecht, Edward. *Merely Players*. Norman, Oklahoma: Oklahoma University Press, 1966.

Wagner, Leopold. *How to Get on the Stage and How to Succeed There*. London: Chatto and Windus, 1899.

———. *The Stage With the Curtain Raised*. London: John Heywood, [1881].

Walkley, Arthur B. *Playhouse Impressions*. London: T. Fisher and Unwin, 1892.

Walkup, Fairfax. *Dressing the Part*. New York: Appleton-Century-Crofts, 1950.

Walsh, Townsend. *The Career of Dion Boucicault*. New York: Dunlap Society, 1915.

Watson, Ernest B. *Sheridan to Robertson: A Study of the Nineteenth-century London Stage*. Cambridge, Massachusetts: Harvard University Press, 1926.

Weales, Gerald. *Religion in Modern English Drama*. Philadelphia: University of Pennsylvania Press, [1961].

Webster, Benjamin N. *Acting National Drama*. 18 vols. London: Chapman and Hall, 1837–1859.

Wey, Francis. *A Frenchman Among Victorians*. Translated by Valerie Pirie. New Haven, Connecticut: Yale University Press, 1936.

White, Henry A. *Scott's Novels on the Stage*. New Haven: Yale University Press, 1927.

Whyte, Frederic. *Actors of the Century*. London: George Bell, 1898.

Williams, Michael. *Some London Theatres Past and Present*. London: Sampson Low and Co., 1883.

Willis, Frederick. *A Book of London Yesterdays*. London: Phoenix House, [1960].

Wilson, Albert E. *East-end Entertainment*. London: Arthur Barker, [1954].

———. *Penny Plain, Two Pence Coloured: A History of the Juvenile Drama*. London: Harrap and Co., Ltd., [1932].

Winter, Marian H. *Theatre of Marvels*. Translated by Charles Meldon. New York: Benjamin Blom, 1964.

Wyndham, Henry Saxe. *Annals of the Covent Garden Theatre.* London: Chatto and Windus, 1906.

Young, G. M., editor. *Early Victorian England, 1830–1865.* 2 vols. London: Oxford University Press, 1934.

Young, Julian C. *A Memoir of Charles Mayne Young, Tragedian.* London: Macmillan and Co., 1871.

Young, Stark. *Theatre Practice.* New York: Charles Scribner, [1926].

Periodicals

Actors by Gaslight; or, Boz in the Boxes. (21 April–29 December 1838.)

Altick, Richard. "Dion Boucicault Stages *Mary Barton.*" *Nineteenth-century Fiction* 14, no. 1 (June 1959): 129–41.

Armstrong, William. "The Art of the Minor Theatres in 1860." *Theatre Notebook* 10, no. 3 (April–June 1956): 89–94.

Baker, Henry B. "The Old Melodrama." *Belgravia* 50 (May 1883): 331–39.

Barker, Kathleen. "The Theatre Proprietors' Story." *Theatre Notebook* 18, no. 3 (Spring 1964): 79–91.

Bispham, David. "Melodrama, or Recitation with Music." *Harper's Bazaar* 43, no. 1 (January 1909): 21–25.

Bligh, N. M. "Mirror Curtains." *Theatre Notebook* 15, no. 2 (Winter 1960–61): 56.

Booth, Michael R. "The Drunkard's Progress—Nineteenth-century Temperance Melodrama." *Dalhousie Review* 44 (Summer 1964): 205–12.

Boucicault, Dion. "The Debut of a Dramatist." *North American Review* 148 (April 1889): 454–63.

———. "The Decline of the Drama." *North American Review* 125 (September 1877): 235–245.

———. "Early Days of a Dramatist." *North American Review* 148 (May 1889): 584–93.

———. "Leaves from a Dramatist's Diary." *North American Review* 149 (August 1889): 228–36.

———. "Theatres, Halls, and Audiences." *North American*

Review 149 (October 1889): 428–36.

Browne, Porter. "Mellowdrammer." *Everybody's Magazine* 21 (September 1909): 347–54.

Coleman, Antony. "Mossop as Wolsey." *Theatre Notebook* 25, no. 1 (Autumn 1970): 11–14.

Coolidge, Archibald. "Dickens and the Philosophic Bases of Melodrama." *Victorian Newsletter*, no. 20 (Fall 1961), pp. 1–6.

Craig, Edward G. "Melodrama." *Yale Review*, n.s. 20 (12 November 1930): 212–16.

Davis, J. F. "Tom Shows." *Scribner's Magazine* 77 (April 1925): 350–60.

"Decay of Melodrama." *Living Age* 265 (16 April 1910): 182–84.

Dent, A. "Boost for Melodrama." *Drama* no. 75 (Winter 1964), pp. 40–42.

Dickens, Charles. "The Amusements of the People," *Household Words* 1 (30 March 1850): 13–15.

Downer, Alan S. "The Case of Mr. Lee Moreton." *Theatre Notebook* 4, no. 2 (January–March 1950): 44–45.

———. "Player and Painted Stage: Nineteenth-century Acting." *PMLA* 61, no. 2 (June 1946): 522–76.

———. "A Preface to Melodrama: 1. The Less Eminent Victorians." *Player's Magazine* 21, no. 4 (January 1945): 9–10.

———. "A Preface to Melodrama: 2. Three Types of Melodrama." *Player's Magazine* 21, no. 5 (February 1945): 9–10, 20.

———. "A Preface to Melodrama: 3. Nautical Melodrama." *Player's Magazine* 21, no. 6 (March 1945): 9–10, 14–15.

———. "A Preface to Melodrama: 4. Domestic Drama." *Player's Magazine* 21, no. 7 (April 1945): 13–14, 16.

———. "A Preface to Melodrama: 5. The Revival of Victorian Melodrama." *Player's Magazine* 21, no. 8 (May 1945): 12–14.

"The Dramatic Register for 1853." *Quarterly Review* 95 (July 1854): 37–46.

Dramatic Magazine (March 1829–April 1831).

Eaton, Walter P. "Is Melodramatic Rubbish Increasing?" *American Magazine* 82 (December 1916): 34, 114, 116.

Faulkner, Seldon. "The Great Train Scene Robbery." *Quarterly Journal of Speech* 1 (February 1964): 24–28.

Ganzel, Dewey. "Patent Wrongs and Patent Theatre: Drama and Law in the Early Nineteenth Century." *PMLA* 76, no. 4 (September 1961): 384–96.

Glossop, Joseph. "Attempt to Suppress the Minor Drama." *Theatrical Inquisitor* 16 (May 1820): 201–204.

Griffin, Martin. "Melodrama." *Catholic World* 141 (August 1935): 564–68.

Halliday, E. "Curses, Foiled Again!" *American Heritage* 15, no. 1 (December 1963): 12–23.

Hamilton, Clayton. "Melodramas and Farces." *Forum* 41 (January 1909): 25–32.

Heilman, Robert. "Tragedy and Melodrama: Speculations on Generic Form." *Texas Quarterly* 3, no. 1 (Summer 1960): 36–50.

Illustrated London News, 26 October 1844, 13 April 1861, 4 May 1861.

Johnson, Albert. "Fabulous Boucicault." *Theatre Arts* 37, no. 3 (March 1953): 26–30, 90–93.

Klingberg, Frank. "Harriet Beecher Stowe and Social Reform in England." *American Historical Review* 43, no. 3 (April 1938): 542–52.

Krutch, J. "What is Melodrama?" *Nation* 138 (9 May 1934): 544, 546.

Landa, M. "Grandfather of Melodrama." *Cornhill Magazine* 132 (October 1925): 476–84.

Lawrence, James. "Dramatic Emancipation." *Pamphleteer* 2, no. 4 (December 1813): 370–95.

Lawrence, W. "Sensation Scenes," *Gentleman's Magazine* 261 (October 1886): 400–405.

–———. "Water in Dramatic Art." *Gentleman's Magazine* 262 (June 1887): 540–553.

Literary Gazette, 20 July 1833.

McIntyre, C. "The Word Universality as Applied to Drama."

PMLA 44, no. 3 (September 1929): 927–29.

McNeill, W. "The Beginning of Melodrama." *Queen's Quarterly* 24 (October–December 1916): 215–27.

Marshal, J. "Non-stop Show: *The Drunkard.*" *Colliers* 108 (27 December 1941): 28, 69.

"Master of Melodrama: The Centenary of Thomas Dibdin from Gothic to the Crime Play." [*London*] *Times Literary Supplement* (20 September 1941), p. 470.

Matthews, B. "Tragedies with Happy Endings." *North American Review* 211 (March 1920): 355–65.

Morris, C. "Memory of Dion Boucicault." *Cosmopolitan* 38, no. 3 (January 1905): 273–78.

Morley, Malcolm. "Dickens's Contribution to *Sweeney Todd.*" *Dickensian*, 58 (Spring 1962): 92–95.

———. "The First Strand Theatre." *Theatre Notebook* 18, no. 3 (Spring 1964): 100–102.

———. "The Minor Theatre in Catherine Street." *Theatre Notebook* 18, no. 4 (Summer 1964): 117–20.

Nitchie, Elizabeth. "The Stage History of *Frankenstein.*" *South Atlantic Quarterly* 41, no. 4 (October 1942): 384–98.

Northend, Marjorie. "Henry Arthur Jones and the Development of Modern English Drama." *Review of English Studies* 18 (October 1942): 448–63.

Norton, M. "The Plays of Joanna Baille." *Review of English Studies* 23 (April 1947): 131–43.

Paston, George. "Apostle of Melodrama." *Fortnightly Review* 100 (November 1913): 962–75.

Pennell, Elizabeth. "The Decline and Fall of Dr. Faustus." *Contemporary Review*, n.s. 51 (March 1887): 394–407.

Philo-Dramaticus [pseud.] "A Letter to Charles Kemble, Esq., and R. W. Elliston, Esq. on the Present State of the Stage." *Blackwood's Magazine* 17 (June 1825): 727–31.

Pritchett, V. S. "Blood and Thunder." *New Statesman* 70 (10 December, 1965): 934.

Quinn, A. H. "In Defense of Melodrama." *Bookman* 16 (June 1925): 413–17.

Rahill, Frank. "Dion Boucicault and the Royalty Payment for

Playwrights." *Theatre Arts* 23, no. 11 (November 1939): 807–13.

————. "Melodrama." *Theatre Arts* 16 (April 1932): 285–94.

Rhodes, Raymond. "The Early Nineteenth-century Drama." *Library* 26, no. 1 (June 1935): 91–112.

————. "The Early Nineteenth-century Drama." *Library* 26, no. 2 (September 1935): 210–31.

Smith, H. J. "Melodrama." *Atlantic Monthly* 99 (March 1907): 320–28.

Stoakes, J. P. "English Melodrama: Forerunner of Modern Social Drama." *Florida State University Studies*, no. 3 (1951), pp. 53–62.

Sypher, Wylie. "Aesthetic of Revolution: The Marxist Melodrama." *Kenyon Review* 10, no. 3 (Summer 1948): 431–44.

The Theatrical Inquisitor. (1812–21)

Thompson, Alan. "Melodrama and Tragedy." *PMLA* 43, no. 3 (September 1928): 810–35.

Thomson, Fred. "A Crisis in Early Victorian Drama: John Westland Marston and the Syncretics." *Victorian Studies* 9, no. 4 (June 1966): 375–98.

Woods, A. "Producing Spine Thrillers." *Literary Digest* 45 (10 August 1912): 222–23.

INDEX

DATE DUE

FACULTY			